PRODUCT DESIGN AND DEVELOPMENT

PRODUCT DESIGN AND DEVELOPMENT

Karl T. Ulrich
The Wharton School, University of Pennsylvania

Steven D. Eppinger
Massachusetts Institute of Technology

McGraw-Hill, Inc.
New York St. Louis San Francisco Auckland Bogotá Caracas
Lisbon London Madrid Mexico City Milan Montreal New Delhi
San Juan Singapore Sydney Tokyo Toronto

PRODUCT DESIGN AND DEVELOPMENT

This book is printed on acid-tree paper.

7 8 9 0   DOC/DOC   9 9 8 7

ISBN 0-07-065811-0

This book was set in Baskerville by Better Graphics, Inc.
The editors were Bonnie K. Binkert, John J. Corrigan, and Sheila H. Gillams;
the production supervisor was Richard A. Ausburn.
The cover was designed by Nadine Flowers and Julie Townsend of Barrett Design, Inc.
The photo editor was Anne Manning.
R. R. Donnelley & Sons Company was printer and binder.

MicroTAC and DynaTAC are trademarks of Motorola, Inc.
Rollerblade and Bravoblade are trademarks of Rollerblade, Inc.
Sinterstation, SLS, and DTM are trademarks of DTM Corporation.

Library of Congress Cataloging-in-Publication Data

Ulrich, Karl T.
    Product design and development / Karl T. Ulrich, Steven D. Eppinger.
        p.   cm.
    Includes bibliographical references and index.
    ISBN 0–07–065811–0
    1. Industrial management.   2. Production management.
3. Industrial engineering.   4. New products—Management.
I. Eppinger, Steven D.   II. Title.
HD31.U47   1995
658.5'752—dc20

94–20358

ABOUT THE AUTHORS

KARL T. ULRICH is an associate professor at The Wharton School at the University of Pennsylvania, and also holds a secondary appointment in the Department of Mechanical Engineering and Applied Mechanics. He received his S.B., S.M., and Sc.D. degrees in Mechanical Engineering from MIT. Professor Ulrich has participated as a member of development teams for dozens of products ranging from snack foods to surgical instruments. His current research is aimed at better coordination of design, manufacturing, and marketing decisions in the product development process.

STEVEN D. EPPINGER is an associate professor at the Massachusetts Institute of Technology Sloan School of Management where he is a member of the Operations Management Group. He holds S.B., S.M., and Sc.D. degrees in Mechanical Engineering from MIT, and teaches and conducts research in the field of manufacturing, with a focus on product design and development. Professor Eppinger specializes in the study of large product development projects and has advised development teams at many firms in the automotive, electronics, and consumer products industries.

To the professionals who shared their experiences with us and to the product development teams we hope will benefit from those experiences.

CONTENTS

PREFACE

This book contains material developed for use in an interdisciplinary graduate course on product development that we have been teaching at MIT. Participants in this course include MBA students at the MIT Sloan School of Management, graduate students from the MIT School of Engineering, and industrial design students from the Rhode Island School of Design. While we aimed the book at interdisciplinary graduate-level audiences such as this, many faculty teaching graduate and undergraduate courses in engineering design have also found the material useful. *Product Design and Development* is also for practicing professionals. Indeed, we could not avoid writing for a professional audience because most of our students are themselves professionals who have worked either in product development or in closely related functions.

This book blends the perspectives of marketing, design, and manufacturing into a single approach to product development. As a result, we provide students of all kinds an appreciation for the realities of industrial practice and for the complex and essential roles played by the various members of product development teams. For industrial practitioners, in particular, we provide a set of product development methodologies that can be put into immediate practice on development projects.

A debate currently rages in the engineering design community as to whether design should be taught primarily by establishing a foundation of theory or by engaging students in loosely supervised practice. For the broader activity of product design and development, we reject both approaches when taken to their extremes. Theory without practice is ineffective because there are many nuances, exceptions, and subtleties to be learned in practical settings and because some necessary tasks simply lack any theoretical underpinnings. Practice without guidance can too easily result in frustration and fails to exploit the knowledge that successful product development professionals and researchers have accumulated over time. Product development, in this respect, is like sailing: proficiency is gained through practice, but some theory of how sails work and some instruction in the mechanics (and even tricks) of operating the boat help tremendously.

We attempt to strike a balance between theory and practice through our emphasis on *methodologies*. A methodology is a step-by-step procedure for completing a task, but it rarely embodies a clean and concise theory. In some cases, the methodologies are supported in part by a long tradition of research and practice, as in the chapter on the economics of product development projects. In other cases, the methodologies are a distillation of relatively recent and ad hoc techniques, as in the chapter on design for manufacturing. In all cases, the methodologies provide a concrete approach to solving a product development problem. In our experience, product development is best learned by applying structured methodologies to ongoing project work in either industrial or academic settings. Therefore, we intend this book to be used as a guide to completing development tasks either in the context of a course project or in industrial practice.

Every methodology in the book is illustrated by an industrial example or case study. We chose to use different products as the examples for each chapter rather than carrying the same example through the entire book. We provide this variety because we think it makes the book more interesting and because we hope to illustrate that the methodologies can be applied to a wide range of products, from bowling equipment to syringes.

We designed the book to be extremely modular—it consists of 12 independent chapters. Each chapter presents a development methodology for a specific portion of the product development process. The primary benefit of the modular approach is that each chapter can be used independently of the rest of the book. This way, faculty, students, and practitioners can easily access only the material they find most useful. To facilitate the selective use of one or a few chapters of the book, McGraw-Hill publishes this material in three formats: (1) as a traditional integrated volume containing twelve chapters, (2) as a collection of separately bound chapters which can be ordered individually or in any combination, and (3) as a "custom-published" volume from the McGraw-Hill Primis system, which can be specified by an instructor to contain excerpts from other books, case studies, or articles.

The application of structured methodologies to product development also facilitates the study and improvement of development processes. We hope, in fact, that readers will use the ideas in this book as seeds for the creation of their own development methodologies, uniquely suited to their personalities, talents, and company environments. We encourage readers to share their experiences with us and to provide suggestions for improving this material. Please write to us with your ideas and comments: Massachusetts Institute of Technology, Sloan School of Management, 50 Memorial Drive, Cambridge, Massachusetts, 02139; internet: ulrich@mit.edu, eppinger@mit.edu.

ACKNOWLEDGMENTS

Hundreds of people contributed to this book in large and small ways. We are grateful to the many industrial practitioners who provided data, examples, and insights. We appreciate the assistance we have received from numerous academic colleagues, research assistants, and support staff, from our sponsors, and from the McGraw-Hill team. Indeed we could not have completed this project without the cooperation and collaboration of many professionals, colleagues, and friends. Thank you all.

Financial support for much of the development of this textbook has come from the Alfred P. Sloan Foundation and from the MIT Leaders for Manufacturing Program.

Many industrial practitioners helped us in gathering data and developing examples. We would particularly like to acknowledge the following: Richard Ahern (Herbst LaZar Bell), Liz Altman (Motorola), Lindsay Anderson (Boeing), Mario Belsanti (Castronics), Scott Beutler (Motorola), Michael Carter (General Motors), Pat Casey (Polaroid), Victor Cheung (Product Genesis), David Cutherell (DTM), Tom Davis (Hewlett Packard), George Favaloro (Product Genesis), David Fitzpatrick (Boeing), Marc Filerman (Hewlett-Packard), Anthony Giordano (Fitch), David Gordon (Cumberland Foundry), Matt Haggerty (Product Genesis), Matthew Hern (Product Genesis), Alan Huffenus (Brainin Advance Industries), Art Janzen and the Enterprise Design Group (Eastman Kodak), Randy Jezowski (Ramco), Carol Keller (Polaroid), Edward Kreuzer (Brainin Advance Industries), David Lauzun (Chrysler), Peter Lawrence (Corporate Design Foundation), Brian Lee (Product Genesis), David Levy (Apple Computer), Albert Lucchetti (Cumberland Foundry), Doug Miller (Rollerblade), Leo Montagna (Lee Plastics), Al Nagle (Motorola), Hossain Nivi (Ford Motor), E. Timothy Pawl (Pawl Inventioneering), Amy Potts (Design Continuum), Earl Powell (Design Management Institute), Virginia Runkle (General Motors), David Shea (General Motors), Leon Soren (Motorola), Michael Stephens (AMF Bowling), Scott Stropkay (IDEO), Kamala Sundaram (Black & Decker), Malcom Taylor (Foster-Miller), David Webb (Stanley Tools), Bob Weisshappel (Motorola), and Mark Winter (Specialized Bicycle Components).

We have received tremendous assistance from our MIT colleagues. In the Sloan School, our senior colleagues Gabriel Bitran, Charlie Fine, Steve Graves, and Tom Magnanti have offered frequent encouragement and support for our somewhat unusual approach to teaching and research, some of which is reflected in this book. We are especially indebted to the MIT Leaders for Manufacturing (LFM) Program, a unique partnership involving thirteen major US manufacturing firms and MIT's engineering and management schools. We have benefited from collaboration with the faculty and staff associated with the program, especially Kent Bowen, Don Clausing, Tom Eagar, Don Rosenfield, Warren Seering, Shoji Shiba, and Dan Whitney. We have received financial support from LFM and its partner companies; however, most important, LFM companies have provided us with unparalleled access to industrial projects and research problems in product development and manufacturing.

Several faculty members have helped us by reviewing chapter drafts and providing feedback from their in-class trials in teaching with this material. We are particularly grateful to these reviewers and "beta testers": Alice Agogino (University of California, Berkeley), Don Brown (University of Utah), Charles Burnette (University of the Arts), Gary Cadenhead (University of Texas at Austin), Kim Clark (Harvard Business School), Morris Cohen (University of Pennsylvania, Wharton School), Michael Duffey (George Washington University), William Durfee (University of Minnesota), Josh Eliashberg (University of Pennsylvania, Wharton School), Woodie Flowers (MIT), Gary Gabriele (Rensselaer Polytechnic Institute), Abbie Griffin (University of Chicago), Marc Harrison (Rhode Island School of Design), Rebecca Henderson (MIT), Tim Hight (Santa Clara University), Mike Houston (University of Minnesota), Marco Iansiti (Harvard Business School), Kos Ishii (Ohio State University), R. T. Johnson (Wichita State University), Viswanathan Krishnan (University of Texas at Austin), Richard Locke (MIT), Bill Lovejoy (Stanford University), Farrokh Mistree (Georgia Institute of Technology), Wanda Orlikowski (MIT), Warren Seering (MIT), Robert Smith (University of Washington), Carl Sorensen (Brigham Young University), Mark Steiner (University of Louisville), Chuck Turtle (University of Rhode Island), Marcie Tyre (MIT), Dan Whitney (MIT), Kristin Wood (University of Texas at Austin), and Khim-Teck Yeo (Nanyang Technological University).

Several industrial practitioners and training experts have also assisted us by reviewing and commenting on draft chapters: Wesley Allen (CWA Engineering), Geoffrey Boothroyd (Boothroyd Dewhurst), Gary Burchill (US Navy), Eugene Cafarelli (Center for Concept Development), James Carter (United Technologies), David Cutherell (DTM), Gerard Furbershaw (Lunar Design), Jack Harkins (Roche Harkins), Gerhard Jünemann (Daimler Benz), David Meeker (Digital Equipment), Ulrike Närger (Daimler Benz), B. Joseph Pine II (Strategic Horizons), William Townsend (Barrett Technology), Brian Vogel (Product Genesis), and John Wesner (AT&T Bell Laboratories).

We also wish to acknowledge the several hundred students in the classes in which we have tested these teaching materials over the past few years. These students have been in several teaching programs at MIT, STOA (Italy), The University of Pennsylvania, and Nanyang Technological University (Singapore). Many students provided constructive comments for improving the structure and delivery of the material finally contained here. Also, our experiences in observing the students' use of these methodologies in product development projects have greatly helped us to refine the material.

Several MIT students served as research assistants to help investigate many of the development methodologies, examples, and data contained in this book. These students kept the project moving along for the first three years. The students are credited in each individual chapter and we also list them here: Paul

Brody (Chapter 8), Tom Foody (Chapter 11), Amy Greenlief (Chapter 10), Eric Howlett (Chapter 6), Tom Pimmler (Chapter 9 Appendices), Stephen Raab (Chapter 12), Jonathan Sterrett (Chapter 3), and Gavin Zau (Chapter 5).

Other research students have also contributed by assisting with data collection and by offering comments and stimulating criticisms related to some of the chapters: Tom Abell, E. Yung Cha, Matthew Fein, Daniel Hommes, and Vikas Sharma. We also appreciate the cheerful and able assistance of our MIT support staff, Kristin Rocheleau and Anna Piccolo.

The staff throughout the McGraw-Hill organization has been superb. We are particularly grateful for the enduring efforts of our editor Bonnie Binkert, who has encouraged, supported, and rewarded us with her enthusiasm over more than three years. We also appreciate the efforts of senior engineering editor John Corrigan, senior editing supervisor Sheila Gillams, copy editor Linda Biemiller, photo editor Anne Manning, and photographer Stuart Cohen. We are also fortunate to have been able to work with cover designers Nadine Flowers and Julie Townsend at Barrett Design.

Finally, we thank our families for their love and support. Our parents provided much encouragement. Our wives gave us constant support (our children tried too) during many long days of this four-year project.

Karl T. Ulrich
Steven D. Eppinger

PRODUCT DESIGN AND DEVELOPMENT

INTRODUCTION

EXHIBIT 1   Examples of engineered, discrete, physical products (*clockwise from top left*): Stanley Tools Jobmaster Screwdriver (Stuart Cohen), Hewlett-Packard DeskJet 500 Printer (courtesy of Hewlett-Packard), Boeing 777 Airplane (courtesy of *Aviation Weekly*), Chrysler Concorde Automobile (courtesy of Chrysler Corp.), and Rollerblade Bravoblade In-Line Skate (courtesy of Rollerblade, Inc.).

The economic success of manufacturing firms depends on their ability to identify the needs of customers and to quickly create products that meet these needs and can be produced at low cost. Achieving these goals is not solely a marketing problem, nor is it solely a design problem or a manufacturing problem; it is a product development problem involving all of these functions. This book is a collection of methodologies intended to enhance the abilities of cross-functional teams to work together to develop products.

A *product* is something sold by an enterprise to its customers. *Product development* is the set of activities beginning with the perception of a market opportunity and ending in the production, sale, and delivery of a product. Although much of the material in this book is useful in the development of any product, we explicitly focus on products that are engineered, discrete, and physical. Exhibit 1 displays several examples of products from this category. Because we focus on engineered products, the book applies better to the development of power tools and computer peripherals rather than teddy bears or sweaters. Our focus on discrete goods makes the book less applicable to the development of products such as gasoline, nylon, and paper. Because of the focus on physical products, we do not emphasize the specific issues involved in developing services or software. Even with these restrictions, the methodologies presented apply well to a broad range of products, including, for example, consumer electronics, scientific instruments, machine tools, and medical devices.

The goal of this book is to present in a clear and detailed way a set of product development methodologies aimed at bringing together the marketing, design, and manufacturing functions of the enterprise. In this introductory chapter we describe some aspects of the industrial practice of product development and provide a road map of the book.

CHARACTERISTICS OF SUCCESSFUL PRODUCT DEVELOPMENT

From the perspective of the investors in a for-profit enterprise, successful product development results in products that can be produced and sold profitably, yet profitability is often difficult to assess quickly and directly. Five more specific dimensions, all of which ultimately relate to profit, are commonly used to assess the performance of a product development effort:

- *Product quality:* How good is the product resulting from the development effort? Does it satisfy customer needs? Is it robust and reliable? Product quality is ultimately reflected in market share and the price that customers are willing to pay.

- *Product cost:* What is the manufacturing cost of the product? This cost includes spending on capital equipment and tooling as well as the incremental cost of producing each unit of the product. Product cost determines how much profit accrues to the firm for a particular sales volume and a particular sales price.

- *Development time:* How quickly did the team complete the product development effort? Development time determines how responsive the firm can be to competitive forces and to technological developments, as well as how quickly the firm receives the economic returns from the team's efforts.

- *Development cost:* How much did the firm have to spend to develop the product? Development cost is usually a significant fraction of the investment required to achieve the profits.

- *Development capability:* Are the team and the firm better able to develop future products as a result of their experience with a product development project? Development capability is an asset the firm can use to develop products more effectively and economically in the future.

High performance along these five dimensions should ultimately lead to economic success; however, other performance criteria are also important. These criteria arise from interests of other stakeholders in the enterprise, including the members of the development team, other employees, and the community in which the product is manufactured. Members of the development team may be interested in creating an inherently exciting product. Members of the community in which the product is manufactured may be concerned about the degree to which the product creates jobs. Both production workers and users of the product hold the development team accountable for high safety standards, whether or not these standards can be justified on the strict basis of profitability. Other individuals, who may have no direct connection to the firm or the product, may demand that the product make ecologically sound use of resources and create minimal dangerous waste products.

WHO DESIGNS AND DEVELOPS PRODUCTS?

Product development is an interdisciplinary activity requiring contributions from nearly all the functions of a firm; however, three functions are almost always central to a product development project:

- *Marketing:* The marketing function mediates the interactions between the firm and its customers. Marketing often facilitates the identification of product opportunities, the definition of market segments, and the identification of customer needs. Marketing also typically arranges for communication between the firm and its customers, sets prices, and oversees the launch and promotion of the product.

- *Design:* The design function leads the definition of the physical form of the product to best meet customer needs. In this context, the design function includes engineering design (mechanical, electrical, software, etc.) and industrial design (aesthetics, ergonomics, user interfaces).

- *Manufacturing:* The manufacturing function is primarily responsible for designing and operating the production system in order to produce the product. Broadly defined, the manufacturing function also often includes purchasing, distribution, and installation.

Different individuals within these functions often have specific disciplinary training in areas such as market research, mechanical engineering, electrical engineering, materials science, or manufacturing operations. Several other functions, including finance, sales, and legal functions, are frequently involved on a part-time basis in the development of a new product. Beyond these broad functional categories, the specific composition of a development team depends on the particular characteristics of the product.

Few products are developed by a single individual. The collection of individuals developing a product form the *project team*. This team usually has a single team leader, who could be drawn from any of the functions of the firm. The team can be thought of as consisting of a *core team* and an *extended team*. In order to work together effectively, the core team usually remains small enough to meet in a conference room, while the extended team may consist of dozens, hundreds, or even thousands of other members. (Even though the term *team* is inappropriate for a group of thousands, the word is often used in this context to emphasize that the group must work toward a common goal.) In most cases, a team within the firm will be supported by individuals or teams at partner companies, suppliers, and consulting firms. Sometimes, as is the case for the development of a new airplane, the number of external team members may be even greater than that of the team within the company whose name will appear on the final product. The composition of a team for the development of an electromechanical product of modest complexity is shown in Exhibit 2.

Throughout this book we assume that the team is situated within a firm. In fact, a for-profit manufacturing company is the most common institutional setting for product development, but other settings are possible. Product development teams sometimes work within consulting firms, universities, government agencies, and nonprofit organizations.

DURATION AND COST OF PRODUCT DEVELOPMENT

Most people without experience in product development are astounded by how much time and money is required to develop a new product. The reality is that very few products can be developed in less than one year, many require three to five years, and some take as long as ten years. Exhibit 1 shows five engineered, discrete products. Exhibit 3 is a table showing the approximate scale of the associated product development efforts along with some distinguishing characteristics of the products.

The cost of product development is roughly proportional to the number of people on the project team and to the duration of the project. In addition to expenses for development effort, a firm will almost always have to make some investment in the tooling and equipment required for production. This expense is often as large as the rest of the product development budget; however, it is sometimes useful to think of these expenditures as part of the *fixed costs* of pro-

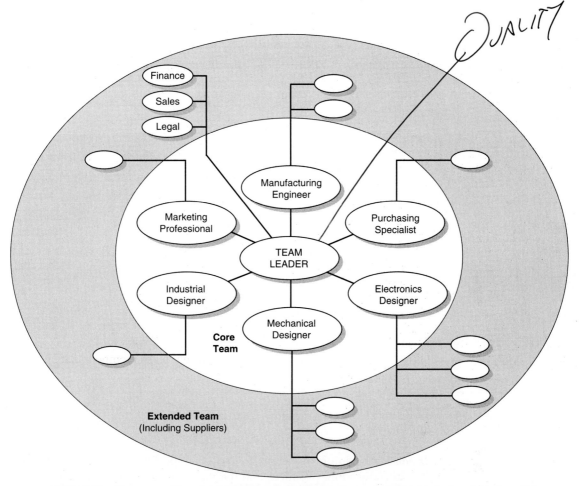

EXHIBIT 2 The composition of a product development team for an electromechanical product of modest complexity.

duction. For reference purposes, this production investment is listed in Exhibit 3 along with the development expenditures.

THE CHALLENGES OF PRODUCT DEVELOPMENT

Developing great products is hard. Few companies are highly successful more than half the time. These odds present a significant challenge for a product development team. Some of the characteristics that make product development challenging are:

- *Trade-offs:* An airplane can be made lighter, but this action will probably increase manufacturing cost. One of the most difficult aspects of product development is recognizing, understanding, and managing such trade-offs in a way that maximizes the success of the product.

	Stanley Tools Jobmaster Screwdriver	Rollerblade Bravoblade In-Line Skates	Hewlett-Packard DeskJet 500 Printer	Chrysler Concorde Automobile	Boeing 777 Airplane
Annual-production volume	100,000 units/year	100,000 units/year	1.5 million units/year	250,000 units/year	50 units/year
Sales lifetime	40 years	3 years	3 years	6 years	30 years
Sales price	$3	$200	$365	$19,000	$130 million
Number of unique parts (part numbers)	3 parts	35 parts	200 parts	10,000 parts	130,000 parts
Development time	1 year	2 years	1.5 years	3.5 years	4.5 years
Internal development team (peak size)	3 people	5 people	100 people	850 people	6,800 people
External development team (peak size)	3 people	10 people	100 people	1400 people	10,000 people
Development cost	$150,000	$750,000	$50 million	$1 billion	$3 billion
Production investment	$150,000	$1 million	$25 million	$600 million	$3 billion

EXHIBIT 3 Attributes of five products and their associated development efforts. All figures are approximate, based on publicly available information and company sources.

- *Dynamics:* Technologies improve, customer preferences evolve, competitors introduce new products, and the macroeconomic environment shifts. Decision making in an environment of constant change is a formidable task.

- *Details:* The choice between using screws or snap-fits on the enclosure of a computer printer can have economic implications of millions of dollars. Developing a product of even modest complexity may require thousands of such decisions.

- *Time pressure:* Any one of these difficulties would be easily manageable by itself given plenty of time, but product development decisions must usually be made quickly and without complete information.

For many people, product development is interesting precisely because it is challenging. For others, several intrinsic attributes also contribute to its appeal:

- *Creation:* The product development process begins with an idea and ends with the production of a physical artifact. When viewed both in its entirety and at the level of individual activities, the product development process is intensely creative.

- *Satisfaction of societal and individual needs:* All products are aimed at satisfying needs of some kind. Individuals interested in developing new products can almost always find institutional settings in which they can develop products satisfying what they consider to be important needs.
- *Team diversity:* Successful development requires many different skills and talents. As a result, development teams involve people with a wide range of different training, experience, perspectives, and personalities.
- *Team spirit:* Product development teams are often highly motivated, cooperative groups. The team members may be co-located so they can focus their collective energy on creating the product. This situation can result in lasting camaraderie among team members.

STANDARDS? QUALITY

APPROACH OF THIS BOOK

We focus on product development activities that benefit from the participation of all of the core functions of the firm. For our purposes, we define the core functions as marketing, design, and manufacturing. We expect that team members have competence in one or more specific disciplines such as mechanical engineering, electrical engineering, industrial design, market research, or manufacturing operations. For this reason, we do not discuss, for example, how to perform a stress analysis or to create a conjoint survey. These are disciplinary skills we expect someone on the development team to possess. The integrative methodologies in this book are intended to facilitate problem solving and decision making among people with different disciplinary perspectives.

We also focus on a limited segment of the product development process. We specifically exclude the very early phases of product development, including the development of basic technologies and market strategy. We assume that the team begins with a mission statement identifying a target market and the core benefit the product will provide to that market. The methodologies in the book are those we believe are required to integrate different functional perspectives in order to transform this mission into a tangible product.

Structured Methodologies

The book consists of *methodologies*—procedures for completing development activities. The methodologies are structured, which means we generally provide a step-by-step approach and often provide templates for the key information systems used by the team. We believe structured methodologies are valuable for three reasons: First, they make the decision process explicit, allowing everyone on the team to understand the decision rationale and reducing the possibility of moving forward with unsupported decisions. Second, by acting as "checklists" of the key steps in a development activity they ensure that important issues are not forgotten. Third, structured methodologies are largely self-documenting; in the process of executing the methodology the team creates a record of the decision-making process for future reference and for educating newcomers.

Although the methodologies are structured, they are not intended to be applied blindly. The methodologies are a starting point for continuous improvement. Teams should adapt and modify the approaches to meet their own needs and to reflect the unique character of their institutional environment.

Industrial Examples

Each remaining chapter is built around an example drawn from industrial practice. The major examples include the following: a line of bowling equipment, a cordless screwdriver, a mountain bike suspension fork, a power nailer, a dose-metering syringe, a rapid prototyping machine, a cellular telephone, an automobile engine, a trackball for a notebook computer, a computer printer, and a microfilm cartridge. In most cases we use as examples the simplest products we have access to that illustrate the important aspects of the methodologies. When a screwdriver illustrates an idea as well as a jet engine, we use the screwdriver. However, every methodology in this book has been used successfully in industrial practice on both large and small projects.

Although built around examples, the chapters are not intended to be historically accurate case studies. We have used the examples as a way to illustrate development methodologies and in doing so have recast some historical details in a way that improves the presentation of the material. We have also disguised much of the quantitative information in the examples, especially financial data.

Organizational Realities

We have deliberately chosen to present the methodologies with the assumption that the development team operates in an organizational environment conducive to success. In reality, some organizations exhibit characteristics that lead to dysfunctional product development teams. These characteristics include:

- *Lack of empowerment of the team:* General managers or functional managers may engage in continual intervention in the details of a development project without a full understanding of the basis for the team's decisions.
- *Functional allegiances transcending project goals:* Representatives of marketing, design, or manufacturing may influence decisions in order to increase the political standing of themselves or their functions without regard for the overall success of the product.
- *Inadequate resources:* A team may be unable to complete development tasks effectively because of a lack of staff, a mismatch of skills, or a lack of money, equipment, or tools.

- *Lack of cross-functional representation on the project team:* Key development decisions may be made without involvement of marketing, design, manufacturing, or other critical functions.

While most organizations exhibit one or more of these characteristics to some degree, the significant presence of these problems can be so stifling that sound development methodologies are rendered ineffective. While recognizing the importance of basic organizational issues, we assume, for clarity of explanation, that the development team operates in an environment in which the most restrictive organizational barriers have been removed.

Road Map of the Book

We divide the product development process into five phases, as shown in Exhibit 4. (These phases are described in more detail in the chapter "Development Processes and Organizations.") This book describes the concept development phase in its entirety and the remaining phases less completely, because we do

EXHIBIT 4 The product development process. The diagram shows where each of the integrative methodologies presented in the remaining chapters is most applicable.

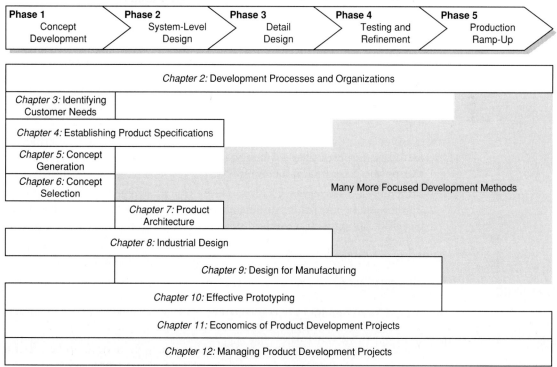

not provide methodologies for the more focused development activities that are applied later in the process. Each of the remaining chapters in this book can be read, understood, and applied independently.

- Chapter 2, "Development Processes and Organizations," presents a generic product development process and shows how variants of this process are used in different industrial situations. The chapter also discusses the way individuals are organized into groups in order to undertake product development projects.

- Chapters 3 through 6, "Identifying Customer Needs," "Establishing Product Specifications," "Concept Generation," and "Concept Selection," present the four key activities of the concept development phase. These methodologies guide a team from a mission statement through a selected product concept.

- Chapter 7, "Product Architecture," discusses the implications of product architecture on product change, product variety, component standardization, product performance, manufacturing cost, and project management; it then presents a methodology for establishing the architecture of a product.

- Chapter 8, "Industrial Design," discusses the role of the industrial designer and how human interaction issues, including aesthetics and ergonomics, are treated in product development.

- Chapter 9, "Design for Manufacturing," discusses techniques used to reduce manufacturing cost. These techniques are primarily applied during the system-level and detail-design phases of the process.

- Chapter 10, "Effective Prototyping," presents a methodology to assure that prototyping efforts, which occur throughout the process, are applied effectively.

- Chapter 11, "Economics of Product Development Projects," describes a methodology for understanding the influence of internal and external factors on the economic value of a project.

- Chapter 12, "Managing Product Development Projects," presents some fundamental concepts for understanding and representing interacting project tasks, along with a methodology for planning and executing a development project.

REFERENCES AND BIBLIOGRAPHY

Two large industry studies were conducted by MIT in the 1980s. They highlighted management practices believed to have caused many important U.S. industries to decline in the 1970s and 1980s. They suggest several remedies to these problems, including a renewed focus on improving product development practices.

Dertouzos, Michael L., Richard K. Lester, Robert M. Solow, and The MIT Commission on Industrial Productivity, *Made in America: Regaining the Productive Edge*, MIT Press, Cambridge, MA, 1989. ISBN 0-262-04100-6.

Womack, James P., Daniel T. Jones, and Daniel Roos, *The Machine That Changed the World*, Rawson Associates, New York, 1990. ISBN 0-89256-350-8.

Wheelwright and Clark devote much of their book to the very early stages of product development, which we do not discuss.

Wheelwright, Stephen C., and Kim B. Clark, *Revolutionizing Product Development: Quantum Leaps in Speed, Efficiency, and Quality*, The Free Press, New York, 1992. ISBN 0-02-905515-6.

Katzenbach and Smith write about teams in general, but most of their insights apply to product development teams as well.

Katzenbach, Jon R., and Douglas K. Smith, *The Wisdom of Teams: Creating the High-Performance Organization*, Harvard Business School Press, Boston, MA, 1993. ISBN 0-87584-367-0.

Kidder effectively communicates the excitement of product development for a technology-dominated product, a computer workstation.

Kidder, Tracy, *The Soul of a New Machine*, Avon Books, New York, 1981. ISBN 0-380-59931-7.

EXERCISES

1 Estimate what fraction of the price of a pocket calculator is required to cover the cost of developing the product. To do this you might start by estimating the information needed to fill out Exhibit 3 for the pocket calculator.
2 Create a set of scatter charts by plotting each of the rows in Exhibit 3 against the development cost row. For each one, explain why there is or is not any correlation. (For example, you would first plot "annual production volume" versus "development cost" and explain why there seems to be no correlation. Then repeat for each of the remaining rows.)

THOUGHT QUESTION

1 Each of the chapters listed in Exhibit 4 presents a methodology for a portion of the product development process. For each one, consider what types of skills and expertise might be required. Can you make an argument for staffing the development team from start to finish with individuals possessing all of these skills and areas of expertise?

DEVELOPMENT PROCESSES AND ORGANIZATIONS

EXHIBIT 1   A ball return, one of AMF Bowling's products.   (Arthur Stephens)

The Capital Equipment Division of AMF Bowling is the leading manufacturer of bowling equipment, including pin spotters, ball returns, and scoring equipment. An AMF ball return product is shown in Exhibit 1. The general manager of the division asked the engineering manager to establish a well-defined product development process and to propose a product development organization that would allow AMF to compete effectively over the next decade. Some of the questions AMF faced were:

- Is there a "standard" development process that will work for every company?
- What role do experts from different functional areas play in the development process?
- What milestones can be used to divide the overall development process into phases?
- Should the development organization be divided into groups corresponding to projects or to development functions?

This chapter helps to answer these and related questions by presenting a generic development process and showing how this process can be adapted to meet the needs of particular industrial situations. We highlight the activities and contributions of different functions of the company during each phase of the development process. The chapter also explains what constitutes a product development organization and discusses why different types of organizations are appropriate for different settings.

A GENERIC DEVELOPMENT PROCESS

A process is a sequence of steps that transforms a set of inputs into a set of outputs. Most people are familiar with the idea of physical processes, such as those used to bake a cake or to assemble an automobile. A *product development process* is the sequence of steps or activities that an enterprise employs to conceive, design, and commercialize a product. Many of these steps and activities are intellectual and organizational rather than physical. Some organizations define and follow a precise and detailed development process, while others may not even be able to describe their processes. Furthermore, every organization employs a process at least slightly different from that of every other organization. In fact, the same enterprise may follow different processes for each of several different types of development projects.

A well-defined development process is useful for the following reasons:

- *Quality assurance:* A development process specifies the phases a development project will pass through and the checkpoints along the way. Assuming that these phases and checkpoints are chosen wisely, following the development process is one way of assuring the quality of the resulting product.

Concept Development	System-Level Design	Detail Design	Testing and Refinement	Production Ramp-Up
Marketing				
• Define market segments. • Identify lead users. • Identify competitive products.	• Develop plan for product options and extended product family.	• Develop marketing plan.	• Develop promotion and launch materials. • Facilitate field testing.	• Place early production with key customers.
Design				
• Investigate feasibility of product concepts. • Develop industrial design concepts. • Build and test experimental prototypes.	• Generate alternative product architectures. • Define major sub-systems and interfaces. • Refine industrial design.	• Define part geometry. • Choose materials. • Assign tolerances. • Complete industrial design control documentation.	• Do reliability testing, life testing, and performance testing. • Obtain regulatory approvals. • Implement design changes.	• Evaluate early production output.
Manufacturing				
• Estimate manufacturing cost. • Assess production feasibility.	• Identify suppliers for key components. • Perform make-buy analysis. • Define final assembly scheme.	• Define piece-part production processes. • Design tooling. • Define quality assurance processes. • Begin procurement of long-lead tooling.	• Facilitate supplier ramp-up. • Refine fabrication and assembly processes. • Train work force. • Refine quality assurance processes.	• Begin operation of entire production system.
Other Functions				
• Finance: Facilitate economic analysis. • Legal: Investigate patent issues.	• Finance: Facilitate make-buy analysis. • Service: Identify service issues.		• Sales: Develop sales plan.	

EXHIBIT 2   A generic development process. Five phases are shown, including the tasks and responsibilities of the key functions of the organization.

- *Coordination:* A clearly articulated development process acts as a master plan which defines the roles of each of the players on the development team. This plan informs the members of the team when their contributions will be needed and with whom they will need to exchange information and materials.

- *Planning:* A development process contains natural milestones corresponding to the completion of each phase. The timing of these milestones anchors the schedule of the overall development project.

- *Management:* A development process is a benchmark for assessing the performance of an ongoing development effort. By comparing the actual events to the established process, a manager can identify possible problem areas.

- *Improvement:* The careful documentation of an organization's development process often helps to identify opportunities for improvement.

A generic product development process is illustrated in Exhibit 2. The process consists of five phases. The input to the process is a mission statement and the output of the process is the product launch. The mission statement identifies the target market for the product, provides a basic functional description of the product, and specifies the business goals of the effort. (The mission statement is described in more detail in the introduction to the chapter "Identifying Customer Needs.") The product launch occurs when the product becomes available for purchase in the marketplace.

One way to think about the development process is as the initial creation of a wide set of alternative product concepts and then the subsequent narrowing of alternatives and increasing specification of the product until the product can be reliably and repeatably produced by the production system. Note that most of the phases of development are defined in terms of the state of the product, although the production process and marketing plans, among other tangible outputs, are also evolving as development progresses.

Exhibit 2 also identifies the key activities and responsibilities of the different functions of the organization during each development phase. Because of their continual involvement in the process, we choose to articulate the roles of marketing, design, and manufacturing. Representatives from other functions, such as research, finance, field service, documentation, and sales, also play key roles at particular points in the process.

The five phases of the generic development process are:

1 *Concept development:* In the concept development phase, the needs of the target market are identified, alternative product concepts are generated and evaluated, and a single concept is selected for further development. A concept is a description of the form, function, and features of a product and is usually accompanied by a set of specifications, an analysis of competitive products, and an economic justification of the project. Because this

book contains several methodologies for the concept development phase, we expand this phase into each of its constitutive activities in the next section.

2 *System-level design:* The system-level design phase includes the definition of the product architecture and the division of the product into subsystems and components. The final assembly scheme for the production system is usually defined during this phase as well. The output of this phase is usually a geometric "layout" of the product, a functional specification of each of the product's subsystems, and a preliminary process flow diagram for the final assembly process. (See the chapter "Product Architecture" for a discussion of some of the important activities during system-level design.)

3 *Detail design:* The detail design phase includes the complete specification of the geometry, materials, and tolerances of all of the unique parts in the product and the identification of all of the standard parts to be purchased from suppliers. A process plan is established and tooling is designed for each part to be fabricated within the production system. The output of this phase is the *control documentation* for the product—the drawings or computer files describing the geometry of each part and its production tooling, the specifications of the purchased parts, and the process plans for the fabrication and assembly of the product. (See the chapter "Design for Manufacturing" for a discussion of a few of the issues faced in the detail design phase.)

4 *Testing and refinement:* The testing and refinement phase involves the construction and evaluation of multiple preproduction versions of the product. Early (*alpha*) prototypes are usually built with *production-intent* parts—parts with the same geometry and material properties as intended for the production version of the product but not necessarily fabricated with the actual processes to be used in production. Alpha prototypes are tested to determine whether or not the product will work as designed and whether or not the product satisfies the key customer needs. Later (*beta*) prototypes are usually built with parts supplied by the intended production processes but may not be assembled using the intended final assembly process. Beta prototypes are extensively evaluated internally and are also typically tested by customers in their own use environment. The goal for the beta prototypes is usually to answer questions about performance and reliability in order to identify necessary changes for the final product. (See the chapter "Effective Prototyping" for a more thorough discussion of the nature and use of prototypes.)

5 *Production ramp-up:* In the production ramp-up phase the product is made using the intended production system. The purpose of the ramp-up is to train the work force and to work out any remaining problems in the production processes. The artifacts produced during production ramp-up are sometimes supplied to preferred customers and are carefully evaluated to

identify any remaining flaws. The transition from production ramp-up to ongoing production is usually gradual and continuous. At some point in this transition, the product is *launched* and becomes available for widespread distribution.

CONCEPT DEVELOPMENT: THE FRONT-END PROCESS

Because the concept development phase of the development process demands perhaps more coordination among functions than any other, many of the integrative development methodologies presented in this book are concentrated here. In this section we expand the concept development phase into what we call the *front-end process*. The front-end process generally contains the following distinct activities, ordered roughly as shown in Exhibit 3.

- *Identifying customer needs:* The goal of this activity is to understand customers' needs and to effectively communicate them to the development team. The output of this step is a set of carefully constructed customer need statements, organized in a hierarchical list, with importance weightings for each need. (A methodology for this activity is contained in the chapter "Identifying Customer Needs.")

- *Establishing target specifications:* Specifications are a precise description of what a product has to do. They are the translation of the customer needs into technical terms. Targets for the specifications are set early in the process and represent the hopes of the development team. Later these specifications are refined to be consistent with the constraints imposed by the team's choice of a product concept. The output of this stage is a list of specifications. Each specification consists of a metric and a target value for that metric. (A methodology for the specification activity is contained in the chapter "Establishing Product Specifications.")

EXHIBIT 3 Concept development: the front-end activities.

- *Analysis of competitive products:* An understanding of competitive products is critical to successful positioning of a new product and can provide a rich source of ideas for the product and production process design. Analysis of competitive products is also called *competitive benchmarking.* Competitive benchmarking is performed in support of the specifications activity as well as in support of concept generation and concept selection. (The chapters "Establishing Product Specifications," "Concept Generation," and "Concept Selection" each discuss the role of competitive benchmarking.)

- *Concept generation:* The goal of concept generation is to explore thoroughly the space of product concepts that may be applied to meeting the customer needs. Concept generation includes a mix of external search, creative problem solving within the team, and systematic exploration of the various solution fragments the team generates. The result of this activity is usually a set of 10 to 20 concepts, each typically represented by a sketch and brief descriptive text. (The chapter "Concept Generation" describes this activity in detail.)

- *Concept selection:* Concept selection is the activity in which various product concepts are analyzed and sequentially eliminated to identify one preferred concept. The process usually requires several iterations and may initiate additional concept generation and refinement. (A methodology for this activity is described in the chapter "Concept Selection.")

- *Refinement of specifications:* The target specifications set earlier in the process are revisited after a concept has been selected. At this point, the team must commit to specific values of the metrics reflecting the constraints inherent in the product concept, limitations identified through technical modeling, and trade-offs between cost and performance. (The chapter "Establishing Product Specifications" explains the details of this activity.)

- *Economic analysis:* The team, often with the support of a financial analyst, builds an economic model for the new product. This model is used to justify continuation of the overall development program and to resolve specific trade-offs among, for example, development costs and manufacturing costs. While economic analysis is shown as one of the later activities in the concept development phase, an early economic analysis will almost always be performed before the project even begins. (A methodology for this activity is presented in the chapter "Economics of Product Development Projects.")

- *Project planning:* In this final activity of concept development, the team creates a detailed development schedule, devises a strategy to minimize development time, and identifies the resources required to complete the project. The major results of the front-end activities can be usefully captured in a *contract book* that contains the mission statement, the customer needs, the details of the selected concept, the product specifications, the economic analysis of the product, the development schedule, the project staffing, and the budget. The contract book serves to document the agreement (contract) between the team and the senior management of the enterprise. (A project planning methodology is presented in the chapter "Managing Product Development Projects.")

ADAPTING THE GENERIC PRODUCT DEVELOPMENT PROCESS

The development process described by Exhibits 2 and 3 is generic, and particular processes will differ in accordance with a firm's unique context. The generic process is most like the process used in a *market-pull* situation: a firm begins product development with a market opportunity and then seeks out whatever technologies are required to satisfy the market need (that is, the market pulls the development decisions). In addition to the market-pull process outlined in Exhibits 2 and 3, several variants are common and correspond to the following: *technology-push* products, *platform* products, *process-intensive* products, and *customized* products. Each of these situations is described below. The characteristics of these situations and the resulting deviations from the generic process are summarized in Exhibit 4.

EXHIBIT 4 Summary of variants of generic development process.

	Generic (Market Pull)	Technology-Push	Platform Products	Process-Intensive	Customized
Description	The firm begins with a market opportunity, then finds an appropriate technology to meet customer needs.	The firm begins with a new technology, then finds an appropriate market.	The firm assumes that the new product will be built around the same technological sub-system as an existing product.	Characteristics of the product are highly constrained by the production process.	New products are slight variations of existing configurations.
Distinctions with respect to generic process		Additional initial activity of matching technology and market. Concept development assumes a given technology.	Concept development assumes a technology platform.	Both process and product must be developed together from the very beginning, or an existing production process must be specified from the beginning.	Similarity of projects allows for a highly structured development process. Development process is almost like a production process.
Examples	Sporting goods, furniture, tools.	Gore-Tex rainwear, Tyvek envelopes.	Consumer electronics, computers, printers.	Snack foods, cereal, chemicals, semiconductors.	Switches, motors, batteries, containers.

Technology-Push Products

In developing technology-push products the firm begins with a new proprietary technology and looks for an appropriate market in which to apply this technology (that is, the technology pushes development). Gore-Tex, an expanded Teflon sheet manufactured by W. L. Gore Associates, is a striking example of technology push. The company has developed dozens of products incorporating Gore-Tex, including artificial veins for vascular surgery, insulation for high-performance electric cables, fabric for outerwear, dental floss, and liners for bagpipe bags.

Many successful technology-push products involve basic materials or basic process technologies. This may be because basic materials and processes are deployed in thousands of applications, and there is therefore a high likelihood that new and unusual characteristics of materials and processes can be matched with an appropriate application.

The generic product development process can be used with minor modifications for technology-push products. The technology-push process begins with an additional phase to match a given technology with a market opportunity. Once this matching has occurred, the generic process can be carried out. The team simply makes the assumption in the mission statement that the firm's proprietary technology will be embodied in the product concepts considered by the team. Although there are many extremely successful products that have arisen from technology-push development, this approach can be perilous. Unless the assumed technology offers a clear competitive advantage in meeting customer needs, the product is unlikely to succeed. This risk can be minimized by simultaneously considering the merit of a broader set of concepts which do not necessarily incorporate the new technology. In this way the team verifies that the product concept embodying the new technology is superior to the alternatives.

Platform Products

A platform product is built around a pre-existing technological subsystem (a technology *platform*). Examples of such platforms include the tape transport mechanism in the Sony Walkman, the Apple Macintosh operating system, and the instant film used in Polaroid cameras. Huge investments were made in developing these platforms, and therefore every attempt is made to incorporate them into several different products. In some sense, platform products are very similar to technology-push products in that the team begins the development effort with an assumption that the product concept will embody a particular technology. The primary difference is that a technology platform has already demonstrated its usefulness in the marketplace in meeting customer needs. The firm can in many cases assume that the technology will also be useful in related markets. Products built on technology platforms are much simpler to develop than if the technology were developed from scratch. For this reason, and because of the possible sharing of costs across several products, a firm may be able to offer a platform product in markets that could not justify the development of a unique technology.

Process-Intensive Products

Examples of process-intensive products include semiconductors, foods, chemicals, and paper. For these products, the production process places strict constraints on the properties of the product, so that the product design cannot be separated, even at the concept phase, from the production process design. In many cases, process-intensive products are produced in very high volumes and are bulk, as opposed to discrete, goods.

In some situations, a new product and new process are developed simultaneously. For example, creating a new shape of breakfast cereal or snack food will require both product and process development activities. In other cases, a specific existing process for making the product is chosen in advance, and the product design is constrained by the capabilities of this process. This might be true of a new paper product to be made in a particular paper mill or a new semiconductor device to be made in an existing wafer fabrication facility.

Customized Products

Examples of customized products include switches, motors, batteries, and containers. Customized products are slight variations of standard configurations and are typically developed in response to a specific order by a customer. Development of customized products consists primarily of setting values of design variables such as physical dimensions and materials. When a customer requests a new product, the firm executes a structured design and development process to create the product to meet the customer's needs. Such firms typically have created highly detailed development processes involving dozens of steps that, because of the structured flow of information and well-defined sequence of steps, are quite similar to production processes. For customized products, the generic process is augmented with a detailed description of the specific information processing activities required within each of the five phases. Such development processes may consist of hundreds of carefully defined activities.

THE AMF DEVELOPMENT PROCESS

AMF Bowling is a market-pull enterprise. AMF generally drives its development process with a market need and seeks out whatever technology is required to meet that need. Its competitive advantage arises from strong marketing channels, strong brand recognition, and a large installed base of equipment, and not from any single proprietary technology. For this reason, the technology-push approach would not be appropriate. AMF products are assembled from components fabricated with relatively conventional processes such as molding, casting, and machining. So the AMF product is clearly not process intensive in the way a food product or a chemical is. Bowling equipment is rarely customized for a particular customer; most of the product development at AMF is aimed at new models of products, rather than at the customization of existing models. For this reason, the customization approach is also inappropriate.

AMF chose to establish a development process similar to the generic process. The process proposed by the AMF engineering manager is illustrated in Exhibit 5. The representation of the development process used by AMF is a hybrid of those used in Exhibits 2 and 3, in that it shows the individual activities in the development process as well as the roles of the different development functions in those activities. Note that AMF defines the key functions in new product development as marketing, engineering/design, manufacturing, quality assurance, purchasing, and customer service. Also note that there are three major milestones in the process: the project approval, the beginning of tooling fabrication, and "production release." Each of these milestones follows a major review.

Although AMF established a standard process, its managers realized that this process would not necessarily be suitable in its entirety for all AMF products. For example, a few of AMF's new products are based on technology platforms. When platform products are developed, the team assumes the use of an existing technology platform during concept development. Nevertheless, the standard development process is the baseline from which a particular project plan begins.

PRODUCT DEVELOPMENT ORGANIZATIONS

In addition to crafting an effective development process, successful firms must organize their product development staffs effectively. In this section, we describe several types of organizations used for product development and offer guidelines for choosing among these options.

Organizations Are Formed by Establishing Links Among Individuals

A product development organization is the scheme by which individual designers and developers are linked together into groups. The links among individuals may be formal or informal and include, among others, these types:

- *Reporting relationships:* Reporting relationships give rise to the classic notion of *supervisor* and *subordinate.* These are the formal links most frequently shown on an organization chart.

- *Financial arrangements:* Individuals are linked by being part of the same financial entity, such as that defined by a particular budget category or profit-and-loss statement.

- *Physical layout:* Links are created between individuals when they share the same office, floor, building, or site. These links are often informal, arising from spontaneous encounters while at work.

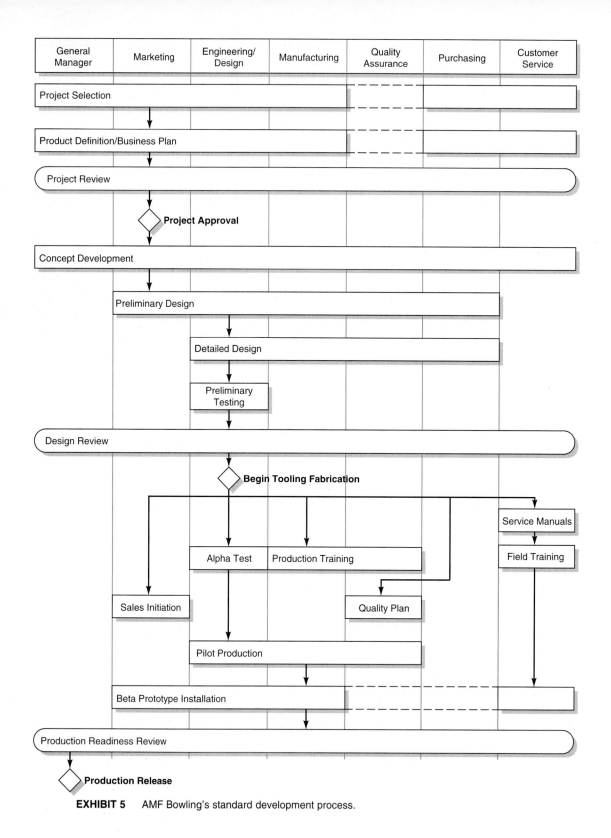

EXHIBIT 5   AMF Bowling's standard development process.

Any particular individual may be linked in several different ways to other individuals. For example, an engineer may be linked by a reporting relationship to another engineer in a different building, while being linked by physical layout to a marketing person sitting in the next office. The strongest organizational links are typically those involving performance evaluation, budgets, and other resource allocations.

Organizational Links May Be Aligned with Functions, Projects, or Both

Regardless of their organizational links, particular individuals can be classified in two different ways: according to their *function* and according to the *projects* they work on.

- A function (in organizational terms) is an area of responsibility usually involving specialized education, training, or experience. The classic functions in product development organizations are marketing, design, and manufacturing. Finer divisions than these are also possible and may include, for example, market research, market strategy, stress analysis, industrial design, human factors engineering, process development, and operations management.
- Regardless of their functions, individuals apply their expertise to specific projects. In product development, a project is the set of activities in the development process for a particular product and includes, for example, identifying customer needs, generating product concepts, etc.

Note that these two classifications must overlap: individuals from several different functions will work on the same project. Also, while most individuals are associated with only one function, they may contribute to more than one project. Two classic organizational structures arise from aligning the organizational links according to function or according to projects. In *functional organizations*, the organizational links are primarily among those who perform similar functions. In *project organizations*, the organizational links are primarily among those who work on the same project.

For example, a strict functional organization might include a group of marketing professionals, all sharing similar training and expertise. These people would all report to the same manager who would evaluate them and set their salaries. The group would have its own budget and the people would sit in the same part of a building. This marketing group would be involved in many different projects, but there would be no strong organizational links to the other members of each project team. There would be similarly arranged groups corresponding to design and to manufacturing.

A strict project organization would be made up of groups of people from several different functions, with each group focused on the development of a specific product (or product line). These groups would each report to an experienced project manager, who might be drawn from any of the functional areas. Performance evaluation would be handled by the project manager, and the team would typically be co-located as much as possible so that they all work in the same office or part of a building. New ventures, or "start-ups," are among the most extreme examples of project organizations: every individual, regardless of function, is linked together by a single project—the growth of the new company and the creation of its product(s). In these settings, the president or CEO can be viewed as the project manager.

The *matrix organization* was conceived as a hybrid of functional and project organizations. In the matrix organization, each individual is linked to others according to both the project they work on and their function. Typically each individual has two supervisors, one a project manager and one a functional manager. The practical reality is that either the project or the function tends to have stronger links. This is because, for example, both functional and project managers cannot have independent budget authority, they cannot independently evaluate and determine the salaries of their subordinates, and both functional and project organizations cannot easily be grouped together physically. As a result, either the functional or the project organization tends to dominate.

Two variants of the matrix organization are called the *heavyweight project organization* and *lightweight project organization* (Hayes et al., 1988). A heavyweight project organization contains strong project links. The heavyweight project manager has complete budget authority, is heavily involved in performance evaluation of the team members, and makes most of the major resource allocation decisions. Although each participant in a project also belongs to a functional organization, the functional managers have relatively little authority and control. A lightweight project organization contains weaker project links and relatively stronger functional links. In this scheme, the project manager is more of a coordinator and administrator. The lightweight project manager updates schedules, arranges meetings, and facilitates coordination, but the manager has no real authority and control in the project organization. The functional managers are responsible for budgets, hiring and firing, and performance evaluation. Exhibit 6 illustrates the pure functional and project organizations, along with the heavyweight and lightweight variants of the matrix organization.

In this book we refer to the project *team* as the primary organizational unit. In this context, the team is the set of all people involved in the project, regardless of the organizational structure of the product development staff. In a functional organization, the team consists of individuals distributed throughout the functional groups without any organizational linkages other than their common involvement in a project. In the other organizations, the team corresponds to a formal organizational entity, the project group, and has a formally appointed manager. For this reason the notion of a team has much more meaning in matrix and project organizations than it does in functional organizations.

Choosing an Organizational Structure

The most appropriate choice of organizational structure depends on which organizational performance factors are most critical to success. Functional organiza-

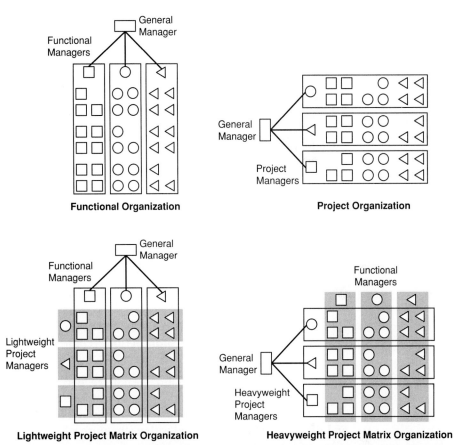

EXHIBIT 6   Various product development organizations. For simplicity, three functions and three projects are shown. (Adapted from Hayes, Robert H., Steven C. Wheelwright, and Kim B. Clark, *Dynamic Manufacturing: Creating the Learning Organization,* The Free Press, New York, 1988.)

tions tend to breed specialization and deep expertise in the functional areas. Project organizations tend to enable rapid and effective coordination among diverse functions. Matrix organizations, being hybrid, have the potential to exhibit some of each of these characteristics. The following questions help guide the choice of organizational structure:

- *How important is cross-functional integration?* Functional organizations may exhibit difficulty in coordinating project decisions which span the functional areas. Project organizations tend to enable strong cross-functional integration because of the organizational links of the team members across the functions.

- *How critical is cutting-edge functional expertise to business success?* When disciplinary expertise must be developed and retained over several product generations, then some functional links are necessary. For example, in some aerospace companies, computational fluid dynamics is so critical that the fluid dynamicists are organized functionally to ensure the firm will have the best possible capability in this area.

- *Can individuals from each function be fully utilized for most of the duration of a project?* For example, a project may only require a portion of an industrial designer's time for a fraction of the duration of a project. In order to use the industrial design resources efficiently, the firm may choose to organize the industrial designers functionally, so that several projects can draw on the industrial design resource in exactly the amount needed for a particular project.

- *How important is product development speed?* Project organizations tend to allow for conflicts to be resolved quickly and for individuals from different functions to coordinate their activities efficiently. Relatively little time is spent transferring information, assigning responsibilities, and coordinating tasks. For this reason, project organizations are usually faster than functional organizations in developing innovative products. For example, portable computer manufacturers almost always organize their product development teams by project. This allows the teams to develop new products within the extremely short periods required by the fast-paced computer market.

Dozens of other issues confound the choice between functional and project organizations. Exhibit 7 summarizes some of the strengths and weaknesses of each organizational type, examples of the types of firms pursuing each strategy, and the major issues associated with each approach.

THE AMF ORGANIZATION

AMF chose to organize its product development staff in a matrix structure. The functions involved in product development at AMF include engineering, manufacturing, marketing, sales, purchasing, and quality assurance. Each of these functions has a manager who reports to the general manager of the division. However, product development projects are led by project managers and project teams are drawn from each of the functional areas. The AMF matrix organization is probably closest to the lightweight project organization. This is because the project managers are not typically the most senior managers in the division and do not have direct control of resources and staffing for the project teams. While in general a lightweight project organization tends to strengthen the functions at the expense of project efficiency, several characteristics of the AMF organization make the lightweight organization a wise choice and have led to good product development performance.

The most significant factor leading to the choice of a lightweight project organization is that AMF carries out many small product development projects along

	Functional Organization	Matrix Organization		Project Organization
		Lightweight Project Organization	Heavyweight Project Organization	
Strengths	Fosters development of deep specialization and expertise.	Coordination and administration of projects is explicitly assigned to a single project manager. Maintains development of specialization and expertise.	Provides integration and speed benefits of the project organization. Some of the specialization of a functional organization is retained.	Resources can be optimally allocated within the project team. Technical and market trade-offs can be evaluated quickly.
Weaknesses	Coordination among different functional groups can be slow and bureaucratic.	Requires more managers and administrators than a nonmatrix organization.	Requires more managers and administrators than a nonmatrix organization.	Individuals may have difficulty maintaining "cutting edge" functional capabilities.
Typical examples	Customization development—firms in which development involves slight variations to a standard design (e.g., custom motors, bearings, packaging),	Traditional automobile, electronics, and aerospace companies.	Many recently successful projects in automobile, electronics, and aerospace companies.	Start-up companies. "Tiger teams" and "skunkworks" intended to achieve breakthroughs. Firms competing in extremely dynamic. markets.
Major issues	How to integrate different functions (e.g., marketing and design) to achieve a common goal.	How to balance functions and projects. How to evaluate simultaneously project and functional performance.		How to maintain functional specialization over product generations. How to share technical learning from one project to another.

EXHIBIT 7 Characteristics of different organizational structures.

with one or two large projects. The result of this mix of projects is that many of the team members on smaller projects contribute on a part-time basis. By having relatively strong functional links among individuals, the assignment of staff to smaller projects and the balancing of work load within a function is more easily accomplished.

Another factor allowing AMF to use a lightweight project organization and still achieve high performance in product development is that AMF is an extraordinarily lean company. The Capital Equipment Division has fewer than 100 salaried employees generating and supporting sales of over $100 million per year. Everyone in the division works in the same building, and most of the key employees earn substantial financial rewards when the division is highly profitable. As a result, members of project teams are motivated to look beyond their own function and work together to develop successful products.

A slight deviation from the standard lightweight project organization also facilitates project completion. The engineering manager is held personally responsible for all aspects of successful completion of projects and not for engineering excellence alone. Although he is responsible for the engineering function, he is primarily responsible for developing successful products. He therefore works daily to ensure that the appropriate coordination occurs, for example, between marketing and engineering.

Finally, the emphasis that the senior management places on product development encourages effective teamwork. The general manager takes a personal interest in every product development project and devotes several days each month to monitoring the progress of these projects. The message communicated to the project teams is that successful products are more important than strong functions.

SUMMARY

An enterprise must make two important decisions about the way it carries out product development. It must define both a product development process and a product development organization.

- A product development process is the sequence of steps an enterprise employs to conceive, design, and commercialize a product.

- A well-defined development process helps to assure product quality, facilitate coordination among team members, plan the development project, and continuously improve the process.

- The generic process presented in this chapter begins with a mission statement and ends with the launch of the product. It includes five phases: concept development, system-level design, detail design, testing and refinement, and production ramp-up.

- The concept development phase requires tremendous integration across the different functions on the development team. This front-end process includes identifying customer needs, analyzing competitive products, establishing target specifications, generating product concepts, selecting a product concept, refining the specifications, performing an economic analysis, and planning the remaining project activities. The results of the concept development phase are documented in a contract book.

- The development process employed by a particular firm may differ somewhat from the generic process described here. The generic process is most appropriate for market-pull products. Other types of products, which may require variants to the generic process, include technology-push products, platform products, process-intensive products, and customized products.

- Regardless of the development process, tasks are completed by individuals residing in organizations. Organizations are defined by linking individuals through reporting relationships, financial relationships, and/or physical layout.

- Functional organizations are those in which the organizational links correspond to the development functions. Project organizations are those in which the organizational links correspond to the development projects. Two types of hybrid, or matrix, organizations are the heavyweight project organization and the lightweight project organization.

- The classic trade-off between functional organizations and project organizations is between deep functional expertise and coordination efficiency.

REFERENCES AND BIBLIOGRAPHY

The concept of heavyweight and lightweight project organizations is articulated by Hayes, Wheelwright, and Clark.

Hayes, Robert H., Steven C. Wheelwright, and Kim B. Clark, *Dynamic Manufacturing: Creating the Learning Organization*, The Free Press, New York, 1988. ISBN 0-02-914211-3.

In addition to reiterating the concept of heavyweight and lightweight project management, Wheelwright and Clark discuss the product strategy activities and technology development activities that precede the product development process described in this chapter.

Wheelwright, Steven C., and Kim B. Clark, *Revolutionizing Product Development: Quantum Leaps in Speed, Efficiency, and Quality*, The Free Press, New York, 1992. ISBN 0-02-905515-6.

Andreasen and Hein provide some good ideas on how to integrate different functions in product development. They also show several conceptual models of product development organizations.

Andreasen, M. Myrup, and Lars Hein, *Integrated Product Development*, Springer-Verlag, New York, 1987. ISBN 0-387-16679-3.

Allen provides strong empirical evidence that physical layout can be used to create significant, although informal, organizational links. He also discusses the use of matrix organizations to mitigate the weaknesses of functional and project organizations.

Allen, Thomas J., *Managing the Flow of Technology: Technology Transfer and the Dissemination of Technological Information within the R&D Organization*, MIT Press, Cambridge, MA, 1977. ISBN 0-262-01048-8; paperback edition 1984, ISBN 0-262-51027-8.

Galbraith's seminal book on organizational design contains much useful information which can be applied to product development. His recent book is an update of his earlier writing.

Galbraith, Jay R., *Designing Complex Organizations*, Addison-Wesley, Reading, MA, 1973. ISBN 0-201-02559-0.

Galbraith, Jay R., *Competing with Flexible Lateral Organizations*, second edition, Addison-Wesley, Reading, MA, 1994. ISBN 0-201-50836-2.

EXERCISES

1 Diagram a process for planning and cooking a family dinner. Does your process resemble the generic product development process? Is cooking dinner analogous to a market-pull, technology-push, process-intensive, or customization process?
2 Define a process for finding a job. For what types of endeavors does a well-defined process enhance performance?
3 What type of development process would you expect to find in an established company successful at developing residential air-conditioning units? How about for a small company that is trying to break into the market for racing wheelchairs?
4 Sketch the organization (in some appropriate graphical representation) of a consulting firm that develops new products for clients on a project-by-project basis. Assume that the individuals in the firm represent all of the different functions required to develop a new product. Would this organization most likely be aligned with functions, be aligned by projects, or be a hybrid?

THOUGHT QUESTIONS

1 What role does basic technological research play in the product development process? How would you amend Exhibit 3 to include the research activity in the front-end process?
2 Is there an analogy between a university and a product development organization? Is a university a functional or project organization?
3 What is the product development organization for students engaged in projects as part of a product development class?
4 Is it possible for some members of a product development organization to be organized functionally, while others are organized by project? If so, which members of the team would be the most likely candidates for the functional organization?

IDENTIFYING CUSTOMER NEEDS

Developed in collaboration with Jonathan Sterrett.

EXHIBIT 1 Existing products used to drive screws: manual screwdrivers, cordless screw-driver, screw gun, cordless drill with driver bit.   (Stuart Cohen)

A successful hand tool manufacturer was exploring the growing market for hand-held power tools. After performing initial research, the firm decided to enter the market with a cordless screwdriver. Exhibit 1 shows several existing products used to drive screws. After some initial concept work, the manufacturer's development team fabricated and field-tested several prototypes. The results were discouraging. Although some of the products were liked better than others, each one had some feature that customers objected to in one way or another. The results were quite mystifying since the company had been successful in related consumer products for years. After much discussion, the team decided that its process for identifying customer needs was inadequate.

This chapter presents a methodology for comprehensively identifying a set of customer needs. The goals of the methodology are to:

- Ensure that the product is focused on customer needs
- Identify latent or hidden needs as well as explicit needs
- Provide a fact base for justifying the product specifications
- Create an archival record of the needs activity of the development process
- Ensure that no critical customer need is missed or forgotten
- Develop a common understanding of customer needs among the development team members

The philosophy behind the methodology is to create a high-quality information channel that runs directly between customers in the target market and the developers of the product. This philosophy is built on the premise that those who directly control the details of the product, including the engineers and industrial designers, must interact with customers and experience the *use environment* of the product. Without this emphasis on direct experience, technical trade-offs are not likely to be made correctly, innovative solutions to customer needs may never be discovered, and the development team may never develop a deep commitment to meeting customer needs.

The process of identifying customer needs is an integral part of the larger product development process and is most closely related to concept generation, concept selection, competitive benchmarking, and the establishment of product specifications. The customer-needs activity is shown in Exhibit 2 in relation to these other early product development activities, which collectively can be thought of as the *concept development* phase.

The concept development phase illustrated in Exhibit 2 implies a distinction between customer needs and product specifications. This distinction is subtle but important. *Needs* are largely independent of any particular product we might develop; they are not specific to the concept we eventually choose to pursue. A team should be able to identify customer needs without knowing if or how it will eventually address those needs. On the other hand, *specifications* do depend on the concept we select. The specifications for the product we finally choose to develop will depend on what is technically and economically feasible and on

EXHIBIT 2   The customer-needs activity in relation to other concept development activities.

what our competitors offer in the marketplace, as well as on customer needs. (See the chapter "Establishing Product Specifications" for a more detailed discussion of this distinction.) Also note that we choose to use the word *need* to label any attribute of a potential product that is desired by the customer; we do not distinguish here between a want and a need. Other terms used in industrial practice to refer to customer needs include *customer attributes* and *customer requirements.*

Identifying customer needs is itself a process, for which we present a six-step methodology. We believe that a little structure goes a long way in facilitating effective product development practices, and we hope and expect that this methodology will not be viewed as a rigid process by those who employ it but rather as a starting point for continuous improvement and refinement. The six steps are:

1 Define the scope of the effort.

2 Gather raw data from customers.

3 Interpret the raw data in terms of customer needs.

4 Organize the needs into a hierarchy of primary, secondary, and (if necessary) tertiary needs.

5 Establish the relative importance of the needs.

6 Reflect on the results and the process.

We treat each of the six steps in turn and illustrate the key points with the cordless screwdriver example. We chose the screwdriver because it is simple enough that the methodology is not hidden by the complexity of the example. However, note that the same methodology, with minor adaptation, has been successfully applied to hundreds of products ranging from kitchen utensils costing less than $10 to machine tools costing hundreds of thousands of dollars.

The cordless screwdriver category of products is already relatively well developed. Such products are particularly well suited to a structured process for gathering customer needs. One could reasonably ask whether a structured methodology is effective for completely new categories of products with which customers have no experience. Satisfying needs is just as important in revolutionary products as in incremental products. A necessary condition for product success is that a product offer perceived benefits to the customer. Products offer benefits when they satisfy needs. This is true whether the product is an incremental variation on an existing product or whether it is a completely new product based on a revolutionary invention. Developing an entirely new category of product is a risky undertaking, and to some extent the only real indication of whether customer needs have been identified correctly is whether customers like the team's first prototypes. Nevertheless, in our opinion, a structured methodology for gathering data from customers remains useful and can lower the inherent risk in developing a radically new product. Whether or not customers are able to fully articulate their latent needs, interaction with customers in the target market will help the development team develop a personal understanding of the user's environment and point of view. This information is always useful, even if it does not result in the identification of every need the new product will address.

STEP 1: DEFINE THE SCOPE OF THE EFFORT

For completeness we include defining the scope of the product development effort as part of the customer needs phase of development, although this step is usually performed as part of a product planning activity preceding formal product development. In defining the scope of the development effort the firm specifies a particular market opportunity and lays out the broad constraints and objectives for the project. This information is frequently formalized as a *mission statement* (also sometimes called a *charter* or a *design brief*). The mission statement specifies which direction to go in but generally does not specify a precise destination or a particular way to proceed. The mission statement for the cordless screwdriver is shown in Exhibit 3. The mission statement may include some or all of the following information:

- *Brief (one-sentence) description of the product:* This description typically includes the key customer benefit of the product but avoids implying a specific product concept.
- *Key business goals:* Often these goals include the timing of the new product introduction, market share targets, and desired financial performance.
- *Target market(s) for the product:* There may be several target markets for the product. This part of the mission statement identifies the primary market as well as any secondary markets that should be considered in the development effort.
- *Assumptions that constrain the development effort:* Assumptions must be made

---

Mission Statement: Screwdriver Project

Product Description	A hand-held, power-assisted device for installing threaded fasteners
Key Business Goals	• Product introduced in fourth quarter of 1997 • 50% gross margin • 10% share of cordless screwdriver market by 1999
Primary Market	• Do-it-yourself consumer
Secondary Markets	• Casual consumer • Light-duty professional
Assumptions	• Hand-held • Power-assisted • Nickel-metal-hydride rechargeable battery technology
Stakeholders	• User • Retailer • Sales force • Service center • Production • Legal department

EXHIBIT 3   Mission statement for the cordless screwdriver.

---

carefully; although they restrict the range of possible product concepts, they help to maintain a manageable project scope. We have already implied one assumption in our example by calling the product a *cordless* screwdriver. The implication is that the screwdriver will be powered but will not use a corded power supply.

• *Stakeholders:* One way to ensure that many of the subtle development issues are addressed is to explicitly list all of the product's *stakeholders*, that is, all of the groups of people who are affected by the product's attributes. The stakeholder list begins with the end user (the ultimate, external customer) and the external customer who makes the buying decision about the product. Stakeholders also include the customers of the product who reside within the firm, such as the sales force, the service organization, and the production departments. Although this chapter is primarily about identifying the needs of external customers, the list of stakeholders serves as a reminder to consider the needs of everyone who will be influenced by the product.

STEP 2: GATHER RAW DATA FROM CUSTOMERS

Consistent with our basic philosophy of creating a high-quality information channel directly from the customer, gathering data involves contact with customers and experience with the use environment of the product. Three methods are commonly used:

1 *Interviews:* One or more development team members discuss needs with a single customer. Interviews are usually conducted in the customer's environment and typically last one to two hours.

2 *Focus groups:* A moderator facilitates a two-hour discussion with a group of 8 to 12 customers. Focus groups are typically conducted in a special room equipped with a two-way mirror allowing several members of the development team to observe the group. The proceedings are usually videotaped. Participants are usually paid a modest fee ($50 to $100 each) for their attendance. The total cost of a focus group, including rental of the room, participant fees, videotaping, and refreshments is about $2,000. In most U.S. cities, firms that rent focus group facilities are listed in the telephone book under "Market Research."

3 *Observing the product in use:* Watching customers use an existing product or perform a task for which a new product is intended can reveal important details about customer needs. For example, a customer painting a house may use a screwdriver to open paint cans in addition to driving screws. Observation may be completely passive, without any direct interaction with the customer, or may involve working side by side with a customer, allowing members of the development team to develop firsthand experience using the product. For some products, such as do-it-yourself tools, actually using the products is simple and natural; for others, such as surgical instruments, the team may have to use the products on surrogate tasks (e.g., cutting fruit instead of human tissue when developing a new scalpel).

Some practitioners also rely on written surveys for gathering raw data. While a mail survey is quite useful later in the process, we cannot recommend this approach for initial efforts to identify customer needs; written surveys simply do not provide enough information about the use environment of the product, and they are ineffective in revealing unanticipated needs.

Research by Griffin and Hauser shows that one 2-hour focus group reveals about the same number of needs as two 1-hour interviews (Griffin and Hauser, 1993). (See Exhibit 4.) Because interviews are usually less costly (per hour) than focus groups and because an interview often allows the product development team to experience the use environment of the product, we recommend that interviews be the primary data collection method. Interviews may be supplemented with one or two focus groups as a way to allow top management to observe a group of customers or as a mechanism for sharing a common customer experience (via videotape) among the members of a larger team. Some practitioners believe that for certain products and customer groups, the interactions among the participants of focus groups can elicit more varied needs than are

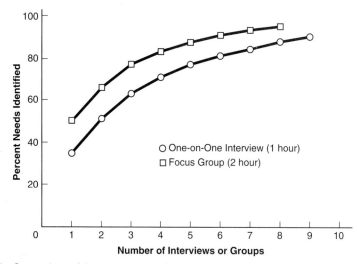

EXHIBIT 4 Comparison of the percentages of customer needs that are revealed for focus groups and interviews as a function of the number of sessions. Note that a focus group lasts two hours, while an interview lasts one hour. (Abbie Griffin and John R. Hauser, "The Voice of the Customer," *Marketing Science*, Vol. 12, No. 1, Winter 1993.)

revealed through interviews, although this belief is not strongly supported by research findings.

Choosing Customers

Griffin and Hauser have also addressed the question of how many customers should be interviewed in order to reveal most of the customer needs. In one study, they estimated that 90 percent of the customer needs for picnic coolers were revealed after 30 interviews. In another study, they estimated that 98 percent of the customer needs for a piece of office equipment were revealed after 25 hours of data collection in both focus groups and interviews. As a practical guideline for most products, conducting fewer than 10 interviews is probably inadequate and 50 interviews are probably too many. However, interviews can be conducted sequentially and the process can be terminated when no new needs are revealed by additional interviews. Teams containing more than 10 people usually collect data from plenty of customers simply by involving everyone in the process. For example, if the team is divided into five pairs and each pair conducts 6 interviews, the team will conduct 30 interviews in total.

Needs can be identified more efficiently by interviewing a class of customers called *lead users*. According to von Hippel, lead users are customers who experience needs months or years ahead of the majority of the marketplace and stand to benefit substantially from product innovations (von Hippel, 1988). These customers are particularly useful sources of data for two reasons: (1) they are often able to articulate their emerging needs, because they have had to struggle with the inadequacies of existing products, and (2) they may have already invented

	Lead Users	Users	Retailer or Sales Outlet	Service Centers
Homeowner (occasional use)	0	5	2	3
Handy person (frequent use)	3	10		
Professional (heavy-duty use)	3	2	2	

EXHIBIT 5   Customer selection matrix for the cordless screwdriver project.

solutions to meet their needs. By focusing a portion of the data collection efforts on lead users, the team may be able to identify needs which, although explicit for lead users, are still latent for the majority of the marketplace. Developing products to meet these latent needs allows a firm to anticipate trends and to leapfrog competitive products.

The choice of which customers to interview is complicated when several different groups of people can be considered "the customer." For many products, one person (the buyer) makes the buying decision and another person (the user) actually uses the product. A good approach is to gather data from the end user of the product in all situations, and in cases where other types of customers and stakeholders are clearly important, to gather data from these as well. Furthermore, if there are multiple market segments to be addressed by the product, it is important to gather data from each segment in order to understand the differences in their respective needs.

A customer selection matrix is useful for planning exploration of both market and customer variety. Burchill suggests that market segments be listed on the left side of the matrix while the different types of customers are listed across the top (Burchill et al., 1992), as shown in Exhibit 5. The number of intended customer contacts is entered in each cell to indicate the depth of coverage.

Actually locating customers is usually a matter of making telephone calls. In developing industrial products within an existing manufacturing firm, a field sales force can often provide names of customers, although the team must be careful about biasing the selection of customers toward those with allegiances to a particular manufacturer. The telephone book can be used to identify names of some types of customers for some classes of products (e.g., building contractors or insurance agents). For industrial products that are integral to a customer's job, getting someone to agree to an interview is usually simple; these customers are anxious to discuss their needs. Also, most consumers are frustrated quite regularly by products that do not fulfill their needs—much more often than they are bothered by surveys and interview requests.

The Art of Eliciting Customer Needs Data

The techniques we present here are aimed primarily at interviewing end users, but these methods do apply to all of the three data-gathering modes and to all types of stakeholders. The basic approach is to be receptive to information provided by customers and to avoid confrontations or defensive posturing. Gathering needs data is very different from a sales call: the goal is to elicit an honest expression of needs, not to convince a customer of what he or she needs. In most cases customer interactions will be verbal; interviewers ask questions and the customer responds. A prepared interview guide is valuable for structuring this dialogue. Some helpful questions and prompts for use after the interviewers introduce themselves and explain the purpose of the interview are:

- Walk us through a typical session using the product.
- What do you like about the existing products?
- What do you dislike about the existing products?
- What issues do you consider when purchasing the product?
- What improvements would you make to the product?

Here are some general hints for effective interaction with customers:

- *Go with the flow.* If the customer is providing interesting information, do not worry about conforming to the interview guide. The goal is to gather interesting and important data on customer needs, not to complete the interview guide in the allotted time.

- *Use visual stimuli and props.* Bring a collection of existing and competitors' products, or even products that are tangentially related to the product under development. At the end of a session, the interviewers might even show some preliminary product concepts to get customers' early reactions to various approaches.

- *Suppress preconceived hypotheses about the product technology.* Frequently customers will make assumptions about the product concept they expect would meet their needs. In these situations, the interviewers should avoid biasing the discussion with assumptions about how the product will eventually be designed or produced. When customers mention specific technologies or product features, the interviewer should probe for the underlying need the customer believes the feature would satisfy.

- *Have the customer demonstrate the product and/or typical tasks related to the product.* If the interview is conducted in the use environment, a demonstration is usually convenient and invariably reveals new information.

- *Be alert for surprises and the expression of latent needs.* If a customer mentions something surprising, pursue the lead with follow-up questions. Frequently, an unexpected line of questioning will reveal latent needs—important dimensions of the customers' needs which are neither fulfilled nor commonly articulated and understood.

- *Watch for nonverbal information.* The process described in the chapter is aimed at developing better physical products. Unfortunately, words are not always the best way to communicate needs related to the physical world. This is particularly true of needs involving the human dimensions of the product, such as comfort, image, or style. The development team must be constantly aware of the nonverbal messages provided by customers. What are their facial expressions? How do they hold competitors' products?

Note that many of our suggested questions and guidelines assume that the customer has some familiarity with products similar to the new product under development. This is almost always true. For example, even before the first cordless screwdriver was developed, people installed fasteners. Developing an understanding of customer needs as they relate to the general fastening task would still have been beneficial in developing the first cordless tool. Similarly, understanding the needs of customers using other types of cordless appliances, such as electric razors, would also have been useful. We can think of no product so revolutionary that there would be no analogous products or tasks from which the development team could learn. However, in gathering needs relating to truly revolutionary products with which customers have no experience, the interview questions should be focused on the task or situation in which the new product will be applied, rather than on the product itself.

Documenting Interactions with Customers

Four methods are commonly used for documenting interactions with customers:

1 *Audiotape recording:* Making an audiotape recording of the interview is very easy. Unfortunately, transcribing the tape into text is very time-consuming, and it can be expensive to hire someone to do it. Also, tape recording has the disadvantage of being intimidating to some customers.

2 *Notes:* Handwritten notes are the most common method of documenting an interview. Designating one person as the primary notetaker allows the other person to concentrate on effective questioning. The notetaker should strive to capture some of the wording of every customer statement verbatim. These notes, if transcribed immediately after the interview, can be used to create a description of the interview that is very close to an actual transcript. This debriefing immediately after the interview also facilitates sharing of insights between the interviewers.

3 *Videotape recording:* Videotape is almost always used to document a focus group session. It is also very useful for documenting observations of the customer in the use environment and/or using existing products. The tape is useful for bringing new team members "up to speed" and is also useful as raw material for presentations to upper management. Multiple viewings of

a video tape of customers in action often facilitate the identification of latent customer needs. Videotaping is also useful for capturing many aspects of the end user's environment.

4 *Still photography:* Taking slides or photographs provides many of the benefits of videotape recording. The primary advantages of still photography are ease of display of the photos, excellent image quality, and readily available equipment. The primary disadvantage is the relative inability to record dynamic information.

The final result of the data-gathering phase of the process is a set of raw data, usually in the form of customer statements but frequently supplemented by videotape or photographs. A data template implemented with a spreadsheet software package is useful for organizing these raw data. Exhibit 6 shows an example of a portion of such a template. We recommend that the template be filled in as soon as possible after the interaction with the customer and edited by the other development team members present during the interaction. The first column in the main body of the template indicates the question or prompt that elicited the customer data. The second column is a list of verbatim statements the customer made or an observation of a customer action (from a videotape or from direct observation). The third column contains the customer need implied by the raw data. Some emphasis should be placed on investigating clues which may identify potential latent needs. Such clues may be in the form of humorous remarks, less serious suggestions, nonverbal information, or observations and descriptions of the use environment. Techniques for interpreting the raw data in terms of customer needs are given in the next section.

The final task in step 2 is to write thank-you notes to the customers involved in the process. Invariably, the team will need to solicit further customer information, so developing and maintaining a good rapport with a set of users is important.

STEP 3: INTERPRET RAW DATA IN TERMS OF CUSTOMER NEEDS

Customer needs are expressed as written statements and are the result of interpreting the need underlying the raw data gathered from the customers. Each statement or observation (as listed in the second column of the data template) may be translated into from zero to several customer needs. Griffin and Hauser found that multiple analysts translate the same interview notes into different needs, so it is useful to have more than one team member conducting the translation process. Below we provide five guidelines for writing need statements. The first two guidelines are fundamental and are critical to effective translation; the remaining three guidelines ensure consistency of phrasing and style among team members. Exhibit 7 provides examples to illustrate each guideline.

- *Express the need in terms of* what *the product has to do, not in terms of* how *it might do it.* Customers often express their preferences by describing a solu-

Customer: Bill Esposito	**Interviewer(s):** Jonathan and Lisa	
Address: 100 Memorial Drive	**Date:** 19 December 1994	
Cambridge, MA 02139		
Telephone: 617-864-1274	**Currently uses:** Craftsman Model A3	
Willing to do	**Type of user:** Building maintenance	
follow-up? Yes		

Question/Prompt	Customer Statement	Interpreted Need
Typical uses	I need to drive screws fast, faster than by hand.	The SD drives screws faster than by hand.
	I sometimes do duct work; use sheet metal screws.	The SD drives sheet metal screws into metal duct work.
	A lot of electrical: switch covers, outlets, fans, kitchen appliances.	The SD can be used for screws on electrical devices.
Likes—current tool	I like the pistol grip; it feels the best.	The SD is comfortable to grip.
	I like the magnetized tip.	The SD tip retains the screw before it is driven.
Dislikes—current tool	I don't like it when the tip slips off the screw.	The SD tip remains aligned with the screw head without slipping.
	I would like to be able to lock it so I can use it with a dead battery.	The user can apply torque manually to the SD to drive a screw.
	Can't drive screws into hard wood.	The SD can drive screws into hard wood.
	Sometimes I strip tough screws.	The SD does not strip screw heads.
Suggested improvements	An attachment to allow me to reach down skinny holes.	The SD can access screws at the end of deep, narrow holes.
	A point so I can scrape paint off of screws.	The SD allows the user to work with screws that have been painted over.
	Would be nice if it could punch a pilot hole.	The SD can be used to create a pilot hole.

EXHIBIT 6   Customer data template filled in with sample customer statements and interpreted needs. SD is an abbreviation for *screwdriver*. (Note that this template represents a partial list from a single interview. A typical interview session may elicit more than 50 customer statements and interpreted needs.)

Guideline	Customer Statement	Need Statement—Right	Need Statement—Wrong
"What" not "how"	"Why don't you put protective shields around the battery contacts?"	The screwdriver battery is protected from accidental shorting.	The screwdriver battery contacts are covered by a plastic sliding door.
Specificity	"I drop my screwdriver all the time."	The screwdriver operates normally after repeated dropping.	The screwdriver is rugged.
Positive not negative	"It doesn't matter if it's raining, I still need to work outside on Saturdays."	The screwdriver operates normally in the rain.	The screwdriver is not disabled by the rain.
An attribute of the product	"I'd like to charge my battery from my cigarette lighter."	The screwdriver battery can be charged from an automobile cigarette lighter.	An automobile cigarette lighter adapter can charge the screwdriver battery.
Avoid "must" and "should"	"I hate it when I don't know how much juice is left in the batteries of my cordless tools."	The screwdriver provides an indication of the energy level of the battery.	The screwdriver should provide an indication of the energy level of the battery.

EXHIBIT 7 Examples illustrating the guidelines for writing need statements.

tion concept or an implementation approach; however, the need statement should be expressed in terms independent of a particular technological solution.

- *Express the need as specifically as the raw data.* Needs can be expressed at many different levels of detail. To avoid loss of information, express the need at the same level of detail as the raw data.

- *Use positive, not negative, phrasing.* Subsequent translation of a need into a product specification is easier if the need is expressed as a positive statement. This is not a rigid guideline, because sometimes positive phrasing is difficult and awkward. For example, one of the need statements in Exhibit 6 is "the screwdriver does not strip screw heads." This need is more naturally expressed in a negative form.

- *Express the need as an attribute of the product.* Wording needs as statements about the product ensures consistency and facilitates subsequent translation into product specifications. Not all needs can be cleanly expressed as attributes of the product, however, and in most of these cases the needs can be expressed as attributes of the user of the product (e.g., "the user can apply torque manually to the screwdriver to drive a screw").

- *Avoid the words* **must** *and* **should.** The words *must* and *should* imply a level of importance for the need. Rather than casually assigning a binary importance rating (must versus should) to the needs at this point, we recommend deferring the assessment of the importance of each need until step 5.

The list of customer needs is the superset of all the needs elicited from all the interviewed customers in the target market. Some of these needs may be contradictory. Some needs may not be technologically realizable. The constraints of technical and economic feasibility are incorporated into the process of establishing product specifications in subsequent development steps. (See the chapter "Establishing Product Specifications.")

STEP 4: ORGANIZE THE NEEDS INTO A HIERARCHY

The result of steps 1 through 3 should be a list of 50 to 300 need statements. Such a large number of detailed needs is awkward to work with and difficult to summarize for use in subsequent development activities. The goal of step 4 is to organize these needs into a hierarchical list. The list will typically consist of a set of primary needs, each one of which will be further characterized by a set of secondary needs. In cases of very complex products, the secondary needs may be broken down into tertiary needs as well. The primary needs are the most general needs, while the secondary and tertiary needs express needs in more detail. Exhibit 8 shows the resulting hierarchical list of needs for the screwdriver example. For the screwdriver, there are 15 primary needs and 49 secondary needs. Note that two of the primary needs have no associated secondary needs.

The procedure for organizing the needs into a hierarchical list is intuitive, and many teams can successfully complete the task without detailed instructions. For completeness, we provide a step-by-step procedure here. This activity is best performed on a large table by a group of six or fewer team members.

1 *Print or write each need statement on a separate card or self-stick note.* (A print macro can be easily written to print the need statements directly from the data template. A nice feature of this approach is that the need can be printed in a large font in the center of the card and then the original customer statement and other relevant information can be printed in a small font at the bottom of the card for easy reference. Four "cards" can be cut from a standard printed sheet.)

2 *Eliminate redundant statements.* Those cards expressing redundant need statements can be stapled together and treated as a single card. Be careful to consolidate only those statements that are identical in meaning.

3 *Group the cards according to the similarity of the needs they express.* At this point, the team should attempt to create groups of roughly three to seven cards that express similar needs. The logic by which groups are created deserves special attention. Novice development teams often create groups according to a technological perspective, clustering needs relating to, for example, materials, packaging, or power. Or, they create groups according to assumed physical components such as enclosure, bits, switch, and battery. Both of these approaches are dangerous. Recall that the goal of the process is to create a description of the needs of the customer. For this reason, the groupings should be consistent with the way customers think about their

The SD provides plenty of power to drive screws.

3   The SD maintains power for several hours of heavy use.

3   The SD can drive screws into hardwood.

      The SD drives sheet metal screws into metal duct work.

      The SD drives screws faster than by hand.

The SD makes it easy to start a screw.

3   The SD retains the screw before it is driven.

3   The SD can be used to create a pilot hole.

The SD works with a variety of screws.

4   The SD can turn phillips, torx, socket, and hex head screws.

4   The SD can turn many sizes of screws.

The SD can access most screws.

      The SD can be maneuvered in tight areas.

4   The SD can access screws at the end of deep, narrow holes.

The SD turns screws that are in poor condition.

      The SD can be used to remove grease and dirt from screws.

      The SD allows the user to work with painted screws.

The SD feels good in the user's hand.

      The SD is comfortable when the user pushes on it.

      The SD is comfortable when the user resists twisting.

      The SD is balanced in the user's hand.

      The SD is equally easy to use in right or left hands.

      The SD weight is just right.

2   The SD is warm to touch in cold weather.

      The SD remains comfortable when left in the sun.

The SD is easy to control while turning screws.

      The user can easily push on the SD.

      The user can easily resist the SD twisting.

2   The SD can be locked "on."

4   The SD speed can be controlled by the user while turning a screw.

      The SD remains aligned with the screw head without slipping.

      The user can easily see where the screw is.

      The SD does not strip screw heads.

      The SD is easily reversible.

The SD is easy to set-up and use.

      The SD is easy to turn on.

      The SD prevents inadvertent switching off.

3   The maximum torque of the SD can be set by the user.

      The SD provides ready access to bits or accessories.

      The SD can be attached to the user for temporary storage.

The SD power is convenient.

      The SD is easy to recharge.

3   The SD can be used while recharging.

5   The SD recharges quickly.

2   The SD batteries are ready to use when new.

      The user can apply torque manually to the SD to drive a screw.

The SD lasts a long time.

      The SD tip survives heavy use.

2   The SD can be hammered.

      The SD can be dropped from a ladder without damage.

The SD is easy to store.

      The SD fits in a toolbox easily.

      The SD can be charged while in storage.

2   The SD resists corrosion when left outside or in damp places.

3   The SD maintains its charge after long periods of storage.

      The SD maintains its charge when wet.

The SD prevents damage to the work.

      The SD prevents damage to the screw head.

      The SD prevents scratching of finished surfaces.

3 **The SD has a pleasant sound when in use.**

The SD looks like a professional quality tool.

The SD is safe.

      The SD can be used on electrical devices.

      The SD does not cut the user's hands.

EXHIBIT 8   Hierarchical list of primary and secondary customer needs for the cordless screwdriver. Importance ratings are shown for some of the needs (using the ranking scheme given in Exhibit 9).

needs and not with the way the development team thinks about the product. The groups should correspond to needs customers would view as similar. In fact, some practitioners argue that customers should be the ones to organize the need statements.

4 *For each group, choose a label.* The label is itself a statement of need that generalizes all of the needs in the group. It can be selected from one of the needs in the group, or the team can write a new need statement.

5 *Consider creating "supergroups" consisting of two to five groups.* If there are fewer than 20 groups, then a two-level hierarchy is probably sufficient to organize the data. In this case, the group labels are primary needs and the group members are secondary needs. However, if there are more than 20 groups, the team may consider creating supergroups, and therefore a third level in the hierarchy. The process of creating supergroups is identical to the process of creating groups. As with the previous step, cluster groups according to similarity of the need they express and then create or select a supergroup label. These supergroup labels become the primary needs, the group labels become the secondary needs, and the members of the groups become tertiary needs.

6 *Review and edit the organized needs statements.* The arrangement of needs in a hierarchy is not unique in terms of being "correct." At this point, the team may wish to consider alternative groupings or labels.

STEP 5: ESTABLISH THE RELATIVE IMPORTANCE OF THE NEEDS

The hierarchical list of needs does not provide any information on the relative importance that customers place on different needs. Yet the development team will have to make trade-offs and allocate resources in designing the product. A sense of the relative importance of the various needs is essential to making these trade-offs correctly. Step 5 in the needs process establishes the relative importance of the customer needs identified in steps 1 through 4. The outcome of this step is a numerical importance weighting for a subset of the needs. There are two basic approaches to the task: (1) relying on the consensus of the team members based on their experience with customers, or (2) basing the importance assessment on further customer surveys. The obvious trade-off between the two approaches is cost versus accuracy: the team can make an educated assessment of the relative importance of the needs in one meeting, while a customer survey takes a minimum of two weeks and more realistically one or two months. In general, we believe the customer survey is important and worth the time required to complete it. Other development tasks, such as concept generation and analysis of competitive products, can begin before the relative importance surveys are complete.

The team should at this point have developed a rapport with a group of customers. These same customers can be surveyed to rate the relative importance of the needs. The survey can be done in person, by telephone, or by mail. Few customers will respond to a survey asking them to evaluate the importance of 100 needs, so typically the team will work with only a subset of the needs. A practical limit on how many needs can be addressed in a customer survey is 20 to 30. This limitation is not too severe, however, because many of the needs are either obvi-

---

Cordless Screwdriver Survey

For each of the following cordless screwdriver features, please indicate on a scale of 1 to 5 how important the feature is to you. Please use the following scale:

1. Feature is undesirable. I would not consider a product with this feature.
2. Feature is not important, but I would not mind having it.
3. Feature would be nice to have, but is not necessary.
4. Feature is highly desirable, but I would consider a product without it.
5. Feature is critical. I would not consider a product without this feature.

_____ The screwdriver can drive screws into hardwood.

_____ The screwdriver can turn phillips, torx, socket, and hex head screws.

_____ The screwdriver can access screws at the end of deep, narrow holes.

And so forth.

EXHIBIT 9   Example importance survey (partial).

ously important (e.g., the user can easily see where the screw is) or are easy to implement (e.g., the screwdriver prevents inadvertent switching off). The team can therefore limit the scope of the survey by only querying customers about needs that are likely to give rise to difficult technological trade-offs or costly features in the product design. Such needs would include the need to vary speed, the need to drive screws into hardwood, and the need to have the screwdriver emit a pleasant sound. Alternatively the team could develop a set of surveys to ask a variety of customers each about different subsets of the needs list. There are many survey designs for establishing the relative importance of customer needs. One good design is illustrated by the portion of the cordless screwdriver survey shown in Exhibit 9.

The survey responses for each need statement can be characterized in a variety of ways: by the mean, by standard deviation, or by the number of responses in each category. The responses can then be used to assign an importance weighting to the need statements. The same scale of 1 to 5 can be used to summarize the importance data. Some of the needs in Exhibit 8 are weighted according to the survey data.

STEP 6: REFLECT ON THE RESULTS AND THE PROCESS

The final step in the methodology is to reflect on the results and the process. While the process of identifying customer needs can be usefully structured, it is not a science. The team must continually challenge its results to verify that they are consistent with the knowledge and intuition the team has developed through many hours of interaction with customers. Some questions to ask include:

- Have we interacted with all of the important types of customers in our target market?
- Are we able to see beyond needs related only to existing products in order to capture the latent needs of our target customers?
- Are there areas of inquiry we should pursue in follow-up interviews or surveys?
- Which of the customers we spoke to would be good participants in our ongoing development efforts?
- What do we know now that we didn't know when we started? Are we surprised by any of the needs?
- Did we involve everyone within our own organization who needs to deeply understand customer needs?
- How might we improve the process in future efforts?

SUMMARY

Identifying customer needs is an integral part of the concept development phase of the product development process. The resulting customer needs are used to guide the team in establishing product specifications, generating product concepts, and selecting a product concept for further development.

- The process of identifying customer needs includes six steps:
  1 Define the scope of the product development effort.
  2 Gather raw data from customers.
  3 Interpret the raw data in terms of customer needs.
  4 Organize the needs into a hierarchy of primary, secondary, and tertiary needs.
  5 Establish the relative importance of the needs.
  6 Reflect on the results and the process.
- Creating a high-quality information channel from customers to the product developers ensures that those who directly control the details of the product, including the product designers, fully understand the needs of the customer.
- Lead users are a good source of customer needs because they experience new needs months or years ahead of the bulk of the marketplace and because they stand to benefit substantially from new product innovations. Furthermore, they are frequently able to articulate their needs more clearly than typical customers.
- Latent needs are frequently as important as explicit needs in determining customer satisfaction. Latent needs are those that many customers recognize as important in a final product but do not or are not able to articulate in advance.

- Customer needs should be expressed in terms of what the product has to do, not in terms of how the product might be implemented. Adherence to this principle leaves the development team with maximum flexibility to generate and select product concepts.

- The key benefits of the methodology are: ensuring that the product is focused on customer needs and that no critical customer need is forgotten; developing a clear understanding among members of the development team of the needs of the customers in the target market; developing a fact base to be used in generating concepts, selecting a product concept, and establishing product specifications; and creating an archival record of the needs phase of the development process.

REFERENCES AND BIBLIOGRAPHY

Concept engineering is a methodology developed by the Center for Quality Management. This chapter benefits from our observations of the development and application of concept engineering. For a complete and detailed description of concept engineering, see:

Burchill, Gary, et al., *Concept Engineering: The Key to Operationally Defining Your Customer's Requirements,* Center for Quality Management, Cambridge, MA, Document No. 7I, September 1992.

The research by Griffin and Hauser is one of the only rigorous efforts to validate different methods for extracting needs from interview data. Their study of the fraction of needs identified as a function of the number of customers interviewed is particularly interesting.

Griffin, Abbie, and John R. Hauser, "The Voice of the Customer," *Marketing Science,* Vol. 12, No. 1, Winter 1993.

Kinnear and Taylor thoroughly discuss data collection methods and survey design in:

Kinnear, Thomas C., and James R. Taylor, *Marketing Research: An Applied Approach,* McGraw-Hill, New York, NY, 1991. ISBN 0-07-034757-3.

Payne's book is a detailed and interesting discussion of how to pose questions in surveys.

Payne, Stanley L., *The Art of Asking Questions,* Princeton University Press, Princeton, NJ, 1951.

Total quality management (TQM) provides a valuable perspective on how identifying customer needs fits into an overall effort to improve the quality of goods and services.

Shiba, Shoji, Alan Graham, and David Walden, *A New American TQM: Four Practical Revolutions in Management,* Productivity Press, Cambridge, MA, and The Center for Quality Management, Cambridge, MA, 1993. ISBN 1-56327-032-3.

Urban and Hauser provide a thorough discussion of how to create hierarchies of needs (along with many other topics).

Urban, Glen L., and John R. Hauser, *Design and Marketing of New Products,* second edition, Prentice-Hall, Englewood Cliffs, NJ, 1993. ISBN 0-13-201567-6.

von Hippel describes many years of research on the role of lead users in innovation. He provides useful guidelines for identifying lead users.

von Hippel, Eric, *The Sources of Innovation,* Oxford University Press, New York, NY, 1988. ISBN 0-19-504085-6.

EXERCISES

1 Translate the following customer statements about a student book bag into proper needs statements:
   a "See how the leather on the bottom of the bag is all scratched; it's ugly."
   b "When I'm standing in line at the cashier trying to find my checkbook while balancing my bag on my knee, I feel like a stork."
   c "This bag is my life; if I lose it I'm in big trouble."
   d "There's nothing worse than a banana that's been squished by the edge of a textbook."
   e "I never use both straps on my knapsack; I just sling it over one shoulder."
2 Using a camera, document user frustration with an everyday task of your own choice.
3 Choose a product that continually annoys you. Identify the needs the developers of this product missed. Why do you think these needs were not met? Do you think the developers deliberately ignored these needs?

THOUGHT QUESTIONS

1 How would the needs methodology change if a development team wished to pursue two very different market segments with the same product?
2 One of the reasons the methodology is effective is that it involves the entire development team. Unfortunately, the methodology can become unwieldy with a team of more than six people. How might you modify the methodology to maximize involvement yet maintain a focused and decisive effort given a development team of 12 or more people?
3 Can the process of identifying customer needs lead to the creation of innovative product concepts? In what ways? Could a structured process of identifying customer needs lead to a fundamentally new product concept like the Post-It note?

ESTABLISHING PRODUCT SPECIFICATIONS

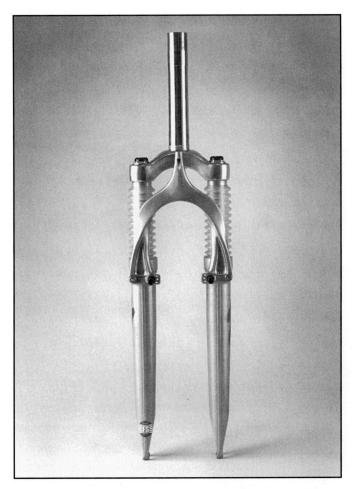

EXHIBIT 1   One of Specialized's existing suspension forks.   (Stuart Cohen)

Specialized Bicycle Components was interested in developing a front fork and suspension for the growing mountain bike market. Although the firm was already selling a suspension fork (Exhibit 1), it was successful primarily in the extremely performance-oriented segment of the market—racing cyclists with less concern for cost or long-term durability. The firm wished to broaden the sales of suspension forks and therefore was interested in developing a product that would provide high value for the recreational cyclist.

The development team had spent a great deal of time identifying customer needs. In addition to logging many hours of riding on suspended bikes themselves, the members of the team had interviewed lead users at mountain bike races and recreational cyclists on local trails, and they also had spent time working with dealers in their stores. As a result of this process they had assembled a list of customer needs. They now faced several challenges:

- How could the relatively subjective customer needs be translated into precise targets for the remaining development effort?
- How could the team and its senior management agree on what would constitute success or failure of the resulting product design?
- How could the team develop confidence that its intended product would garner a substantial share of the suspension fork market?
- How could the team resolve the inevitable trade-offs among product characteristics like cost and weight?

This chapter presents a methodology for establishing product specifications. We assume that the customer needs are already documented as described in the chapter "Identifying Customer Needs." The methodology employs several simple information systems, all of which can be constructed using conventional spreadsheet software. These information systems guide the team in making what remain subjective decisions about the specifications for a new product.

WHAT ARE SPECIFICATIONS?

Customer needs are generally expressed in the "language of the customer." The primary customer needs for the suspension fork are listed in Exhibit 2. Customer needs such as "the suspension is easy to install" or "the suspension enables high-speed descents on bumpy trails" are typical in terms of the subjective quality of the expressions. While such expressions are helpful in developing a clear sense of the issues of interest to customers, they provide little specific guidance about how to design and engineer the product. They simply leave too much margin for subjective interpretation. For this reason, development teams usually establish a set of specifications, which spell out in precise, measurable detail *what* the product has to do. Product specifications do not tell the team *how* to address the customer needs, but they do represent an unambiguous agreement on what the team will attempt to achieve in order to satisfy the customer needs. For example,

54

No.		Need	Imp.
1	The suspension	reduces vibration to the hands.	3
2	The suspension	allows easy traversal of slow, difficult terrain.	2
3	The suspension	enables high-speed descents on bumpy trails.	5
4	The suspension	allows sensitivity adjustment	3
5	The suspension	preserves the steering characteristics of the bike.	4
6	The suspension	remains rigid during hard cornering.	4
7	The suspension	is lightweight.	4
8	The suspension	provides stiff mounting points for the brakes.	2
9	The suspension	fits a wide variety of bikes, wheels, and tires.	5
10	The suspension	is easy to install.	1
11	The suspension	works with fenders.	1
12	The suspension	instills pride.	5
13	The suspension	is affordable for an amateur enthusiast.	5
14	The suspension	is not contaminated by water.	5
15	The suspension	is not contaminated by grunge.	5
16	The suspension	can be easily accessed for maintenance.	3
17	The suspension	allows easy replacement of worn parts.	1
18	The suspension	can be maintained with readily available tools.	3
19	The suspension	lasts a long time.	5
20	The suspension	is safe in a crash.	5

EXHIBIT 2   Customer needs for the suspension fork and their relative importance (shown in a convenient spreadsheet format).

in contrast to the customer need that "the suspension is easy to install," the corresponding specification might be that "the average time to assemble the fork to the frame is less than 75 seconds."

We intend the term *product specifications* to mean the precise description of what the product has to do. Some firms use the terms "product requirements" or "engineering characteristics" in this way. Other firms use "specifications" or "technical specifications" to refer to key design variables of the product such as the oil viscosity or spring constant of the suspension system. These are just differences in terminology. For clarity, let us be precise about a few definitions. A *specification* (singular) consists of a *metric* and a *value.* For example, "average time to assemble" is a metric, while "less than 75 seconds" is the value of this metric. Note that the value may take on several forms, including a particular number, a range, or an inequality. Values are always labeled with the appropriate units (e.g., seconds, kilograms, joules). Together, the metric and value form a specification. The *product specifications* (plural) are simply the set of the individual specifications.

WHEN ARE SPECIFICATIONS ESTABLISHED?

In the ideal world, the team would establish the product specifications once early in the development process and then proceed to design and engineer the product to exactly meet those specifications. For some products, such as soap or soup, this approach works quite well; the technologists on the team can reliably concoct a formulation that satisfies almost any reasonable specifications. However, for technology-intensive products this is rarely possible. For such products, specifications are established at least twice. Immediately after identifying the customer needs, the team sets *target specifications*. These specifications represent the hopes and aspirations of the team, but they are established before the team knows what constraints the product technology will place on what can be achieved. The team's efforts may fail to meet some of these specifications and may exceed others, depending on the product concept the team eventually selects. For this reason, the target specifications must be refined after a product concept has been selected. The team revisits the specifications while assessing the actual technological constraints and the expected production costs. To set the *refined specifications*, the team must frequently make hard trade-offs among different desirable characteristics of the product.

The two stages in which specifications are established are shown as part of the concept development process in Exhibit 3. Note that the refined specifications are one of the key elements of the development plan, which is usually documented in the project's *contract book*. The contract book (described in the chapter "Managing Product Development Projects") specifies what the team agrees to achieve, the project schedule, the required resources, and the economic implications for the business. The list of product specifications is also one of the key information systems used by the team throughout the development process.

This chapter presents two four-step methodologies; the first is for establishing the target specifications and the second is for refining the specifications after the product concept has been selected.

EXHIBIT 3 The concept development process. The target specifications are set early in the process, but refinement of the specifications must wait until after the product concept has been selected.

ESTABLISHING TARGET SPECIFICATIONS

As Exhibit 3 illustrates, the target specifications are established after the customer needs have been identified but before product concepts have been generated and the most promising one selected. An arbitrary setting of the specifications may not be technically feasible. For example, in designing a suspension fork, the team cannot assume in advance that it will be able to achieve simultaneously a mass of 1 kilogram, a manufacturing cost of $30, and the best descent time on the test track, as these are three quite aggressive specifications. Actually meeting the specifications established at this point is contingent upon the details of the product concept the team eventually selects. For this reason, such preliminary specifications are labeled "target specifications." They are the goals of the development team, describing a product that the team believes would succeed in the marketplace. Later these specifications will be refined to suit the limitations of the product concept actually selected.

The process of establishing the target specifications contains four steps:

1 Prepare the list of metrics, using the needs-metrics matrix, if necessary.

2 Collect the competitive benchmarking information.

3 Set *ideal* and *marginally acceptable* target values for each metric.

4 Reflect on the results and the process.

Step 1: Prepare the List of Metrics

The most useful metrics are those that reflect as directly as possible the degree to which the product satisfies the customer needs. The relationship between needs and metrics is central to the entire concept of specifications. The working assumption is that a translation from customer needs to a set of precise, measurable specifications is possible and that meeting specifications will therefore lead to satisfaction of the associated customer needs.

A list of metrics is shown in Exhibit 4. The best way to generate the list of metrics is to contemplate each need in turn and to consider what precise, measurable characteristic of the product will reflect the degree to which the product satisfies that need. In the ideal case, there is one and only one metric for each need. In practice, this is frequently not possible.

For example, consider the need that the suspension be "easy to install." The team may conclude that this need is largely captured by measuring the time required for assembly of the fork to the frame. However, note the possible subtleties in this translation. Is assembly time really identical to ease of installation? The installation could be extremely fast but require an awkward and painful set of finger actions which ultimately may lead to worker harm or dealer frustration. Because of the imprecise nature of the translation process, those establishing the specifications should have been directly involved in identifying the customer needs. In this way the team can rely on its understanding of the meaning of each need statement derived from firsthand interactions with customers.

Metric No.	Need Nos.	Metric	Imp.	Units
1	1, 3	Attenuation from dropout to handlebar at 10 Hz	3	dB
2	2, 6	Spring preload	3	N
3	1, 3	Maximum value from the Monster	5	g
4	1, 3	Minimum descent time on test track	5	s
5	4	Damping coefficient adjustment range	3	N-s/m
6	5	Maximum travel (26 in. wheel)	3	mm
7	5	Rake offset	3	mm
8	6	Lateral stiffness at the tip	3	kN/m
9	7	Total mass	4	kg
10	8	Lateral stiffness at brake pivots	2	kN/m
11	9	Headset sizes	5	in
12	9	Steertube length	5	mm
13	9	Wheel sizes	5	list
14	9	Maximum tire width	5	in
15	10	Time to assemble to frame	1	s
16	11	Fender compatibility	1	list
17	12	Instills pride	5	subj.
18	13	Unit manufacturing cost	5	US$
19	14	Time in spray chamber without water entry	5	s
20	15	Cycles in mud chamber without contamination	5	k-cycles
21	16, 17	Time to disassemble/assemble for maintenance	3	s
22	17, 18	Special tools required for maintenance	3	list
23	19	UV test duration to degrade rubber parts	5	hours
24	19	Monster cycles to failure	5	cycles
25	20	Japan Industrial Standards test	5	binary
26	20	Bending strength (frontal loading)	5	kN

EXHIBIT 4 List of metrics for the suspension. The relative importance of each metric and the units for the metric are also shown.

The need for the fork to reduce vibration to the user's hands may be even more difficult to translate into a single metric, because there are many different conditions under which vibration can be transmitted, including small bumps on level roads and big bumps on steep hills. The team may conclude that several metrics are required to capture this need, including, for example, the metrics "attenuation from dropout to handlebar at 10 Hz" and "maximum value from the Monster." (The "Monster" is a shock test used by *Mountain Bike* magazine.)

Need	1 Attenuation from dropout to handlebar at 10 Hz	2 Spring preload	3 Maximum value from the Monster	4 Minimum descent time on test track	5 Damping coefficient adjustment range	6 Maximum travel (26 in. wheel)	7 Rake offset	8 Lateral stiffness at the tip	9 Total mass	10 Lateral stiffness at brake pivots	11 Headset sizes	12 Steertube length	13 Wheel sizes	14 Maximum tire width	15 Time to assemble to frame	16 Fender compatibility	17 Instills pride	18 Unit manufacturing cost	19 Time in spray chamber without water entry	20 Cycles in mud chamber without contamination	21 Time to disassemble/assemble for maintenance	22 Special tools required for maintenance	23 UV test duration to degrade rubber parts	24 Monster cycles to failure	25 Japan Industrial Standards test	26 Bending strength (frontal loading)
1 Reduces vibration to the hands	•		•	•																						
2 Allows easy traversal of slow, difficult terrain		•																								
3 Enables high-speed descents on bumpy trails	•		•	•																						
4 Allows sensitivity adjustment					•																					
5 Preserves the steering characteristics of the bike						•	•																			
6 Remains rigid during hard cornering		•						•																		
7 Is lightweight									•																	
8 Provides stiff mounting points for the brakes										•																
9 Fits a wide variety of bikes, wheels, and tires											•	•	•	•												
10 Is easy to install															•											
11 Works with fenders																•										
12 Instills pride																	•									
13 Is affordable for an amateur enthusiast																		•								
14 Is not contaminated by water																			•							
15 Is not contaminated by grunge																				•						
16 Can be easily accessed for maintenance																					•					
17 Allows easy replacement of worn parts																					•	•				
18 Can be maintained with readily available tools																						•				
19 Lasts a long time																							•	•		
20 Is safe in a crash																									•	•

EXHIBIT 5 The needs-metrics matrix.

A simple needs-metrics matrix represents the relationship between needs and metrics and assures that all of the customer needs are considered. An example needs-metrics matrix is shown in Exhibit 5. The rows of the matrix correspond to the customer needs, and the columns of the matrix correspond to the metrics. A mark in a cell of the matrix means that the need and the metric associated with the cell are related; performance relative to the metric will influence the degree to which the product satisfies the customer need. This matrix is a key element of the recently popular *House of Quality*, a graphical technique used in *Quality Function Deployment*, or *QFD* (Hauser and Clausing, 1988). In many cases, we find the information in the needs-metrics matrix is just as easily communicated by listing the numbers of the needs related to each metric alongside the list of metrics (the second column in Exhibit 4). There are some cases, however, in which the mapping from needs to metrics is complex, and the matrix can be quite useful for representing this mapping.

A few caveats should be considered when constructing the list of metrics:

- *Metrics should be **dependent, not** independent, variables.* Designers use many types of variables in product development; some are *dependent*, such as the mass of the fork, and some are *independent*, such as the material used for the fork. In other words, designers cannot control mass directly, because it arises from other independent decisions the designers will make, such as dimensions and materials choices. Metrics specify the overall performance of a product and should therefore be the dependent variables in the design problem.

- *Metrics should be practical.* It does not serve the team to devise a metric for a bicycle suspension that can only be measured by a scientific laboratory at a cost of $100,000. Ideally, metrics will be directly observable or analyzable properties of the product that can be easily evaluated by the team.

- *Some needs cannot easily be translated into quantifiable metrics.* The need that the suspension instills pride may be quite critical to success in the fashion-conscious mountain bike market, but how can pride be quantified? In these cases, the team simply repeats the need statement as a specification and notes that evaluation of the metric is subjective. (We indicate this by entering "subj." in the units column.)

- *The metrics should include the popular criteria for comparison in the marketplace.* Many customers in many markets buy products based on independently published evaluations. Such evaluations are found in, for example, *Popular Science, Consumer Reports*, or, in our case, *Bicycling* and *Mountain Bike* magazines. If the team knows that its product will be evaluated by the trade media and knows what the evaluation criteria will be, then it should include metrics corresponding to these criteria. *Mountain Bike* magazine uses a test machine called the Monster, which measures the vertical acceleration (in g's) of the handlebars as a bicycle equipped with the fork runs over a block 50 millimeters tall. For this reason, the team included "maximum value from the Monster" as a metric. If the team cannot find a relationship between the criteria used by the media and the customer needs it has identified, then it should ensure that a need has not been overlooked and/or should work with the media to revise the criteria. In a few cases, the team may conclude that high performance in the media evaluations is in itself a customer need and choose to include a metric used by the media that has little intrinsic technical merit.

In addition to denoting the needs related to each metric, Exhibit 4 contains the units of measurement and an importance rating for each metric. The units of measurement are most commonly conventional engineering units such as kilograms and seconds. However, some metrics will not lend themselves to numerical values. The need that the suspension "works with fenders" is best translated into a specification listing the models of fenders the fork is compatible with. In this case, the value of the metric is actually a list of fenders rather than a number. For the metric involving the standard safety test, the value is pass/fail. (We indicate these two cases by entering "list" and "binary" in the units column.)

The importance rating of a metric is derived from the importance ratings of the needs it reflects. For cases in which a metric maps directly to a single need, the importance rating of the need becomes the importance rating of the metric. For cases in which a metric is related to more than one need, the importance of the metric is determined by considering the importances of the needs to which it relates and the nature of these relationships. We believe that there are enough subtleties in this process that importance weightings can best be determined through discussion among the team members, rather than through a formal algorithm.

Step 2: Collect the Competitive Benchmarking Information

Unless the team expects to enjoy a total monopoly, the relationship of the new product to competitive products is paramount in determining commercial success. While the team will have entered the product development process with some idea of how it wishes to compete in the marketplace, the target specifications are the language the team uses to discuss and agree on the detailed positioning of its product relative to existing products, both its own and competitors'. Information on competing products must be gathered in order to support these positioning decisions.

An example of a competitive benchmarking chart is shown in Exhibit 6. The columns of the chart correspond to the competitive products and the rows are the metrics established in step 1. Note that the competitive benchmarking chart can be constructed as a simple appendage to the spreadsheet containing the list of metrics. This information is one of the "rooms" in the *House of Quality*, described by Hauser and Clausing.

The benchmarking chart is conceptually very simple. For each competitive product, the values of the metrics are simply entered down a column. Gathering these data can be very time-consuming, involving (at the least) purchasing, testing, disassembling, and estimating the production costs of the most important competitive products. However, this investment of time is essential, as no product development team can expect to succeed without having this type of information. A word of warning: Sometimes the data contained in competitors' cata-

Metric No.	Need Nos.	Metric	Imp.	Units	ST Tritrack	Maniray 2	Rox Tahx Quadra	Rox Tahx Ti 21	Tonka Pro	Gunhill Head Shox
1	1, 3	Attenuation from dropout to handlebar at 10 Hz	3	dB	8	15	10	15	9	13
2	2, 6	Spring preload	3	N	550	760	500	710	480	680
3	1, 3	Maximum value from the Monster	5	g	3.6	3.2	3.7	3.3	3.7	3.4
4	1, 3	Minimum descent time on test track	5	s	13	11.3	12.6	11.2	13.2	11
5	4	Damping coefficient adjustment range	3	N-s/m	0	0	0	200	0	0
6	5	Maximum travel (26 in. wheel)	3	mm	28	48	43	46	33	38
7	5	Rake offset	3	mm	41.5	39	38	38	43.2	39
8	6	Lateral stiffness at the tip	3	kN/m	59	110	85	85	65	130
9	7	Total mass	4	kg	1.409	1.385	1.409	1.364	1.222	1.100
10	8	Lateral stiffness at brake pivots	2	kN/m	295	550	425	425	325	650
11	9	Headset sizes	5	in	1.000 1.125	1.000 1.125 1.250	1.000 1.125	1.000 1.125 1.250	1.000 1.125	NA
12	9	Steertube length	5	mm	150 180 210 230 255	140 165 190 215	150 170 190 210	150 170 190 210 230	150 190 210 220	NA
13	9	Wheel sizes	5	list	26 in	26 in	26 in	26 in 700C	26 in	26 in
14	9	Maximum tire width	5	in	1.5	1.75	1.5	1.75	1.5	1.5
15	10	Time to assemble to frame	1	s	35	35	45	45	35	85
16	11	Fender compatibility	1	list	Zefal	none	none	none	none	all
17	12	Instills pride	5	subj.	1	4	3	5	3	5
18	13	Unit manufacturing cost	5	US$	65	105	85	115	80	100
19	14	Time in spray chamber without water entry	5	s	1300	2900	>3600	>3600	2300	>3600
20	15	Cycles in mud chamber without contamination	5	k-cycles	15	19	15	25	18	35
21	16, 17	Time to disassemble/assemble for maintenance	3	s	160	245	215	245	200	425
22	17, 18	Special tools required for maintenance	3	list	hex	hex	hex	hex	long hex	hex, pin wrench
23	19	UV test duration to degrade rubber parts	5	hours	400+	250	400+	400+	400+	250
24	19	Monster cycles to failure	5	cycles	500k+	500k+	500k+	480k	500k+	330k
25	20	Japan Industrial Standards test	5	binary	pass	pass	pass	pass	pass	pass
26	20	Bending strength (frontal loading)	5	kN	5.5	8.9	7.5	7.5	6.2	10.2

EXHIBIT 6 Competitive benchmarking chart based on metrics.

No.	Need	Imp.	ST Tritrack	Maniray 2	Rox Tahx Quadra	Rox Tahx Ti 21	Tonka Pro	Gunhill Head Shox
1	Reduces vibration to the hands	3	•	••••	••	•••••	••	•••
2	Allows easy traversal of slow, difficult terrain	2	••	••••	•••	•••••	•••	••••••
3	Enables high-speed descents on bumpy trails	5	•	•••••	••	•••••	••	•••
4	Allows sensitivity adjustment	3	•	••••	••	•••••	••	•••
5	Preserves the steering characteristics of the bike	4	••••	••	•	••	•••••••	
6	Remains rigid during hard cornering	4	•	•••	•	•••••	•	•••••
7	Is lightweight	4	•	•••	•	•••	••••	•••••
8	Provides stiff mounting points for the brakes	2	•	••••	•••	•••	•••••••	
9	Fits a wide variety of bikes, wheels, and tires	5	••••	•••••	•••	•••••	•••	•
10	Is easy to install	1	••••	•••••	••••	••••	•••••	•
11	Works with fenders	1	•••	•	•	•	•	•••••
12	Instills pride	5	•	••••	•••	•••••	•••	•••••
13	Is affordable for an amateur enthusiast	5	•••••	•	•••	•	•••	••
14	Is not contaminated by water	5	•	•••	••••	••••	••	•••••
15	Is not contaminated by grunge	5	•	•••	•	••••	••	•••••
16	Can be easily accessed for maintenance	3	••••	•••••	••••	••••	•••••	•
17	Allows easy replacement of worn parts	1	••••	•••••	••••	••••	•••••	•
18	Can be maintained with readily available tools	3	•••••	•••••	•••••	•••••	••	•
19	Lasts a long time	5	•••••	•••••	•••••	•••	•••••	•
20	Is safe in a crash	5	•••••	•••••	•••••	•••••	•••••	•••••

EXHIBIT 7 Competitive benchmarking chart based on perceived satisfaction of needs. (Scoring more "dots" corresponds to greater perceived satisfaction of the need.)

logs and supporting literature are not accurate. Where possible, values of the key metrics should be verified by independent testing or observation.

An alternative competitive benchmarking chart can be constructed with rows corresponding to the customer needs and columns corresponding to the competitive products (see Exhibit 7). This chart is used to compare customers' perceptions of the relative degree to which the products satisfy their needs. Constructing this chart requires collecting customer perception data, which can also be very expensive and time-consuming. Some techniques for measuring customers' perceptions of satisfaction of needs are contained in a book by Urban and Hauser (1993). Both charts can be useful; at a minimum, a chart showing the competitive values of the metrics (Exhibit 6) should be created.

Step 3: Set Ideal and Marginally Acceptable Target Values for Each Metric

In this step, the team synthesizes the available information in order to actually set the target values for the metrics. Two types of targets are useful: an *ideal target* and a *marginally acceptable target*. The ideal target is the best result the team could hope for. The marginally acceptable target is the value of the metric that would just barely make the product commercially viable. Both of these targets are useful in guiding the subsequent stages of concept generation and concept selection, and for refining the specifications after the product concept has been selected.

There are five ways to express the values of the metrics:

- *At least X:* These specifications establish targets for the lower bound on a metric, but higher is still better. For example, the value of the brake mounting stiffness is specified to be at least 325 kilonewtons/meter.

- *At most X:* These specifications establish targets for the upper bound on a metric, with smaller values being better. For example, the value for the mass of the suspension fork is set to be at most 1.4 kilograms.

- *Between X and Y:* These specifications establish both upper and lower bounds for the value of a metric. For example, the value for the spring preload is set to be between 480 and 800 newtons. Any more and the suspension is harsh; any less and the suspension is too bouncy.

- *Exactly X:* These specifications establish a target of a particular value of a metric, with any deviation degrading performance. This type of specification is to be avoided and should be used only when absolutely necessary. Often, upon reconsideration, the team realizes that what initially appears as an "exactly X" specification can be expressed as a "between X and Y" specification. For example, the ideal value for the rake offset metric is set to 38 millimeters.

- *A set of discrete values:* Some metrics will have values corresponding to several discrete choices. For example, the headset diameters are 1.000, 1.125, or 1.250 inches. (Industry practice is to use English units for these and several other critical bicycle dimensions.)

The desirable range of values for one metric may depend on another. In other words, we may wish to express a target as, for example, "the fork tip lateral stiffness is no more than 20 percent of the lateral stiffness at the brake pivots." In applications where the team feels this level of complexity is warranted, such targets can easily be included, although we recommend that this level of complexity not be introduced until the refinement phase of the specifications process.

Using these five different types of expressions for values of the metrics, the team sets the target specifications. The team simply proceeds down the list of metrics and assigns both the marginally acceptable and ideal target values for each metric. These decisions are facilitated by the metric-based competitive benchmarking chart shown in Exhibit 6. To set the target values, the team has many considerations, including the capability of competing products available at the time, competitors' future product capabilities (if these are predictable), and the product's mission statement and target market segment. Exhibit 8 shows the targets assigned for the suspension fork.

Because most of the values are expressed in terms of bounds (upper or lower or both), the team is establishing the boundaries of the competitively viable product space. The team hopes that the product will meet some of the ideal targets but is confident that a product can be commercially viable even if it exhibits one or more marginally acceptable characteristics. Note that these specifications are preliminary because until a product concept is chosen and some of the design details are worked out, many of the exact trade-offs are quite uncertain.

Step 4: Reflect on the Results and the Process

The team may require some iteration to agree on the targets. Reflection after each iteration helps to ensure that the results are consistent with the goals of the project. Questions to consider include:

- Are members of the team "gaming"? For example, is the key marketing representative insisting that an aggressive value is required for a particular metric in the hopes that by setting a high goal, the team will actually achieve more than if his or her true, and more lenient, beliefs were expressed?
- Should the team consider offering multiple products or at least multiple options for the product in order to best match the particular needs of more than one market segment, or will one "average" product suffice?
- Are any specifications missing? Do the specifications reflect the characteristics that will dictate commercial success?

Once the targets have been set, the team can proceed to generate solution concepts. The target specifications then can be used to help the team select a concept and will help the team know when a concept is commercially viable. (See the chapters "Concept Generation" and "Concept Selection.")

REFINING THE SPECIFICATIONS

As the team finalizes the choice of a concept and prepares for subsequent design and development, the specifications are revisited. Specifications which

Metric No.	Need Nos.	Metric	Imp.	Units	Marginal Value	Ideal Value
1	1, 3	Attenuation from dropout to handlebar at 10 Hz	3	dB	>10	>15
2	2, 6	Spring preload	3	N	480–800	650–700
3	1, 3	Maximum value from the Monster	5	g	<3.5	<3.2
4	1, 3	Minimum descent time on test track	5	s	<13.0	<11.0
5	4	Damping coefficient adjustment range	3	N-s/m	0	>200
6	5	Maximum travel (26 in. wheel)	3	mm	33–50	45
7	5	Rake offset	3	mm	37–45	38
8	6	Lateral stiffness at the tip	3	kN/m	>65	>130
9	7	Total mass	4	kg	<1.4	<1.1
10	8	Lateral stiffness at brake pivots	2	kN/m	>325	>650
11	9	Headset sizes	5	in	1.000 1.125	1.000 1.125 1.250
12	9	Steertube length	5	mm	150 170 190 210	150 170 190 210 230
13	9	Wheel sizes	5	list	26 in	26 in 700C
14	9	Maximum tire width	5	in	>1.5	>1.75
15	10	Time to assemble to frame	1	s	<60	<35
16	11	Fender compatibility	1	list	none	all
17	12	Instills pride	5	subj.	>3	>5
18	13	Unit manufacturing cost	5	US$	<85	<65
19	14	Time in spray chamber without water entry	5	s	>2300	>3600
20	15	Cycles in mud chamber without contamination	5	k-cycles	>15	>35
21	16, 17	Time to disassemble/assemble for maintenance	3	s	<300	<160
22	17, 18	Special tools required for maintenance	3	list	hex	hex
23	19	UV test duration to degrade rubber parts	5	hours	>250	>450
24	19	Monster cycles to failure	5	cycles	>300k	>500k
25	20	Japan Industrial Standards test	5	binary	pass	pass
26	20	Bending strength (frontal loading)	5	kN	>7.0	>10.0

EXHIBIT 8 The target specifications. Like the other information systems, this one is easily encoded with a spreadsheet as a simple extension to the list of specifications.

originally were only targets expressed as broad ranges of values are now refined and made more precise.

Refining the specifications is difficult because of trade-offs—inverse relationships between two specifications that are inherent in the selected product concept. Trade-offs frequently occur between different technical performance metrics and almost always occur between technical performance metrics and cost. For example, one trade-off is between brake mounting stiffness and mass of the fork. Because of the basic mechanics of the fork structure, these specifications are inversely related, assuming other factors are held constant. Another trade-off is between cost and mass. For a given concept, the team may be able to reduce the mass of the fork by making the parts out of magnesium instead of aluminum. Unfortunately, decreasing the mass in this way will most likely increase the manufacturing cost of the product. The difficult part of refining the specifications is choosing how such trade-offs will be resolved.

Again, we propose a four-step process:

1 Develop technical models of the product.

2 Develop a cost model of the product.

3 Refine the specifications, making trade-offs where necessary.

4 Reflect on the results and the process.

Step 1: Develop Technical Models of the Product

A *technical model* of the product is a tool for predicting the values of the metrics for a particular set of design decisions. We intend the term *models* to refer to both analytical and physical approximations of the product. (See the chapter "Effective Prototyping" for further discussion of such models.)

At this point, the team had chosen an oil-damped coil spring concept for the suspension fork. The design decisions facing the team included details such as the materials for the structural components, the orifice diameter and oil viscosity for the damper, and the spring constant. Three models linking such design decisions to the performance metrics are shown in conceptual form in Exhibit 9. Such models can be used to predict the product's performance along a number of dimensions. The inputs to these models are the design variables associated with the product concept, such as oil viscosity, orifice diameter, spring constant, and geometry. The outputs of the model are the values of the metrics, such as attenuation, stiffness, and fatigue life.

Ideally, the team will be able to accurately model the product analytically, perhaps by implementing the model equations in a spreadsheet or computer simulation. Such a model allows the team to predict rapidly what type of performance can be expected from a particular choice of design variables, without costly physical experimentation. In most cases, such analytical models will be available for only a small subset of the metrics. For example, the team was able to model attenuation analytically, based on the engineers' knowledge of dynamic systems.

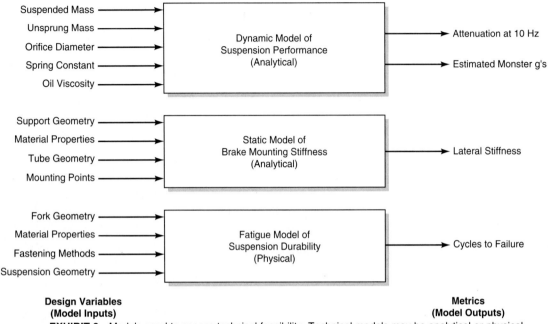

Suspended Mass →
Unsprung Mass →
Orifice Diameter → | Dynamic Model of Suspension Performance (Analytical) | → Attenuation at 10 Hz
Spring Constant →
Oil Viscosity → | | → Estimated Monster g's

Support Geometry →
Material Properties → | Static Model of Brake Mounting Stiffness (Analytical) | → Lateral Stiffness
Tube Geometry →
Mounting Points →

Fork Geometry →
Material Properties → | Fatigue Model of Suspension Durability (Physical) | → Cycles to Failure
Fastening Methods →
Suspension Geometry →

Design Variables (Model Inputs)　　　　　　　　　　　　　　　**Metrics (Model Outputs)**

EXHIBIT 9　Models used to assess technical feasibility. Technical models may be analytical or physical approximations of the product concept.

Several independent models, each corresponding to a subset of the metrics, may be more manageable than one large integrated model. For example, the team developed a separate analytical model for the brake mounting stiffness that was completely independent of the dynamic model used to predict vibration attenuation. In some cases, no analytical models will be available at all. For example, the team was not able to model analytically the fatigue performance of the suspension, so physical models were built and tested. It is generally necessary to actually build a variety of different physical mock-ups or prototypes in order to explore the implications of several combinations of design variables. When physical models must be constructed, it is often useful to use design-of-experiments (DOE) techniques, which can minimize the number of mock-ups that must be tested to explore the design space (Box and Bisgaard, 1988).

Armed with these technical models, the team can predict whether or not any particular set of specifications (such as the ideal target values) is technically feasible by exploring different combinations of design variables. This type of modeling and analysis prevents the team from setting a combination of specifications that cannot be achieved using the available latitude in the product concept.

Note that a technical model is almost always unique to a particular product concept. One of the models illustrated in Exhibit 9 is for an oil-damped suspension system; the model would be substantially different if the team had selected a concept employing a rubber suspension element. Thus, the modeling step can only be performed after the concept has been chosen.

Step 2: Develop a Cost Model of the Product

The goal of this step of the process is to make sure that the product can be produced at a reasonable cost. It is at this point that the team attempts to discover, for example, how much it will have to sacrifice in manufacturing cost to save 50 grams of mass.

For most products, the first estimates of manufacturing costs are completed by drafting a bill of materials (a list of all the parts) and estimating a purchase price or fabrication cost for each part. At this point in the development process the team does not generally know all of the components that will be in the

EXHIBIT 10 A bill of materials with cost estimates. This simple cost model allows early cost estimates to facilitate realistic trade-offs in the product specifications.

Component	Qty/Fork	High ($ ea.)	Low ($ ea.)	High Total ($/fork)	Low Total ($/fork)
Steer tube	1	2.50	2.00	2.50	2.00
Crown	1	4.00	3.00	4.00	3.00
Boot	2	1.00	0.75	2.00	1.50
Lower tube	2	3.00	2.00	6.00	4.00
Lower tube top cover	2	2.00	1.50	4.00	3.00
Main lip seal	2	1.50	1.40	3.00	2.80
Slide bushing	4	0.20	0.18	0.80	0.72
Slide bushing spacer	2	0.50	0.40	1.00	0.80
Lower tube plug	2	0.50	0.35	1.00	0.70
Upper tube	2	5.50	4.00	11.00	8.00
Upper tube top cap	2	3.00	2.50	6.00	5.00
Upper tube adjustment knob	2	2.00	1.75	4.00	3.50
Adjustment shaft	2	4.00	3.00	8.00	6.00
Spring	2	3.00	2.50	6.00	5.00
Upper tube orifice cap	1	3.00	2.25	3.00	2.25
Orifice springs	4	0.50	0.40	2.00	1.60
Brake studs	2	0.40	0.35	0.80	0.70
Brake brace bolt	2	0.25	0.20	0.50	0.40
Brake brace	1	5.00	3.50	5.00	3.50
Oil (liters)	0.1	2.50	2.00	0.25	0.20
Misc. snap rings, o-rings	10	0.15	0.10	1.50	1.00
Decals	4	0.25	0.15	1.00	0.60
Assembly at $20/hr		30 min	20 min	10.00	6.67
Overhead at 25% of direct cost				20.84	15.74
Total				$104.19	$78.68

product, but the team nevertheless makes an attempt to list the components it expects will be required. While early estimates generally focus on the cost of components, the team will usually make a rough estimate of assembly and other manufacturing costs (e.g., overhead) at this point a well. Efforts to develop these early cost estimates involve soliciting cost estimates from vendors and estimating the production costs of the components the firm will make itself. This process is often facilitated by a purchasing expert and a production engineer. A bill-of-materials cost model is shown in Exhibit 10 for the suspension fork. (See the chapter "Design for Manufacturing" for more details on estimating manufacturing cost.)

A useful way to record cost information is to list figures for the high and low estimates of each item. This helps the team to understand the range of uncertainty in the estimates. The bill of materials is typically used iteratively: the team performs a "what if" cost analysis for a set of design decisions and then revises these decisions based on what it learns. The bill of materials is itself a kind of performance model, but instead of predicting the value of a technical performance metric, it predicts cost performance. The bill of materials remains useful throughout the development process and is updated regularly (as frequently as once each week) to reflect the current status of the estimated manufacturing cost.

At this point in the development process, teams developing complex products containing hundreds or thousands of parts will not generally be able to include every part in the bill of materials. Instead, the team will list the major components and subsystems and place bounds on their costs based on past experience or on the judgment of suppliers.

Step 3: Refine the Specifications, Making Trade-offs Where Necessary

Once the team has constructed technical performance models where possible and constructed a preliminary cost model, these tools can be used to develop refined specifications. Refining specifications can be accomplished in a group session in which feasible combinations of values are determined through the use of the technical models and then the cost implications are explored. In an iterative fashion, the team converges on the specifications which will most favorably position the product relative to the competition and will best satisfy the customer needs.

One important tool for supporting this decision-making process is the *competitive map*. An example competitive map is shown in Exhibit 11. A map is simply a scatter plot of the competitive products along two dimensions selected from the set of metrics. The map displayed in Exhibit 11 shows estimated manufacturing cost versus g's on the Monster test. The regions defined by the marginal and ideal values of the specifications are shown on the map. This map is particularly useful in showing that all of the high-performance suspensions (low Monster scores) have high estimated manufacturing costs. Armed with their technical

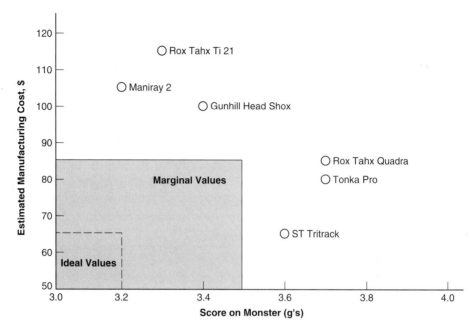

EXHIBIT 11 A competitive map showing estimated manufacturing cost versus score on the "Monster" test.

performance models and cost model, the team can assess whether or not it will be able to "beat the trade-off" exhibited in the competitive map.

These maps can be constructed directly from the data contained in the competitive benchmarking chart using the plotting feature of the spreadsheet software. Generally the team will prepare three or four such maps corresponding to a handful of critical metrics. Additional maps may be created as needed to support subsequent decision making.

The competitive map is used to position the new product relative to the competition. Using the technical and cost models of the product and the competitive maps, the team can refine the specifications in order to both satisfy the inherent constraints of the product concept and make the trade-offs in a way that will provide a performance advantage relative to the competitive products. The refined specifications for the suspension fork are shown in Exhibit 12.

Step 4: Reflect on the Results and the Process

As always, the final step in the methodology is to reflect on the outcome and the process. Some questions the team may want to consider are:

- Is the product a winner? The product concept should allow the team to actually set the specifications in a way that the product will meet the cus-

No.	Metric	Unit	Value
1	Attentuation from dropout to handlebar at 10 Hz	dB	>12
2	Spring preload	N	600–650
3	Maximum value from the Monster	g	<3.4
4	Minimum descent time on test track	s	<11.5
5	Damping coefficient adjustment range	N-s/m	>100
6	Maximum travel (26 in. wheel)	mm	43
7	Rake offset	mm	38
8	Lateral stiffness at the tip	kN/m	>75
9	Total mass	kg	<1.4
10	Lateral stiffness at brake pivots	kN/m	>425
11	Headset sizes	in	1.000 1.125
12	Steertube length	mm	150 170 190 210 230
13	Wheel sizes	list	26 in
14	Maximum tire width	in	>1.75
15	Time to assemble to frame	s	<45
16	Fender compatibility	list	Zefal
17	Instills pride	subj.	>4
18	Unit manufacturing cost	US$	<80
19	Time in spray chamber without water entry	s	>3600
20	Cycles in mud chamber without contamination	k-cycles	>25
21	Time to disassemble/assemble for maintenance	s	<200
22	Special tools required for maintenance	list	hex
23	UV test duration to degrade rubber parts	hours	>450
24	Monster cycles to failure	cycles	>500k
25	Japan Industrial Standards test	binary	pass
26	Bending strength (frontal loading)	kN	>10.0

EXHIBIT 12   The refined specifications.

tomer needs and excel competitively. If not, then the team should return to the concept generation and selection phase or abandon the project.

- How much uncertainty is there in the technical and cost models? If competitive success is dictated by metrics around which much uncertainty remains, the team may wish to refine the technical or cost models in order to increase confidence in meeting the specifications.

- Is the concept chosen by the team best suited to the target market, or could it be best applied in another market (say the low end or high end instead of the middle)? The selected concept may actually be too good. If the team has generated a concept that is dramatically superior to the competitive products, it may wish to consider employing the concept in a more demanding, and potentially more profitable, market segment.

- Should the firm initiate a formal effort to develop better technical models of some aspect of the product's performance for future use? Sometimes the team will discover that it does not really understand the underlying product technology well enough to create useful performance models. In such circumstances, an engineering effort to develop better understanding and models may be useful in subsequent development projects.

SUMMARY

Customer needs are generally expressed in the "language of the customer." In order to provide specific guidance about how to design and engineer a product, development teams establish a set of specifications, which spell out in precise, measurable detail what the product has to do in order to be commercially successful. The specifications must reflect the customer needs, differentiate the product from the competitive products, and be technically and economically realizable.

- Specifications are typically established at least twice. Immediately after identifying the customer needs, the team sets *target specifications*. After concept selection, the team develops *refined specifications*.

- Target specifications represent the hopes and aspirations of the team, but they are established before the team knows the constraints the product technology will place on what can be achieved. The team's efforts may fail to meet some of these specifications and may exceed others, depending on the details of the product concept the team eventually selects.

- The process of establishing the target specifications contains four steps:
  1 Prepare the list of metrics, using the needs-metrics matrix, if necessary.
  2 Collect the competitive benchmarking information.
  3 Set *ideal* and *marginally acceptable* target values for each metric.
  4 Reflect on the results and the process.

- Refined specifications are developed by assessing the actual technological constraints and the expected production costs using analytical and physical models. During this refinement phase the team must make difficult trade-offs among various desirable characteristics of the product.

- The four-step process for refining the specifications is:
  1 Develop technical models of the product.
  2 Develop a cost model of the product.
  3 Refine the specifications, making trade-offs where necessary.
  4 Reflect on the results and the process.

- The specifications process is facilitated by several simple *information systems* which can easily be created using conventional spreadsheet software. Tools such as the list of metrics, the needs-metrics matrix, the competitive benchmarking charts, and the competitive maps all support the team's decision making by providing the team with a way to represent and discuss the specifications.

- Because of the need to utilize the best possible knowledge of the marketplace, the customers, the core product technology, and the cost implications of design alternatives, the specifications process requires active participation from team members representing the marketing, design, and manufacturing functions of the enterprise.

REFERENCES AND BIBLIOGRAPHY

The process of translating customer needs into a set of specifications is also accomplished by the Quality Function Deployment (QFD) methodology. The key ideas behind QFD and the House of Quality are clearly presented by Hauser and Clausing in a popular article.

Hauser, John, and Don Clausing, "The House of Quality," *Harvard Business Review*, Vol. 66, No. 3, 1988, pp. 63–73.

Urban and Hauser present several techniques for selecting combinations of product attributes in order to maximize customer satisfaction. Some of these techniques can serve as powerful analytical support for the general methodology described in this chapter.

Urban, Glen, and John Hauser, *Design and Marketing of New Products*, second edition, Prentice-Hall, Englewood Cliffs, NJ, 1993. ISBN 0-13-201567-6.

Ramaswamy and Ulrich treat the use of engineering models in setting specifications in detail. They also identify some of the weaknesses in the conventional House of Quality methodology.

Ramaswamy, Rajan, and Karl Ulrich, "Augmenting the House of Quality with Engineering Models," *Research in Engineering Design*, Vol. 5, 1994, pp. 70–79.

Box and Bisgaard provide a good overview of the use of designed experiments in improving products.

Box, George, and Soren Bisgaard, "Statistical Tools for Improving Designs," *Mechanical Engineering*, January 1988, pp. 32–40.

EXERCISES

1 List a set of metrics corresponding to the need that a pen write smoothly.
2 Devise a metric and a corresponding test for the need that a roofing material last many years.
3 Some of the same metrics seem to be involved in trade-offs for many different products. Which metrics are these?

THOUGHT QUESTIONS

1 How might you establish precise and measurable specifications for intangible needs such as "the front suspension looks great"?

2 Why are some customer needs difficult to map to a single metric?

3 How might you explain a situation in which customers' perceptions of the competitive products (as in Exhibit 7) are not consistent with the values of the metrics for those same products (as in Exhibit 6)?

4 Can poor performance relative to one specification always be compensated for by high performance on other specifications? If so, how can there ever really be a "marginally acceptable" value for a metric?

5 Why should independent design variables not be used as metrics?

CONCEPT GENERATION

Developed in collaboration with Gavin Zau.

EXHIBIT 1   An existing hand-held nailer for the professional market.   (Courtesy Senco Products.)

The president of a tool manufacturing company commissioned a team to develop a new hand-held nailer for the high-end consumer market. One of several currently available pneumatic tools for the professional market is shown in Exhibit 1. The mission of the team was to consider broadly alternative product concepts, assuming only that the tool would employ conventional nails as the basic fastening technology. After identifying a set of customer needs and establishing target product specifications, the team faced the following questions:

- What existing solution concepts, if any, could be successfully adapted for this application?
- What new concepts might satisfy the established needs and specifications?
- What methods can be used to facilitate the concept generation process?

THE TASK OF CONCEPT GENERATION IN PRODUCT DEVELOPMENT

A product concept is an approximate description of the technology, working principles, and form of the product. It is a concise description of how the product will satisfy the customer needs. A concept is usually expressed as a sketch or as a rough three-dimensional model and is often accompanied by a brief textual description. The degree to which a product satisfies customers and can be successfully commercialized depends to a large measure on the quality of the underlying concept. A good concept is sometimes poorly implemented in subsequent development phases, but a poor concept can rarely be manipulated to achieve commercial success. Fortunately, concept generation is relatively inexpensive and can be done relatively quickly in comparison to the rest of the development process. For example, concept generation had typically consumed less than 5 percent of the budget and 15 percent of the development time in previous nailer development efforts. Because the concept generation activity is not costly, there is no excuse for a lack of diligence and care in executing a sound concept generation methodology.

The concept generation process begins with a set of customer needs and target specifications and results in a set of product concepts from which the team will make a final selection. The relation of concept generation to the other concept development activities is shown in Exhibit 2. In most cases, an effective development team will generate hundreds of concepts, of which 5 to 20 will merit serious consideration during the concept selection activity.

Good concept generation leaves the team with confidence that the full space of alternatives has been explored. Thorough exploration of alternatives early in the development process greatly reduces the likelihood that the team will stumble upon a superior concept late in the development process or that a competitor will introduce a product with dramatically better performance than the product under development.

78

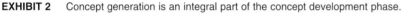

EXHIBIT 2   Concept generation is an integral part of the concept development phase.

Structured Approaches Reduce the Likelihood of Costly Problems

Common dysfunctions exhibited by development teams during concept generation include:

- Consideration of only one or two alternatives, often proposed by the most assertive members of the team
- Failure to consider carefully the usefulness of concepts employed by other firms in related and unrelated products
- Involvement of only one or two people in the process, resulting in lack of confidence and commitment by the rest of the team
- Ineffective integration of promising partial solutions
- Failure to consider entire categories of solutions

A structured approach to concept generation reduces the incidence of these problems by encouraging the gathering of information from many disparate information sources, by guiding the team in the thorough exploration of alternatives, and by providing a mechanism for integrating partial solutions. A structured methodology also provides a step-by-step procedure for those members of the team who may be less experienced in design-intensive activities, allowing them to participate actively in the process.

A Five-Step Methodology

This chapter presents a five-step concept generation methodology. The methodology, outlined in Exhibit 3, breaks a complex problem into simpler subproblems. Solution concepts are then identified for the subproblems by external and internal search procedures. Classification trees and concept combination tables are then used to explore systematically the space of solution concepts and to

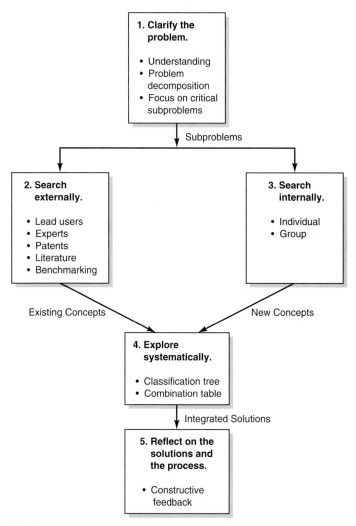

EXHIBIT 3 The five-step concept generation methodology.

integrate the subproblem solutions into a total solution. Finally, the team takes a step back to reflect on the validity and applicability of the results, as well as on the process used.

This chapter will follow the recommended methodology and will describe each of the five steps in detail. Although we present the methodology in a linear sequence, concept generation is almost always iterative. Like our other development methodologies, these steps are intended to be a baseline from which product development teams can develop and refine their own unique problem-solving style.

Our presentation of the methodology is focused primarily on the overall concept for a new product; however, the methodology can and should be used at several different points in the development process. The process is useful not only for overall product concepts but for concepts for subsystems and specific components as well. Also note that while the example in this chapter involves a relatively technical product, the same basic approach can be applied to nearly any product.

STEP 1: CLARIFY THE PROBLEM

Clarifying the problem consists of developing a general understanding and then breaking the problem down into subproblems if necessary.

The mission statement for the product, the customer needs list, and the preliminary product specification are the ideal inputs to the concept generation process, although often these pieces of information are still being refined as the concept generation phase begins. Ideally the team has been involved in both the identification of the customer needs and in the setting of the target product specifications. Those members of the team who were not involved in these preceding steps should become familiar with the processes used and their results before concept generation activities begin. (See the chapters "Identifying Customer Needs" and "Establishing Product Specifications.")

As stated before, the challenge was to "design a better hand-held nailer." The scope of the design problem could have been defined more generally (e.g., "fasten wood together") or more specifically (e.g., "improve the speed of the existing pneumatic tool concept"). Some of the assumptions in the team's mission statement were:

- The nailer will use nails (as opposed to adhesives, screws, etc.).
- The nailer will be compatible with nail magazines on existing tools.
- The nailer will nail into wood.
- The nailer will be hand-held.

Based on the assumptions, the team had identified the customer needs for a hand-held nailer. These included:

- The nailer inserts nails in rapid succession.
- The nailer fits into tight spaces.
- The nailer is lightweight.
- The nailer has no noticeable nailing delay after "tripping" the tool.

The team gathered supplemental information to clarify and quantify the needs, such as the approximate energy and speed of the nailing. These basic needs were subsequently translated into target product specifications. The target specifications included the following:

- Nail lengths from 50 millimeters to 75 millimeters
- Maximum nailing energy of 80 joules per nail
- Nailing forces of up to 2,000 newtons
- Peak nailing rate of 1 nail per second
- Average nailing rate of 4 nails per minute
- Ability to insert nails between standard stud/joists (368 millimeter opening)
- Tool mass less than 4 kilograms
- Maximum trigger delay of 0.25 seconds

Decompose a Complex Problem into Simpler Subproblems

Most design challenges are too complex to solve as a single problem and can be usefully divided into several simpler subproblems. Dividing a problem into simpler subproblems is called *problem decomposition*. There are many schemes by which a problem can be decomposed. Here we demonstrate a *functional* decomposition but then list several other approaches that are frequently useful.

The first step in decomposing a problem functionally is to represent it as a single *black box* operating on material, energy, and signal flows, as shown in Exhibit 4(a). Thin solid lines denote the transfer and conversion of energy, thick solid lines signify the movement of material within the system, and dashed lines represent the exchange of control and feedback signals within the system. This black box represents the overall function of the product.

The next step in functional decomposition is to divide the single black box into subfunctions to create a more specific description of what the elements of the product do in order to implement the overall function of the product. Each subfunction can generally be further divided into even simpler subfunctions. The division process is repeated until the team members agree that each subfunction is simple enough to work with. A good rule of thumb is to create between 3 and 10 subfunctions in the diagram. The end result, shown in Exhibit 4(b), is a function diagram containing subfunctions connected by energy, material, and signal flows.

Note that at this stage the goal is to describe the functional elements of the product without implying a specific technological working principle for the product concept. For example, Exhibit 4(b) includes the subfunction "isolate nail." This subfunction is expressed in such a way that it does not imply any particular physical solution concept, such as indexing the "stick" of nails into a slot or breaking a nail sideways off of the stick. The team should consider each subfunction in turn and ask whether it is expressed in a way that does not imply a particular physical solution principle.

There is no single correct way of creating a function diagram and no single correct functional decomposition of a product. A helpful way to create the dia-

EXHIBIT 4   Function diagram of a hand-held nailer arising from a functional decomposition: (a) overall "black box"; (b) refinement showing subfunctions.

gram is to quickly create several drafts and then work to refine them into a single diagram that the team is comfortable with. Some useful techniques for getting started are:

- Create a function diagram of an existing product.
- Create a function diagram based on an arbitrary product concept already generated by the team or based on a known subfunction technology. Be sure to generalize the diagram to the appropriate level of abstraction.
- Follow one of the flows (for example, material) and determine what operations are required. The details of the other flows can be derived by thinking about their connections to the initial flow.

Note that the function diagram is typically not unique. In particular, subfunctions can often be ordered in different ways to produce different function diagrams. Also note that in some applications the material, energy, and signal flows are difficult to identify. In these cases, a simple list of the subfunctions of the product, without connections between them, is often sufficient.

Functional decomposition is most applicable to technical products, but it can also be applied to simple and apparently nontechnical products. For example, an ice cream scoop has material flow of ice cream being separated, formed, transported, and deposited. These subfunctions could form the basis of a problem decomposition.

Functional decomposition is only one of several possible ways to divide a problem into simpler subproblems. Two other approaches are described below:

- *Decomposition by sequence of user actions:* For example, the nailer problem might be broken down into three user actions: moving the tool to the gross nailing position, positioning the tool precisely, triggering the tool. This approach is often useful for products with very simple technical functions involving a lot of user interaction.

- *Decomposition by key customer needs:* For the nailer, this decomposition might include the following subproblems: fires nails in rapid succession, fits in tight places, and has a large nail capacity. This approach is often useful for products in which form, and not working principles or technology, is the primary problem. Examples of such products include toothbrushes (assuming the basic brush concept is retained) and storage containers.

Focus Initial Efforts on the Critical Subproblems

The goal of all of these decomposition techniques is to divide a complex problem into simpler problems such that these simpler problems can be tackled in a focused way. Once problem decomposition is complete, the team chooses the subproblems that are most critical to the success of the product and that are likely to drive the overall solution to the problem. This approach involves a conscious decision to defer the solution of some of the subproblems. For example, the nailer team chose to focus on the subproblems of storing/accepting energy, converting the energy to translational energy, and applying the translational energy to the nail. The team felt confident that the nail handling and triggering issues could be solved after the energy storage and conversion issues were addressed. The team also deferred most of the user interaction issues of the tool. The team believed that the choice of a basic working principle for the tool would so constrain the eventual form of the tool that they had to begin with the core technology and then proceed to consider how to embody that technology in an attractive and user-friendly form. Teams can usually agree after a few minutes of discussion on which subproblems should be addressed first and which should be deferred for later consideration.

STEP 2: SEARCH EXTERNALLY

External search is aimed at finding existing solutions to both the overall problem and to the subproblems identified during the problem clarification step.

While external search is the second step in the concept generation methodology, this sequential labeling is deceptive; external search occurs continually throughout the development process. Implementing an existing solution is usually quicker and cheaper than developing a new solution. Liberal use of existing solutions allows the team to focus its creative energy on the critical subproblems for which there are no existing solutions. Furthermore, a conventional solution to one subproblem can frequently be combined with a novel solution to another subproblem to yield a superior overall design. For this reason external search includes detailed evaluation not only of directly competitive products but also of technologies used in products with related subfunctions.

The external search for solutions is essentially an information-gathering process. Available time and resources can be optimized by using an expand-and-focus strategy: first *expand* the scope of the search by broadly gathering information that might be related to the problem and then *focus* the scope of the search by exploring the promising directions in more detail. Too much of either approach will make the external search inefficient.

There are at least five good ways to gather information from external sources: lead user interviews, expert consultation, patent searches, literature searches, and competitive benchmarking.

Interview Lead Users

While identifying customer needs, the team may have sought out or encountered lead users. *Lead users* are those users of a class of product who experience needs months or years before the majority of the marketplace and stand to benefit substantially from a product innovation (von Hippel, 1988). Frequently these lead users will have already invented solutions to meet their needs. This is particularly true among highly technical user communities, such as those in the medical or scientific fields. Lead users may be sought out in the market for which the team is developing the new product, or they may be found in markets for products implementing some of the subfunctions of the product.

In the hand-held nailer case, the nailer team consulted with the building contractors from the PBS television series *This Old House* in order to solicit new concepts. These lead users made many interesting observations about the weaknesses in existing tools, but in this case did not provide many new product concepts.

Consult Experts

Experts with knowledge of one or more of the subproblems not only can provide solution concepts directly but also can redirect the search in a more fruitful area. Experts may include professionals at firms manufacturing related products, professional consultants, university faculty, and technical representatives of suppliers. These people can be found by calling universities, by calling companies, and by looking up authors of articles. While finding experts can be hard work, it is almost always less time-consuming than re-creating existing knowledge.

Most experts are willing to talk on the telephone or meet in person for an hour or so without charge. In general, consultants will expect to be paid for time they spend on a problem beyond an initial meeting or telephone conversation. Suppliers are usually willing to provide several days of effort without direct compensation if they anticipate that someone will use their product as a component in a design. Of course, experts at directly competing firms are in most cases unwilling to provide proprietary information about their product designs. A good habit to develop is to always ask people consulted to suggest others who should be contacted. The best information often comes from pursuing these "second generation" leads.

The nailer design team consulted dozens of experts, including a rocket fuel specialist at Morton-Thiokol, electric motor researchers at MIT, and engineers from a vendor of gas springs. Most of this consultation was done on the telephone, although the engineers from the spring vendor made two trips to visit the team, at their company's expense.

Search Patents

Patents are a rich and readily available source of technical information containing detailed drawings and explanations of how many products work. The main disadvantage of patent searches is that concepts found in recent patents are protected (17 years in the United States), so there may be a royalty involved in using them. However, patents are also useful to see what concepts are already protected and must be avoided or licensed. Concepts contained in foreign patents without global coverage and in expired patents can be used without payment of royalties.

The formal indexing scheme for patents is difficult for novices to navigate. Fortunately, several databases (e.g., Lexis/Nexis, Dialog) contain the actual text of all patents. These text databases can be searched electronically by key words. Key word searches can be conducted effectively with only modest practice and are remarkably effective in finding patents relevant to a particular product. Copies of U.S. patents including illustrations can be obtained from the U.S. Patent and Trademark Office for a few dollars (call 703-557-3158).

A U.S. patent search in the area of nailers revealed several interesting concepts. One of the patents described a motor-driven double-flywheel nailer. One of the illustrations from this patent is shown in Exhibit 5. The design in this patent uses the accumulation of rotational kinetic energy in a flywheel which is then suddenly converted into translational energy by a friction clutch. The energy is then delivered to the nail with a single impact of a drive pin.

Search Published Literature

Published literature includes journals; conference proceedings; trade magazines; government reports; market, consumer, and product information; and new product announcements. Literature searches are therefore very fertile sources of existing solutions.

EXHIBIT 5   Concept from motor-driven double-flywheel nailer patent (U.S. Patent 4,042,036). The accompanying text describing the patent is nine pages long.

Electronic database searches are frequently the most efficient way to gather information from published literature. These databases are available from on-line sources or on mass storage devices (e.g., CD-ROM) in the library. Currently, most databases store only abstracts of articles and not the full text and diagrams. A follow-up search for an actual article is often needed for complete information. The two main difficulties in conducting good database searches are determining the key words and limiting the scope of the search. There is a trade-off between the need to use more key words for complete coverage and the need to restrict the number of "matches" to a manageable number.

Handbooks cataloging technical information can also be very useful references for external search. Examples of such engineering references are *Mark's Standard Handbook of Mechanical Engineering, Perry's Chemical Engineers' Handbook,* and *Mechanisms and Mechanical Devices Sourcebook.*

The nailer team found several useful articles related to the subproblems, including articles on energy storage describing flywheel and battery technologies. In a handbook they found an impact tool mechanism that provided a useful energy conversion concept.

Benchmark Related Products

In the context of concept generation, *benchmarking* is the study of existing products with functionality similar to that of the product under development or to the subproblems on which the team is focused. Benchmarking can reveal existing concepts that have been implemented to solve a particular problem, as well as information on the strengths and weaknesses of the competition.

At this point the team will likely already be familiar with the competitive and closely related products. Products in other markets, but with related functionality, are more difficult to find. One of the most useful sources of this information is the *Thomas Register of American Manufacturers*, a directory of manufacturers of industrial products organized by product type. Often the hardest part of using the *Thomas Register* is finding out what related products are actually called and how they are cataloged.

For the nailer, the closely related products included a single-shot gunpowder-actuated tool for nailing into concrete, an electrical solenoid-actuated tacker, a pneumatic nailer for factory use, and a palm-held multi-blow pneumatic nailer. The products with related functionality (in this case, energy storage and conversion) included air bags and the sodium azide propellant used as an energy source, chemical hand warmers for skiing, air rifles powered by carbon dioxide cartridges, and portable computers and their battery packs. The team obtained and disassembled most of these related products in order to discover the general concepts on which they were based, as well as other more detailed information, including, for example, the names of the suppliers of specific components.

External search is an important method of gathering solution concepts. Skill in conducting external searches is therefore a valuable personal and organizational asset. This ability can be developed through careful observation of the world in order to develop a mental database of technologies and through the development of a network of professional contacts. Even with the aid of personal knowledge and contacts, external search remains "detective work" and is completed most effectively by those who are persistent and resourceful in pursuing leads and opportunities.

STEP 3: SEARCH INTERNALLY

Internal search is the use of personal and team knowledge and creativity to generate solution concepts. The search is *internal* in that all of the ideas to emerge from this step are created from knowledge already in the possession of the team. This activity may be the most open-ended and creative of any in new product development. We find it useful to think of internal search as a process of retrieving a potentially useful piece of information from one's memory and then adapting that information to the problem at hand. This process can be carried out by individuals working in isolation or by a group of people working together.

Four guidelines are useful for improving both individual and group internal search:

1 *Suspend judgment.* In most aspects of daily life, success depends on an ability to quickly evaluate a set of alternatives and take action. For example, none of us would be very productive if deciding what to wear in the morning or what to eat for breakfast involved an extensive period of generating alternatives before making a judgment. Because most decisions in our day-to-day lives have implications of only a few minutes or hours, we are accustomed to making decisions quickly and moving on. Concept generation is fundamentally different. We have to live with the consequences of product concept decisions for years. As a result, suspending evaluation for the days or weeks required to generate a large set of alternatives is critical to success. The imperative to suspend judgment is frequently translated into the rule that during group concept generation sessions no criticism of concepts is allowed. A better approach is for individuals perceiving weaknesses in concepts to channel any judgmental tendencies into suggestions for improvements or alternative concepts.

2 *Generate a lot of ideas.* Most experts believe that the more ideas a team generates, the more likely the team is to explore fully the solution space. Striving for quantity lowers the expectations of quality for any particular idea and therefore may encourage people to share ideas they may otherwise view as not worth mentioning. Further, each idea acts as a stimulus for other ideas, so a large number of ideas has the potential to stimulate even more ideas.

3 *Welcome ideas that may seem infeasible.* Ideas which initially appear infeasible can often be improved, "debugged," or "repaired" by other members of the team. The more infeasible an idea, the more it stretches the boundaries of the solution space and encourages the team to think of the limits of possibility. Therefore, infeasible ideas are quite valuable and their expression should be encouraged.

4 *Use graphical and physical media.* Reasoning about physical and geometric information with words is difficult. Text and verbal language are inherently inefficient vehicles for describing physical entities. Whether working as a group or as an individual, abundant sketching surfaces should be available. Foam, clay, cardboard, and other three-dimensional media may also be appropriate aids for problems requiring a deep understanding of form and spatial relationships.

Both Individual and Group Sessions Can Be Useful

Formal studies of group and individual problem solving suggest that a set of people working alone for a period of time will generate more and better concepts than the same people working together for the same time period (McGrath,

1984). This finding is contrary to the actual practices of the many firms that perform most of their concept generation activities in group sessions. Our informal observations confirm the formal studies, and we believe that team members should spend at least some of their concept generation time working alone. We also believe that group sessions are critical for building consensus, communicating information, and refining concepts. In an ideal setting, each individual on the team would spend several hours working alone and then the group would get together to discuss and improve the concepts generated by individuals.

However, we also know that there is a practical reason for holding group concept generation sessions: it is one way to guarantee that the individuals in the group will devote a certain amount of time to the task. Especially in very intense and demanding work environments, without scheduling a meeting, few people will allocate several hours for concentrated individual effort on generating new concepts. The phone rings, people interrupt, urgent problems demand attention. In certain environments, scheduled group sessions may be the only way to guarantee that enough attention is paid to the concept generation activity.

The nailer team used both individual effort and group sessions for internal search. For example, during one particular week each member was assigned one or two subproblems and was expected to develop at least ten solution concepts. This divided the concept generation work among all members. The group then met to discuss and expand on the individually generated concepts. The more promising concepts were investigated further.

Hints for Generating Solution Concepts

Experienced individuals and teams can usually just sit down and begin generating good concepts for a subproblem. Often these people have developed a set of techniques they use to stimulate their thinking, and these techniques have become a natural part of their problem-solving process. Novice product development professionals may be aided by a set of hints that stimulate new ideas or encourage relationships among ideas. VanGundy (1988), von Oech (1983), and McKim (1980) give dozens of helpful suggestions. Here are some hints we have found to be helpful:

- *Make analogies.* Experienced designers always ask themselves what other devices solve a related problem. Frequently they will ask themselves if there is a natural or biological analogy to the problem. They will think about whether their problem exists at a much larger or smaller dimensional scale than that which they are considering. They will ask what devices do something similar in an unrelated area of application. The nailer team, when posing these questions, realized that construction pile drivers are similar to nailers in some respects. In following up on this idea, they developed the concept of a multiblow tool.

- *Wish and wonder.* Beginning a thought or comment with "I wish we could . . ." or "I wonder what would happen if . . ." helps to stimulate oneself or the group to consider new possibilities. These questions cause reflection on the boundaries of the problem. For example, a member of the nailer team, when confronted with the required length of a rail gun (an electromagnetic device for accelerating a projectile) for driving a nail, said, "I wish the tool could be 1 meter long." Discussion of this comment led to the idea that perhaps a long tool could be used like a cane for nailing decking, allowing users to remain on their feet.

- *Use related stimuli.* Most individuals can think of a new idea when presented with a new stimulus. Related stimuli are those stimuli generated in the context of the problem at hand. For example, one way to use related stimuli is for each individual in a group session to generate a list of ideas (working alone) and then pass the list to his or her neighbor. Upon reflection on someone else's ideas, most people are able to generate new ideas. Other related stimuli include customer needs statements and photographs of the use environment of the product.

- *Use unrelated stimuli.* Occasionally, random or unrelated stimuli can be effective in encouraging new ideas. An example of such a technique is to choose, at random, one of a collection of photographs of objects, and then to think of some way that the randomly generated object might relate to the problem at hand. In a variant of this idea, individuals can be sent out on the streets with an instant camera to capture random images for subsequent use in stimulating new ideas. (This may also serve as a good change of pace for a tired group.)

- *Set quantitative goals.* Generating new ideas can be exhausting. Near the end of a session, individuals and groups may find quantitative goals useful as a motivating force. The nailer team frequently issued individual concept generation assignments with quantitative targets of 10 to 20 concepts.

- *Use the gallery method.* The *gallery method* is a way to display a large number of concepts simultaneously for discussion. Sketches, usually one concept to a sheet, are taped or pinned to the walls of the meeting room. Team members circulate and look at each concept. The creator of the concept may offer explanation, and the group subsequently makes suggestions for improving the concept or spontaneously generates related concepts. This method is a good way to merge individual and group efforts.

Exhibit 6 shows some of the solutions the nailer team generated for the subproblems of (1) storing or accepting energy and (2) delivering translational energy to a nail.

STEP 4: EXPLORE SYSTEMATICALLY

As a result of the external and internal search activities, the team will have collected tens or hundreds of concept *fragments*—solutions to the subproblems. Systematic exploration is aimed at navigating the space of possibilities by orga-

(a) **Solutions to Subproblem of Storing or Accepting Energy**	(b) **Solutions to Subproblem of Applying Translational Energy to Nail**
• Self-regulating chemical reaction emitting high-pressure gas	Single Impact
• Carbide (as for lanterns)	
• Combusting sawdust from job site	
• Gun powder	
• Sodium azide (air bag explosive)	
• Fuel-air combustion (butane, propane, acetylene, etc.)	Multiple Impacts (tens or hundreds)
• Compressed air (in tank or from compressor)	
• Carbon dioxide in tank	
• Electric wall outlet and cord	
• High-pressure oil line (hydraulics)	
• Flywheel with charging (spin-up) station	Multiple Impacts (hundreds or thousands)
• Battery pack on tool, belt, or floor	
• Fuel cell	
• Human power: arms or legs	
• Methane from decomposing organic materials	
• "Burning" like that of chemical hand warmers	
• Nuclear reactions	Push
• Cold fusion	
• Solar electric cells	
• Solar-steam conversion	
• Steam supply line	
• Wind	
• Geothermal	Twist-Push

EXHIBIT 6 Some of the solutions to the subproblems of (1) storing or accepting energy and (2) delivering translational energy to a nail.

92

nizing and synthesizing these solution fragments. The nailer team focused on the energy storage, conversion, and delivery subproblems and had generated dozens of concept fragments for each subproblem. One approach to organizing and synthesizing these fragments would be to consider all of the possible combinations of the fragments associated with each subproblem; however, a little arithmetic reveals the impossibility of this approach. Given the three subproblems on which the team focused and an average of 15 fragments for each subproblem, the team would have to consider 3,375 combinations of fragments (15 × 15 × 15). This would be a daunting task for even the most enthusiastic team. Furthermore, the team would quickly discover that many of the combinations do not even make sense. Fortunately, there are two specific tools for managing this complexity and organizing the thinking of the team: the *concept classification tree* and the *concept combination table*. The classification tree helps the team divide the possible solutions into independent categories. The combination table guides the team in selectively considering combinations of fragments.

Concept Classification Tree

The concept classification tree is used to divide the entire space of possible solutions into several distinct classes which will facilitate comparison and pruning. An example of a tree for the nailer example is shown in Exhibit 7. The branches of this tree correspond to different energy sources.

The classification tree provides at least four important benefits:

1 *Pruning of less promising branches:* If by studying the classification tree the team is able to identify a solution approach that does not appear to have much merit, then this approach can be "pruned" and the team can focus its attention on the more promising branches of the tree. Pruning a branch of the tree requires some evaluation and judgment and should therefore be done carefully, but the reality of product development is that there are limited resources and that focusing the available resources on the most promising directions is an important success factor. For the nailer team, the nuclear energy source was pruned from consideration. Although the team had identified some very intriguing nuclear devices for use in powering artificial hearts, they felt that these devices would not be economically practical for at least a decade and would probably be hampered by regulatory requirements indefinitely.

2 *Identification of independent approaches to the problem:* Each branch of the tree can be considered a different approach to solving the overall problem. Some of these approaches may be almost completely independent of each other. In these cases, the team can cleanly divide its efforts among two or more individuals or task forces. When two approaches both look promising, this division of effort can reduce the complexity of the concept generation activities. It also may engender some healthy competition among the approaches under consideration. The nailer team found that both the

EXHIBIT 7   A classification tree for the nailer energy source concept fragments.

chemical/explosive branch and the electrical branch appeared quite promising. They assigned these two approaches to two different subteams and pursued them independently for several weeks.

3 *Exposure of inappropriate emphasis on certain branches:* Once the tree is constructed, the team is able to reflect quickly on whether the effort applied to each branch has been appropriately allocated. The nailer team recognized that they had applied very little effort to thinking about hydraulic energy sources and conversion technologies. This recognition guided them to focus on this branch of the tree for a few days.

4 *Refinement of the problem decomposition for a particular branch:* Sometimes a problem decomposition can be usefully tailored to a particular approach to the problem. Consider the branch of the tree corresponding to the electrical energy source. Based on additional investigation of the nailing process, the team determined that the instantaneous power delivered during the nailing process was about 10,000 watts for a few milliseconds and so exceeds the power which is available from a wall outlet, a battery, or a fuel cell (of reasonable size, cost, and mass). They concluded, therefore, that energy must be accumulated over a substantial period of the nailing cycle (say 100

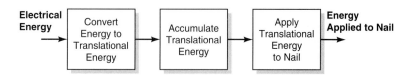

EXHIBIT 8   A new problem decomposition assuming an electrical energy source and the accumulation of energy in the mechanical domain.

milliseconds) and then suddenly released to supply the required instantaneous power to drive the nail. This quick analysis led the team to add a subfunction ("accumulate translational energy") to their function diagram (see Exhibit 8). They chose to add the subfunction after the conversion of electrical energy to mechanical energy, but briefly considered the possibility of accumulating the energy in the electrical domain with a capacitor. This kind of refinement of the function diagram is quite common as the team makes more assumptions about the approach and as more information is gathered.

The classification tree in Exhibit 7 shows the alternative solutions to the energy source subproblem. However, there are other possible trees. The team might have chosen to use a tree classifying the alternative solutions to the energy delivery subproblem, showing branches for single impact, multiple impact, or pushing. Trees can be constructed with branches corresponding to the solution fragments of any of the subproblems, but certain classifications are more useful. In general, a subproblem whose solution highly constrains the possible solutions to the remaining subproblems is a good candidate for a classification tree. For example, the choice of energy source (electrical, nuclear, pneumatic, etc.) constrains whether a motor or a piston-cylinder can be used to convert the energy to translational energy. In contrast, the choice of energy delivery mechanism (single impact, multiple impact, etc.) does not greatly constrain the solutions to the other subproblems. Reflection on which subproblem is likely to most highly constrain the solutions to the remaining subproblems will usually lead to one or two clear ways to construct the classification tree.

Concept Combination Table

The concept combination table provides a way to consider combinations of solution fragments systematically. Exhibit 9 is an example of a combination table that the nailer team used to consider the combinations of fragments for the electrical branch of the classification tree. The columns in the table correspond to the subproblems identified in Exhibit 8. The entries in each column correspond to the solution fragments for each of these subproblems derived from external and internal search. For example, the subproblem of converting electrical energy to translational energy is the heading for the first column. The entries in this column are a rotary motor with a transmission, a linear motor, a solenoid, and a rail gun.

Potential solutions to the overall problem are formed by combining one frag-

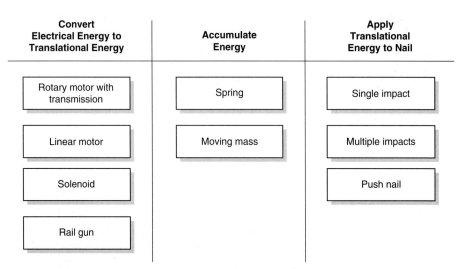

Convert Electrical Energy to Translational Energy	Accumulate Energy	Apply Translational Energy to Nail
Rotary motor with transmission	Spring	Single impact
Linear motor	Moving mass	Multiple impacts
Solenoid		Push nail
Rail gun		

EXHIBIT 9   Concept combination table for the hand-held nailer.

ment from each column. For the nailer example, there are 24 possible combinations ($4 \times 2 \times 3$). Choosing a combination of fragments does not lead spontaneously to a solution to the overall problem. The combination of fragments must usually be developed and refined before an integrated solution emerges. This development may not even be possible or may lead to more than one solution, but at a minimum it involves additional creative thought. In some ways, the combination table is simply a way to make forced associations among fragments in order to stimulate further creative thinking; in no way does the mere act of selecting a combination yield a complete solution.

Exhibit 10 shows a sketch of a concept arising from the combination of the fragments "solenoid," "spring," and "multiple impacts." Exhibit 11 shows some sketches of concepts arising from the combination of the fragments "rotary motor with transmission," "spring," and "single impact." Exhibit 12 shows a sketch of a concept arising from the combination of "rotary motor with transmission," "spring," and "multiple impacts." Exhibit 13 shows some sketches of concepts arising from the combination of "linear motor," "moving mass," "and single impact."

Two guidelines make the concept combination process easier. First, if a fragment can be eliminated as being infeasible before combining it with other fragments, then the number of combinations the team needs to consider is dramatically reduced. For example, if the team could determine that the rail gun would not be feasible under any condition, they could reduce the number of combinations from 24 to 12. Second, the concept combination table should be concentrated on the subproblems that are coupled. Coupled subproblems are those

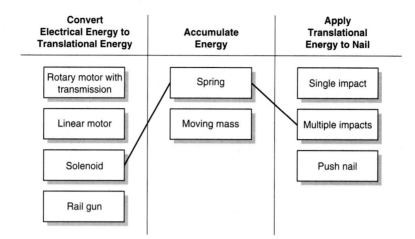

Convert Electrical Energy to Translational Energy	Accumulate Energy	Apply Translational Energy to Nail
Rotary motor with transmission	Spring	Single impact
Linear motor	Moving mass	Multiple impacts
Solenoid		Push nail
Rail gun		

EXHIBIT 10   In this solution concept, a solenoid compresses a spring and then releases it repeatedly in order to drive the nail with multiple impacts.

whose solutions can only really be evaluated in combination with the solutions to other subproblems. For example, the choice of the specific electrical energy source to be used (e.g., battery versus wall outlet), although extremely critical, is somewhat independent of the choice of energy conversion (e.g., motor versus solenoid). Therefore, the concept combination table does not need to contain a column for the different types of electrical energy sources. This reduces the number of combinations the team must consider. As a practical matter, concept combination tables lose their usefulness when the number of columns exceeds three or four.

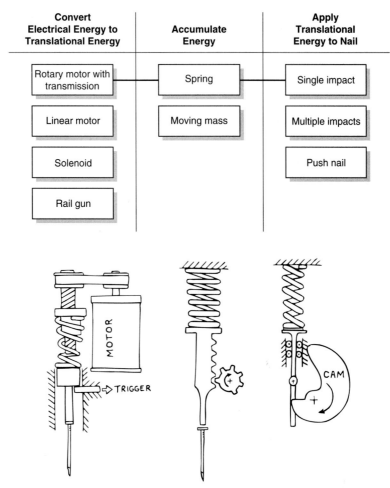

Convert Electrical Energy to Translational Energy	Accumulate Energy	Apply Translational Energy to Nail
Rotary motor with transmission	Spring	Single impact
Linear motor	Moving mass	Multiple impacts
Solenoid		Push nail
Rail gun		

EXHIBIT 11 Multiple solutions arising from the combination of a motor with transmission, a spring, and single impact. The motor winds a spring, accumulating potential energy which is then delivered to the nail in a single blow.

Managing the Exploration Process

The classification tree and combination tables are tools that a team can use somewhat flexibly. They are simple ways to organize thinking and guide the creative energies of the team. Rarely do teams generate only one classification tree and one concept combination table. More typically the team will create several alternative classification trees and several concept combination tables. Interspersed with this exploratory activity may be a refining of the original prob-

EXHIBIT 12   Solution from the combination of a motor with transmission, a spring, and multiple impacts. The motor repeatedly winds and releases the spring, storing and delivering energy over several blows.

lem decomposition or the pursuit of additional internal or external search. The exploration step of concept generation usually acts more as a guide for further creative thinking than as the final step in the process.

Recall that at the beginning of the process the team chooses a few subproblems on which to focus attention. Eventually the team must return to address all of the subproblems. This usually occurs after the team has narrowed the range of alternatives for the critical subproblems. The nailer team narrowed its alternatives to a few chemical and a few electric concepts and then refined them by working out the user interface, industrial design, and configuration issues. One of the resulting concept descriptions is shown in Exhibit 14.

Convert Electrical Energy to Translational Energy	Accumulate Energy	Apply Translational Energy to Nail
Rotary motor with transmission	Spring	Single impact
Linear motor	Moving mass	Multiple impacts
Solenoid		Push nail
Rail gun		

EXHIBIT 13 Solutions from the combination of a linear motor, a moving mass, and single impact. A linear motor accelerates a massive hammer, accumulating kinetic energy which is delivered to the nail in a single blow.

STEP 5: REFLECT ON THE SOLUTIONS AND THE PROCESS

Although the reflection step is placed here at the end for convenience in presentation, reflection should in fact be performed throughout the whole process. Questions to ask include: Is the team developing confidence that the solution space has been fully explored? Have ideas from everyone been accepted and integrated in the process? Are there alternative ways to decompose the problem? Have external sources been thoroughly pursued? Are there alternative function diagrams?

The nailer team members discussed whether they had focused too much

EXHIBIT 14   One of several refined solution concepts. (Illustration courtesy of Product Genesis Inc.)

attention on the energy storage and conversion issues in the tool while ignoring the user interface and overall configuration. They decided that the energy issues remained at the core of the problem and that their decision to focus on these issues first was justified. They also wondered if they had pursued too many branches of the classification tree. Initially they had pursued electrical, chemical, and pneumatic concepts before ultimately settling on an electric concept. In hindsight, the chemical approach had some obvious safety and customer perception shortcomings (they were exploring the use of explosives as an energy source). They decided that although they liked some aspects of the chemical solution they should have eliminated it from consideration earlier in the process, allowing more time to pursue some of the more promising branches in greater detail.

SUMMARY

A product concept is an approximate description of the technology, working principles, and form of the product. The degree to which a product satisfies customers and can be successfully commercialized depends to a large measure on the quality of the underlying concept.

- The concept generation process begins with a set of customer needs and target specifications and results in a set of product concepts from which the team will make a final selection.

- In most cases, an effective development team will generate hundreds of concepts, of which 5 to 20 will merit serious consideration during the subequent concept selection activity.

- The concept generation methodology presented in this chapter consists of five steps:

  1 *Clarify the problem.* Understand the problem and decompose it into simpler subproblems.

  2 *Search externally.* Gather information from lead users, experts, patents, published literature, and related products.

  3 *Search internally.* Use individual and group methods to retrieve and adapt the knowledge of the team.

  4 *Explore systematically.* Use classification trees and combination tables to organize the thinking of the team and to synthesize solution fragments.

  5 *Reflect on the solutions and the process.* Identify opportunities for improvement in subsequent iterations or future projects.

- Although concept generation is an inherently creative process, teams can benefit from using a structured methodology. Such an approach allows full exploration of the design space and reduces the chance of oversight in the types of solution concepts considered. It also acts as a map for those team members who are less experienced in design problem solving.

- Despite the linear presentation of the concept generation process in this chapter, the team will likely return to each step of the process several times. Iteration is particularly common when the team is developing a radically new product.

- Professionals who are good at concept generation seem to always be in great demand as team members. Contrary to popular opinion, we believe concept generation is a skill that can be learned and developed.

REFERENCES AND BIBLIOGRAPHY

Pahl and Beitz were the driving force behind structured design methods in Germany. We adapt many of their ideas for functional decomposition.

Pahl, Gerhard, and Wolfgang Beitz, *Engineering Design*, K. Wallace (ed.), Springer-Verlag, New York, 1984. ISBN 0-387-13601-0.

Hubka and Eder have written in a detailed way about systematic concept generation for technical products.

Hubka, Vladimir, and W. Ernst Eder, *Theory of Technical Systems: A Total Concept Theory for Engineering Design*, Springer-Verlag, New York, 1988. ISBN 0-387-17451-6.

von Hippel reports on his empirical research on the sources of new product concepts. His central argument is that lead users are the innovators in many markets.

von Hippel, Eric, *The Sources of Innovation*, Oxford University Press, New York, 1988. ISBN 0-19-504085-6.

VanGundy presents dozens of methods for problem solving, many of which are directly applicable to product concept generation.

VanGundy, Arthur B., Jr., *Techniques of Structured Problem Solving*, second edition, Van Nostrand Reinhold, New York, 1988. ISBN 0-442-28847-6.

Author von Oech provides dozens of good ideas for improving individual and group creative performance.

von Oech, Roger, *A Whack on the Side of the Head: How to Unlock Your Mind for Innovation*, Warner Books, New York, 1983. ISBN 0-446-38000-8.

McKim presents a holistic approach to developing creative thinking skills in individuals and groups.

McKim, Robert H., *Experiences in Visual Thinking*, second edition, Brooks/Cole Publishing, Monterey, CA, 1980. ISBN 0-818-50411-0.

McGrath presents studies comparing the relative performance of groups and individuals in generating new ideas.

McGrath, Joseph, E., *Groups: Interaction and Performance*, Prentice-Hall, Englewood Cliffs, NJ, 1984. ISBN 0-13-365700-0.

Engineering handbooks are handy sources of information on standard technical solutions. Three good handbooks are:

Avallone, Eugene A., and Theodore Baumeister III (eds.), *Mark's Standard Handbook of Mechanical Engineering*, ninth edition, McGraw-Hill, New York, 1987. ISBN 0-070-04127-X.

Green, Don W. (ed.), *Perry's Chemical Engineers' Handbook*, sixth edition, McGraw-Hill, New York, 1984. ISBN 0-070-49479-7.

Chironis, Nicholas P., *Mechanisms and Mechanical Devices Sourcebook*, McGraw-Hill, New York, 1991. ISBN 0-07-010918-4.

The *Thomas Register* is a categorized listing of manufacturers of all types of industrial products.

Thomas Register of American Manufacturers, Thomas Publishing Company, New York, published annually. ISBN 0362-7721.

EXERCISES

1 Decompose the problem of designing a new barbecue grill. Try a functional decomposition as well as a decomposition based on the user interactions with the product.
2 Generate 20 concepts for the subproblem "prevent fraying of end of rope" as part of a system for cutting lengths of nylon rope from a spool.

3 Prepare an external search plan for the problem of permanently applying serial numbers to plastic products.

THOUGHT QUESTIONS

1 What are the prospects for computer support for concept generation activities? Can you think of any computer tools that would be especially helpful in this process?
2 What would be the relative advantages and disadvantages of involving actual customers in the concept generation process?
3 For what types of products would the initial focus of the concept generation activity be on the form and user interface of the product and not on the core technology? Describe specific examples.
4 Could you apply the five-step methodology to an everyday problem like choosing the food for a picnic?
5 Consider the task of generating new concepts for the problem of dealing with leaves on a lawn. How would the assumptions and problem decomposition differ for a manufacturer of plastic bags, from those of a manufacturer of lawn tools and equipment, from those of a company responsible for maintaining golf courses around the world? Should the context of the firm dictate the way concept generation is approached?

CONCEPT SELECTION

Developed in collaboration with Eric Howlett.

EXHIBIT 1 One of the existing outpatient syringes. (Courtesy of Novo Nordisk
Pharmaceuticals Inc.)

A medical supply company retained a design firm to develop a reusable syringe with precise dosage control for outpatient use. One of the products sold by a competitor is shown in Exhibit 1. To focus the development effort, the supply company identified two major problems with its current product: cost (the existing model was made of stainless steel) and accuracy of dose metering. The company also requested that the product be tailored to the physical capabilities of the elderly, an important segment of the target market. To summarize the needs of its client and of the intended end users, the team established seven criteria on which the choice of a product concept would be based:

- Ease of handling
- Ease of use
- Readability of dose settings
- Dose metering accuracy
- Durability
- Ease of manufacture
- Portability

The team described the concepts under consideration with the sketches shown in Exhibit 2. Although each concept nominally satisfied the key customer needs, the team was faced with choosing the best concept for further design, refinement, and production. The need to select one syringe concept from many raises several questions:

- How can the team choose the best concept, given that the designs are still quite abstract?
- How can a decision be made that is embraced by the whole team?
- How can desirable attributes of otherwise weak concepts be identified and used?
- How can the decision making process be documented?

This chapter uses the syringe example to present a concept selection methodology addressing these and other issues.

Concept Selection Is an Integral Part of the Product Development Process

Early in the development process the product development team identifies a set of customer needs. By using a variety of methods, the team then generates alternative solution concepts in response to these needs. (See the chapters "Identifying Customer Needs" and "Concept Generation" for more detail on these activities.) *Concept selection* is the process of evaluating concepts with respect to customer needs and other criteria, comparing the relative strengths and weaknesses of the concepts, and selecting one or more concepts for further investigation or development. Exhibit 3 illustrates how the concept selection activity is related to the other activities that make up the concept development phase of the product development process. Although this chapter focuses on the selection of an overall product concept at the beginning of the development process, the methodology we present is also useful later in the development process when the team must select subsystem concepts, components, and production processes.

While many stages of the development process benefit from unbounded creativity and divergent thinking, concept selection is the process of narrowing the set of concept alternatives under consideration. Although concept selection is a convergent process, it is frequently iterative and may not produce a dominant concept immediately. A large set of concepts is initially winnowed down to a smaller set, but these concepts may subsequently be combined and improved to temporarily enlarge the set of concepts under consideration. Through several iterations a dominant concept is finally chosen. Exhibit 4 illustrates the successive narrowing and temporary widening of the set of options under consideration during the concept selection activity.

All Teams Use Some Method for Choosing a Concept

Whether or not the concept selection process is explicit, all teams use some method to choose among concepts. (Even those teams generating only one concept are using a method: choosing the first concept they think of.) The methods vary in their effectiveness and include the following:

- *External decision:* Concepts are turned over to the customer, client, or some other external entity for selection.
- *Product champion:* An influential member of the product development team chooses a concept based on personal preference.
- *Intuition:* The concept is chosen by its "feel." Explicit criteria or trade-offs are not used. The concept just "seems" better.
- *Pros and Cons:* The team lists the strengths and weaknesses of each concept and makes a choice based upon group opinion.
- *Prototype and test:* The organization builds and tests prototypes of each concept, making a selection based upon test data.
- *Decision matrices:* The team rates each concept against prespecified selection criteria, which may be weighted.

The concept selection methodology in this chapter is built around the use of decision matrices for evaluating each concept with respect to a set of selection criteria.

Concept A: Master Cylinder

PLUNGER

SEALED FLUID FILLED CAVITY

MODE SELECTOR
NOTE: SLIDE TO SET DOSE, SLIDE TO INSERT.

MEDICINE VIAL

DOSE SETTING

SLEEVE

ROD

PUSHER

NOTE: CROSS SECTIONAL AREA OF ROD $^1/_{11}$ OF CAVITY → PUSHER DISPLACEMENT = $^1/_{11}$ OF PLUNGER DISPLACEMENT

Concept B: Rubber Brake

PUSHNUT GRIPS FLATTED SHAFT.

NOTE: TURN PLUNGER 90° TO SET DOSE OR STORE PLUNGER.

DOSE SETTING

INDICATOR

WINDOW

PLUNGER

RUBBER CLUTCH

VIAL

FLATTED SHAFT

Concept C: Ratchet

CONNECTOR

DRIVE FINGERS

REVERSE CLUTCH FINGERS

WINDOW

DOSE SETTING

INDICATOR

VIAL

PLUNGER

NOTE: TURN PLUNGER 90° AND PULL BACK TO SET DOSE. TURN BACK TO ENGAGE CONNECTOR

EXHIBIT 2
Seven concepts for the outpatient syringe. The product development team generated the seven sketches to describe the basic concepts under consideration.

NOTE: SCREW SLEEVE FORWARD TO SET DOSE. INJECT WITH PLUNGER

SLEEVE WITH INTERNAL THREAD

PLUNGER

Concept D: Plunge Stop

GUIDE

VIAL

NOTE: TO SET DOSE ROTATE DOSE SET RING.
PULL PLUNGER AND PUSH TO INJECT

DOSE SET RING

STROKE IS
SAME FOR
ALL DOSES

PLUNGER

ROTATABLE ANNULUS

SHAFT SUPPORT

VIAL

Concept E: Swash Ring

NOTE: SET DOSE BY PUSHING LEVER
FORWARD. INJECT BY PUSHING
LEVER BACK.

OPERATING
LEVER

INJECT
SET
DOSE

PLUNGER RELEASE

CAM CLUTCH

INDICATOR

RESET RELEASE

PLUNGER

Concept F: Lever Set

STORAGE SPACE

NOTE: SET DOSE BY TURNING
SET KNOB. INJECT BY
PRESSING ACTUATOR

DOSE SET
KNOB

SPACE FOR
NEEDLES
AND VIALS

SPRING

GEAR

PLUNGER

VIAL

ACTUATOR

Concept G: Dial Screw   LEAD SCREW

EXHIBIT 3 Concept selection is part of the overall concept development phase.

EXHIBIT 4 Concept selection is an iterative process leading to a single concept upon which subsequent development activities will be focused.

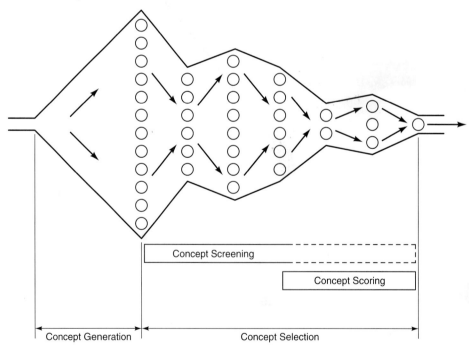

A Structured Methodology Offers Several Benefits

All of the early phases of product development are extremely influential on eventual product success. Certainly the response of the marketplace to a product depends critically on the product concept, but many practitioners and researchers also believe that the choice of a product concept dramatically constrains the eventual manufacturing cost of the product. A structured concept selection process helps to maintain objectivity throughout the concept phase of the development process and guides the product development team through a critical, difficult, and sometimes emotional process. Specifically, a structured concept selection methodology offers the following potential benefits:

- *A customer-focused product:* Because concepts are explicitly evaluated against customer-oriented criteria, the selected concept is likely to be focused on the customer.

- *A competitive design:* By benchmarking concepts with respect to existing designs, designers push the design to match or exceed their competitors' performance along key dimensions.

- *Better product-process coordination:* Explicit evaluation of the product with respect to manufacturing criteria improves the product's manufacturability and helps to match the product with the process capabilities of the firm.

- *Reduced time to product introduction:* A structured methodology becomes a common language among design engineers, manufacturing engineers, industrial designers, marketers, and project managers, resulting in decreased ambiguity, faster communication, and fewer false starts.

- *Effective group decision making:* Within the development team, organizational philosophy and guidelines, willingness of members to participate, and team member experience may constrain the concept selection process. A structured methodology encourages decision making based on objective criteria and minimizes the likelihood that arbitrary or personal factors influence the product concept.

- *Documentation of the decision process:* A structured methodology results in a readily understood archive of the rationale behind concept decisions. This record is useful for assimilating new team members and for quickly assessing the impact of changes in the customer needs or in the available alternatives.

OVERVIEW OF METHODOLOGY

We present a two-stage concept selection methodology, although the first stage may suffice for simple design decisions. The first stage is called *concept screening* and the second stage is called *concept scoring.* Each is supported by a decision matrix which is used by the team to rate, rank, and select the best concept(s). Although the methodology is structured, we emphasize the role of group insight to improve and combine concepts.

Concept selection is often performed in two stages as a way to manage the complexity of evaluating dozens of product concepts. The application of these two methods is illustrated in Exhibit 4. Screening is a quick, approximate evaluation aimed at producing a few viable alternatives. Scoring is a more careful analysis of these relatively few concepts in order to choose the single concept most likely to lead to product success.

During concept screening, rough initial concepts are evaluated relative to a common reference concept using the *screening matrix*. At this preliminary stage, detailed quantitative comparisons are difficult to obtain and may be misleading, so a coarse comparative rating system is used. After some alternatives are eliminated, the team may choose to move on to concept scoring and conduct more detailed analysis and finer quantitative evaluation of the remaining concepts using the *scoring matrix* as a guide. Throughout the screening and scoring process, several iterations may be performed, with new alternatives arising from the combination of the features of several concepts. Exhibits 5 and 7 illustrate the screening and scoring matrices, using the selection criteria and concepts from the syringe example.

While the selection matrices are the most visual components of the method, they are by no means the only important part. Both stages, concept screening and concept scoring, follow a six-step process which leads the team through the concept selection activity. The steps are:

1 Prepare the selection matrix.
2 Rate the concepts.
3 Rank the concepts.
4 Combine and improve the concepts.
5 Select one or more concepts.
6 Reflect on the results and the process.

Although we present a well-defined process, the team, not the methodology, creates the concepts and makes the decisions that determine the quality of the product. Ideally, teams are made up of people from different functional groups within the organization. Each member, representing a constituency, brings unique views that increase the understanding of the problem and thus facilitate the development of a successful, customer-oriented product. The concept selection methodology exploits the matrices as visual guides for consensus building among team members. The matrices focus attention upon the customer needs and other decision criteria and on the product concepts for explicit evaluation, improvement, and selection.

CONCEPT SCREENING

Concept screening is based on a method developed by the late Stuart Pugh in the 1980s and is often called *Pugh concept selection* (Pugh, 1990). The purposes of this stage are to narrow the number of concepts quickly and to improve the concepts. Exhibit 5 illustrates the screening matrix used during this stage.

Step 1: Prepare the Selection Matrix

To prepare the matrix, the team selects a physical medium appropriate to the problem. Individuals and small groups with a short list of criteria may use matrices on paper similar to Exhibit 5 or Appendix A for their selection process. For larger problems or for larger groups a chalkboard or flip chart is desirable to facilitate group discussion.

Next, the inputs (concepts and criteria) are entered on the matrix. Although possibly generated by different individuals, concepts should be presented at the same level of detail for meaningful comparison and unbiased selection. The concepts are best portrayed by both a written description and a graphical representation. A simple one-page sketch of each concept greatly facilitates communication of the key features of the concept. The concepts are entered along the top of the matrix, using graphical or textual labels of some kind.

If the team is considering more than about 12 concepts, the *multivote* technique may be used to quickly choose the dozen or so concepts to be evaluated with the screening matrix. Multivoting is a technique in which members of the team simultaneously vote for three to five concepts by applying "dots" to the sheets describing their preferred concepts. The concepts with the most dots are chosen for the screening phase.

The selection criteria are listed along the left-hand side of the screening matrix as shown in Exhibit 5. These criteria are chosen based on the customer needs the team has identified as well as on the needs of the enterprise, such as low manufacturing cost or minimal risk of product liability. The criteria at this stage are usually expressed at a fairly high level of abstraction and typically include from 5 to 10 dimensions. The selection criteria should be chosen to differentiate among the concepts. However, because each criterion is given equal weight in the concept screening phase, the team should be careful not to list many relatively unimportant criteria in the screening matrix. Otherwise, the differences among the concepts relative to the more important criteria will not be clearly reflected in the outcome.

After careful consideration, the team chooses a concept to become the benchmark or *reference concept* against which all other concepts are rated. The reference is generally either an industry standard or an obvious solution to the problem. It can be a commercially available product, an earlier generation of the product, any one of the concepts under consideration, or a combination of subsystems combined to represent the best features of different products.

Selection Criteria	Concepts						
	A Master Cylinder	**B** Rubber Brake	**C** Ratchet	**D** (reference) Plunge Stop	**E** Swash Ring	**F** Lever Set	**G** Dial Screw
Ease of handling	0	0	−	0	0	−	−
Ease of use	0	−	−	0	0	+	0
Readability of settings	0	0	+	0	+	0	+
Dose metering accuracy	0	0	0	0	−	0	0
Durability	0	0	0	0	0	+	0
Ease of manufacture	+	−	−	0	0	−	0
Portability	+	+	0	0	+	0	0
Sum +'s	2	1	1	0	2	2	1
Sum 0's	5	4	3	7	4	3	5
Sum −'s	0	2	3	0	1	2	1
Net Score	2	−1	−2	0	1	0	0
Rank	1	6	7	3	2	3	3
Continue?	Yes	No	No	Combine	Yes	Combine	Revise

EXHIBIT 5 The concept screening matrix. For the syringe example, the team rated the concepts against the reference concept using a simple code (+ for "better than," 0 for "same as," − for "worse than") in order to identify some concepts for further consideration. Note that the three concepts ranked "3" all received the same score.

Step 2: Rate the Concepts

A relative score of "better than" (+), "same as" (0), or "worse than" (−) is placed in each cell of the matrix depending upon how the concept rates in comparison to the reference concept relative to the particular criterion. Some people find the coarse nature of the relative ratings difficult to work with. However, at this stage in the design process, each concept is only a general notion of the ultimate product, and more detailed ratings are largely meaningless.

When available, objective metrics should be used as the basis for rating a concept. For example, a good approximation of assembly cost is the number of parts in a design. Similarly, a good approximation of ease of use is the number of operations required to use the device. These objective metrics help to minimize the judgmental nature of the rating process. Objective metrics suitable for concept selection may arise from the process of establishing target specifications for the product. (See the chapter "Establishing Product Specifications" for a discussion of metrics.) Absent objective metrics, ratings are established by team consensus, although secret ballot or other methods may also be useful. At this point the team may also wish to note which selection criteria need further investigation and analysis.

Step 3: Rank the Concepts

After rating all the concepts, the team sums the number of "better than," "same as," and "worse than" scores and enters the sum for each category in the lower rows of the matrix. From our example in Exhibit 5, concept A was rated to have two criteria better than, five the same as, and none worse than the reference concept. Next, a net score can be calculated by subtracting the number of "worse than" ratings from the "better than" ratings.

Once the summation is completed, the team rank-orders the concepts. Obviously, in general those concepts with more pluses and fewer minuses are ranked higher. Often at this point the team can identify one or two criteria which really seem to differentiate the concepts.

Step 4: Combine and Improve the Concepts

Having rated and ranked the concepts, the team should verify that the results make sense and then consider if there are ways to combine and improve certain concepts. Two issues to consider are:

- Is there a generally good concept which is degraded by one bad feature? Can a minor modification improve the overall concept and yet preserve a distinction from the other concepts?
- Are there two concepts which can be combined to preserve the "better than" qualities while annulling the "worse than" qualities?

In our example, the team noticed that concepts D and F could be combined to remove several of the "worse than" ratings to yield a new concept, DF, to be considered in the next round. Concept G was also considered for revision. The team decided that this concept was too bulky, so the excess storage space was removed while retaining the injection technique. These revised concepts are shown in Exhibit 6.

Step 5: Select One or More Concepts

Once the team members are satisfied with their understanding of each concept and its relative worth, they decide which concepts are to be selected for further refinement and analysis. During the previous steps, the team will likely develop a clear sense of which are the most promising concepts. The number of concepts selected for further review will be limited by team resources (personnel, money, and time). For our example, the team selected concepts A and E to be considered along with the revised concept G+ and the new concept DF. Having determined the concepts for further analysis, the team must clarify which issues need to be investigated further before a final selection can be made.

The team must also decide whether another round of concept screening will be performed or whether concept scoring will be applied. If the screening matrix is seen as not providing sufficient resolution for the next step of evalua-

Concept G+: Dial Screw+

Concept DF: Lever Stop

EXHIBIT 6   New and revised concepts for the syringe. During the selection process, the syringe team revised concept G and generated a new concept, DF, arising from the combination of D and F.

tion and selection, then the concept scoring stage with its weighted selection criteria and more detailed rating scheme would be used.

Step 6: Reflect on the Results and the Process

All of the team members should be comfortable with the outcome. If an individual is not in agreement with the decision of the team, then perhaps one or more important criteria are missing from the screening matrix, or perhaps a particular rating is in error, or at least is not clear. An explicit consideration of whether the results make sense to everyone reduces the likelihood of making a mistake and increases the likelihood that the entire team will be solidly committed to the subsequent development activities.

CONCEPT SCORING

Concept scoring is used when increased resolution will better differentiate among competing concepts. In this stage, the team weighs the relative importance of the selection criteria and focuses on more refined comparisons with respect to each criterion. The concept scores are determined by the weighted sum of the ratings. Exhibit 7 illustrates the scoring matrix used in this stage. In describing the concept scoring process, we focus on the differences relative to concept screening.

Step 1: Prepare the Selection Matrix

As in the screening stage, the team prepares a matrix and identifies a reference concept. In some cases a computer spreadsheet is the best format to facilitate ranking and sensitivity analysis. The concepts that have been identified for analysis are entered on the top of the matrix. The concepts have typically been refined to some extent since concept screening and may be expressed in more detail. In conjunction with more detailed concepts, the team may wish to add more detail to the selection criteria. The use of hierarchical relations is a useful way to illuminate the criteria. For the syringe example, suppose the team decided that the

EXHIBIT 7   The concept scoring matrix. The team uses a weighted average of the criteria to determine concept ranking.

Selection Criteria	Weight	Concepts							
		A (reference) Master Cylinder		DF Lever Stop		E Swash Ring		G+ Dial Screw+	
		Rating	Weighted Score	Rating	Weighted Score	Rating	Weighted Score	Rating	Weighted Score
Ease of handling	5%	3	0.15	3	0.15	4	0.2	4	0.2
Ease of use	15	3	0.45	4	0.6	4	0.6	3	0.45
Readability of settings	10	3	0.3	3	0.3	5	0.5	5	0.5
Dose metering accuracy	25	3	0.75	3	0.75	2	0.5	3	0.75
Durability	15	3	0.45	5	0.75	4	0.6	3	0.45
Ease of manufacture	20	3	0.6	3	0.6	2	0.4	2	0.4
Portability	10	3	0.3	3	0.3	3	0.3	3	0.3
Total Score			3.00		3.45		3.10		3.05
Rank			4		1		2		3
Continue?			No		Develop		No		No

criterion "ease of use" did not provide sufficient detail to help distinguish among the remaining concepts. "Ease of use" could be broken down, as shown in Exhibit 8, to include "ease of injection," "ease of cleaning," and "ease of loading." The level of criteria detail will depend upon the needs of the team; it may not be necessary to expand the criteria at all. If the team has created a hierarchical list of customer needs, the secondary and tertiary needs are good candidates for more detailed selection criteria. (See the chapter "Identifying Customer Needs" for an explanation of primary, secondary, and tertiary needs, and see Appendixes A and B for examples of hierarchical selection criteria.)

After the criteria are entered, the team adds importance weights to the matrix. Several different schemes can be used to weigh the criteria, such as assigning an importance value from 1 to 5, or allocating 100 percentage points among them, as the team has done in Exhibit 7. There are marketing techniques for empirically determining weights from customer data, and a thorough process of identifying customer needs may result in such weights (Urban and Hauser, 1993). However, for the purpose of concept selection the weights are often determined subjectively by team consensus.

Step 2: Rate the Concepts

As in the screening stage, one way to rate the concepts is to compare them to the reference concept. Because of the need for additional resolution to distinguish among competing concepts, a finer scale is now used. We recommend a scale from 1 to 5:

Relative Performance	Rating
Much worse than reference concept	1
Worse than reference concept	2
Same as reference concept	3
Better than reference concept	4
Much better than reference concept	5

Another scale, such as 1 to 10, may certainly be used, but finer scales sometimes require more time and effort. Our experience suggests that a scale symmetric about the reference concept score is the most useful.

EXHIBIT 8   Hierarchical decomposition of selection criteria. In conjunction with more detailed concepts, the team may need to break down criteria to the level of detail necessary for meaningful comparison.

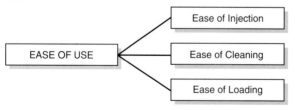

Unless by pure coincidence the reference concept is of average performance relative to all of the criteria, the use of the same reference concept for the evaluation of each criterion will lead to "scale compression" for some of the criteria. For example, if the reference concept happens to be the easiest concept to manufacture, all of the remaining concepts will earn an evaluation of 1, 2, or 3 ("much worse than," "worse than," or "same as") for the ease-of-manufacture criterion, compressing the rating scale from five levels to three levels. In these situations, the team may choose to use different concepts as the reference points for different criteria. Doing so does not prevent the team from designating one concept as the overall reference for the purposes of ensuring that the selected concept is competitive relative to that benchmark. Under such conditions the overall reference concept will simply not receive a neutral score. Exhibit 7 illustrates a scoring matrix with the use of a single reference concept for all criteria, while Appendix B illustrates a scoring matrix in which different reference points are used for the different criteria.

Step 3: Rank the Concepts

Once the ratings are entered for each concept, weighted scores are calculated by multiplying the raw scores by the criteria weights. The total score for each concept is the sum of the weighted scores:

$$s_j = \sum_{i=1}^{n} r_{ij}\, w_i$$

where r_{ij} = raw rating of concept j for the ith criterion
$\quad\quad w_i$ = weighting for ith criterion
$\quad\quad n$ = number of criteria
$\quad\quad s_j$ = total score for concept j

Finally, each concept is given a rank corresponding to its total score, as shown in Exhibit 7.

Step 4: Combine and Improve the Concepts

As in the screening stage, the team looks for changes or combinations that improve concepts. Although the formal concept generation process is typically completed before concept selection begins, some of the most creative refinements and improvements occur during the concept selection process as the team realizes the inherent strengths and weaknesses of certain features of the product concepts.

Step 5: Select One or More Concepts

The final selection is not simply a question of choosing the concept that achieves the highest ranking after the first pass through the process. Rather, the team should explore its initial evaluation by conducting a sensitivity analysis. Using a computer spreadsheet, the team can vary weights and ratings to determine their effect on the ranking.

By investigating how sensitive the ranking is to variations in a particular rating, the team members can assess whether uncertainty about a particular rating has a large impact on their choice. In some cases they may select a lower-scoring concept about which there is little uncertainty instead of a higher-scoring concept that may possibly prove unworkable or less desirable as they learn more about it.

The team may also create two scoring matrices with different weightings to yield the concept ranking for customer groups with different preferences. It may be that one concept is dominant in both cases. The team should also consider carefully the significance of differences in concept scores. Given the resolution of the scoring system, small differences are not generally significant.

For the syringe example, the team agreed that concept DF was the most promising and was likely to lead to a successful product.

Step 6: Reflect on the Results and the Process

As a final step the team reflects on the selected concept and on the concept selection process. In some ways, this is "the point of no return" for the concept development process, so everyone on the team should feel comfortable that all of the relevant issues have been discussed and that the selected concept will satisfy customers and be economically successful.

The organization can also benefit from reflection on the process itself. Two questions are useful in improving the process for subsequent concept selection activities:

- In what way (if at all) did the concept selection methodology facilitate team decision making?
- How can the methodology be modified to improve team performance?

These questions focus the team on the strengths and weaknesses of the methodology in relation to the needs and capabilities of the organization.

CAVEATS

With experience, users of the concept selection methodology will discover several subtleties. Here we discuss some of these subtleties and point out a few areas for caution.

- *Decomposition of concept quality:* The basic theory underlying the concept selection methodology is that selection criteria—and, by implication, customer needs—can be evaluated independently and that concept quality is the sum of the quality of the concept relative to each criterion. The quality of some product concepts may not be easily decomposed into a set of independent criteria, or the performance of the concept relative to the different criteria may be difficult to relate to overall concept quality. For example, the overall appeal or performance of a tennis racquet design may arise in a highly complex way from its weight, ease of swinging, shock transmission, and energy absorption. Simply choosing a concept based on the sum of performance relative to each criterion may fail to capture complex relationships among these criteria. Keeney and Raiffa (1993) discuss the problem of multi-attribute decision making, including the issue of nonlinear relationships among selection criteria.

- *Subjective criteria:* Some selection criteria, particularly those related to aesthetics, are highly subjective. Choices among alternatives based solely on subjective criteria must be made carefully. In general, the development team's collective judgment is not the best way to evaluate concepts on subjective dimensions. Rather, the team should narrow the alternatives to three or four and then solicit the opinions of representative customers from the target market for the product, perhaps using mock-ups or models to represent the concepts.

- *Where to include cost:* Most of the selection criteria are adaptations of the customer needs. However, "ease of manufacturing" and "manufacturing cost" are not customer needs. The only reason customers care about manufacturing cost is that it establishes the lower bound on sale price. Nevertheless, cost is an extremely important factor in choosing a concept, because it is one of the factors determining the economic success of the product. For this reason, we advocate the inclusion of some measure of cost or ease of manufacturing when evaluating concepts, even though these measures are not bona fide customer needs. Similarly, there may be needs of other stakeholders that are not strictly customer needs but are important for economic success.

- *Selecting elements of complex concepts:* Some complex concepts are really aggregations of several simpler concepts. If all of the concepts under consideration are combinations of the same set of simpler concepts, then the simple concepts can be evaluated first and in an independent fashion before the more complex concept is evaluated. For example, if all of the syringes in our example could be used with all of several different needle types, then the selection of a needle concept could be conducted independently of the selection of an overall syringe concept.

- *Applying concept selection throughout the development process:* Although throughout this chapter we have emphasized the application of the methodology to the selection of a basic product concept, concept selection is used again and again at many levels of detail in the design and development process. For example, in the syringe example, concept selection could be used at the very beginning of the development project to decide between a single-use or multiple-use approach. Once the basic approach had been determined, concept selection could be used to choose the basic product concept, as illustrated in this chapter. Finally, concept selection could be used at the most detailed level of design for resolving decisions such as the choice of colors or materials.

SUMMARY

Concept selection is the process of evaluating concepts with respect to customer needs and other criteria, comparing the relative strengths and weaknesses of the concepts, and selecting one or more concepts for further investigation or development.

- All teams use some method, implicit or explicit, for selecting concepts. Decision techniques employed for selecting concepts range from intuitive approaches to structured methods.
- Successful design is facilitated by structured concept selection. We recommend a two-stage process: concept screening and concept scoring.
- Concept screening and concept scoring use a reference concept to evaluate concept variants against selection criteria.
- Concept screening uses a coarse comparison system to narrow the range of concepts under consideration.
- Concept scoring uses weighted selection criteria and a finer rating scale. Concept scoring may be skipped if concept screening produces a dominant concept.
- Both screening and scoring use a matrix as the basis of a six-step selection process. The six steps are:
  1 Prepare the selection matrix.
  2 Rate the concepts.
  3 Rank the concepts.
  4 Combine and improve the concepts.
  5 Select one or more concepts.
  6 Reflect on the results and the process.
- Concept selection is applied not only during concept development but throughout the subsequent design and development process.
- Concept selection is a group process that facilitates the selection of a winning concept, helps build team consensus, and creates a record of the decision-making process.

REFERENCES AND BIBLIOGRAPHY

The concept selection methodology is a decision-making process. Other decision techniques are outlined in:

Souder, William E., *Management Decision Methods for Managers of Engineering and Research*, Van Nostrand Reinhold Co., New York, NY, 1980. ISBN 0-442-27888-8.

For a more formal treatment of multi-attribute decision making, illustrated with a set of eclectic and interesting case studies, see:

Keeney, Ralph L., and Howard Raiffa, *Decisions with Multiple Objectives: Preferences and Value Tradeoffs*, Cambridge University Press, New York, NY, 1993. ISBN 0-521-44185-4.

Pahl and Beitz's influential engineering design textbook contains an excellent set of systematic methods. The book outlines two concept selection methodologies similar to the concept scoring phase.

Pahl, Gerhard, and Wolfgang Beitz, *Engineering Design*, K. Wallace (ed.), The Design Council, London, 1984. ISBN 0-850-72239-X.

For an in-depth treatment of the process of industrial benchmarking, see:

Camp, Robert C., *Benchmarking: The Search for Industry Best Practices that Lead to Superior Performance*, ASQC Quality Press, Milwaukee, WI, 1989. ISBN 0-873-89058-2.

Weighting alternatives for selection is not a new idea. The following is one of the earlier references for using selection matrices with weights:

Alger, J. R., and C. V. Hays, *Creative Synthesis in Design*, Prentice-Hall, Englewood Cliffs, NJ, 1964.

The concept screening phase is based upon a method presented by Stuart Pugh in the following:

Pugh, Stuart, *Total Design*, Addison-Wesley, Reading, MA, 1990. ISBN 0-201-41639-5.

Concept scoring is similar to a method often called the Kepner-Tregoe method. It is described, along with other techniques for problem identification and solution, in:

Kepner, Charles H., and Benjamin B. Tregoe, *The Rational Manager*, McGraw-Hill, New York, NY, 1965.

Urban and Hauser describe techniques for determining the relative importance of different product attributes.

Urban, Glen, L., and John R. Hauser, *Design and Marketing of New Products*, second edition, Prentice Hall, Englewood Cliffs, NJ, 1993. ISBN 0-13-201567-6.

EXERCISES

1 How can the concept selection methods be used to benchmark or evaluate existing products? Perform such an evaluation for five automobiles you might consider purchasing.

2 Propose a set of selection criteria for the choice of a battery technology for use in a portable computer.

3 Perform concept screening for the four pencil holder concepts shown below. Assume the pencil holders are for a member of a product development team who is continually moving from site to site.

| Zip Pouch | Screw Cap | Clam Shell | Slider |

4 Repeat Exercise 3, but use concept scoring.

THOUGHT QUESTIONS

1 How might you use the concept selection methodology to decide whether to offer a single product to the marketplace or to offer several different product options?
2 How might you use the methodology to determine which product features should be standard and which should be optional or add-ons?
3 Can you imagine an interactive computer tool that would allow a large group (say, 20 or more people) to participate in the concept selection process? How might such a tool work?
4 What could cause a situation in which a development team uses the concept selection methodology to agree on a concept that then results in commercial failure?

APPENDIX A: Screening Matrix Example

This matrix was created and used by a development team designing a collar to hold weights onto a barbell.

Concepts

Selection Criteria	Handcuff	Master Lock	Velcro Belt	Rubber Belt	Alligator Clip	4-Part Latch (REF)	Torsional Spring	Screw Type	Wing Nut	Clothes-pin	Hose Clamp	C-Clamp	Spring-Loaded Bar	Magnetic Plates	Threaded Bar
Functionality															
Lightweight	+	0	+	+	+	0	+	–	–	+	0	0	+	+	0
Fits different bars	+	0	+	+	+	0	0	0	0	+	0	+	0	–	0
Weights secured laterally	0	0	–	–	0	0	0	–	+	–	0	0	–	0	+
Convenience															
Tighten from end/side	0	0	0	0	0	0	0	–	–	0	–	0	+	+	–
Does not roll	0	0	0	0	0	0	0	0	0	0	0	0	0	0	0
Change weights without removing collar	0	0	0	0	0	0	0	0	0	0	0	0	+	+	0
Convenience of placement when changing weights	0	0	+	+	0	0	–	–	–	0	–	0	+	+	–
Ergonomics															
Secure/release (1 motion)	+	0	–	–	+	0	–	–	–	0	–	–	+	–	–
Low force to secure/release	0	0	0	0	–	0	–	0	0	0	0	0	+	–	0
RH/LH usage	0	0	0	0	0	0	0	–	–	0	–	0	0	0	–
Not slippery when wet	0	0	+	+	0	0	0	0	0	0	0	0	+	+	0
Use with one hand	+	0	0	0	+	0	0	0	0	0	0	0	+	+	0
Durability															
Longevity	–	–	–	–	0	0	0	+	0	0	+	+	–	–	+
Other															
Cost of raw materials	0	0	+	+	0	0	0	0	–	+	0	0	–	–	–
Manufacturability	0	–	+	+	0	0	0	+	–	+	+	0	–	–	–
Uses existing weight bars	0	0	0	0	0	0	0	0	0	0	0	0	–	0	–
Sum +'s	4	0	6	6	4	0	1	2	1	4	2	2	8	6	2
Sum 0's	11	14	7	7	11	16	11	8	8	11	10	12	3	4	7
Sum –'s	1	2	3	3	1	0	4	6	7	1	4	2	5	6	7
Net Score	3	–2	3	3	3	0	–3	–4	–6	3	–2	0	3	0	–5
Rank	1	10	1	1	1	7	12	13	15	1	10	7	1	7	15

APPENDIX B: Scoring Matrix Example

A development team generated this matrix while selecting a new concept for a spill-proof beverage holder to be used on boats. Note that in this case the team chose not to define a single concept as the reference concept for all of the decision criteria.

Selection Criteria	Weight	Concept A		Concept C		Concept F		Concept I		Concept J		Concept K		Concept O	
		Rating	Weighted Score	Rating	Weighted Score	Rating	Weighted Score	Rating	Weighted Score	Rating	Weighted Score	Rating	Weighted Score	Rating	Weighted Score
Flexible in use	20														
Use in different locations	15	7	105	7	105	8	120	6	90	6	90	5	75	7	105
Holds different beverages	5	5	25	5	25	3	15	4	20	5	25	3	15	3	15
Maintains drink condition	15														
Retains temperature of drink	13	5	65	5	65	5	65	1	13	5	65	5	65	5	65
Prevents water from getting in	2	5	10	7	14	5	10	5	10	5	10	5	10	5	10
Survives boating environment	5														
Doesn't break when dropped	1	6	6	6	6	9	9	7	7	5	5	9	9	6	6
Resists corrosion from sea spray	2	7	14	7	14	8	16	8	16	5	10	9	18	7	14
Floats when it falls in water	2	5	10	6	12	8	16	4	8	5	10	8	16	7	14
Keeps drink container stable	20														
Prevents spilling	7	3	21	4	28	3	21	5	35	5	35	3	21	3	21
Prevents bouncing in waves	6	7	42	8	48	7	42	5	30	5	30	7	42	7	42
Will not slide during pitch/roll	7	5	35	5	35	5	35	5	35	5	35	5	35	5	35
Requires little maintenance	5														
Easily stored when not in use	1	7	7	6	6	8	8	9	9	4	4	8	8	7	7
Easy to maintain a clean appearance	2	6	12	6	12	3	6	4	8	5	10	5	10	6	12
Allows liquid to drain out bottom	2	5	10	5	10	5	10	5	10	5	10	5	10	5	10
Easy to use	15														
Usable with one hand	5	7	35	7	35	7	35	6	30	5	25	7	35	7	35
Easy/comfortable to grip	5	8	40	8	40	6	30	5	25	5	25	6	30	8	40
Easy to exchange beverage containers	2	5	10	5	10	5	10	8	16	5	10	5	10	5	10
Works reliably	3	3	9	3	9	3	9	3	9	4	12	4	12	3	9
Attractive in environment	10														
Doesn't damage boat surface	5	8	40	8	40	8	40	8	40	8	40	6	30	8	40
Attractive to look at	5	7	35	8	40	3	15	4	20	5	25	5	25	8	40
Manufacturing ease	10														
Low-cost materials	4	5	20	4	16	7	28	8	32	4	16	8	32	6	24
Low complexity of parts	3	4	12	3	9	7	21	4	12	3	9	8	24	5	15
Low number of assembly steps	3	5	15	5	15	8	24	3	9	3	9	8	24	6	18
Total Score			578		594		585		484		510		556		587
Rank			**4**		**1**		**3**		**7**		**6**		**5**		**2**

PRODUCT ARCHITECTURE

EXHIBIT 1   The production version of the Sinterstation 2000 System. (Courtesy of DTM Corp.)

T he development team at DTM Corporation, a new venture in Austin, Texas, faced the challenge of transforming a product concept and an early prototype into a production-ready product within 12 months. The product would embody one of several so-called rapid prototyping technologies which emerged in the 1980s to create parts directly from computer-aided design (CAD) files. The core technology of the product, the SLS selective laser sintering process, had been refined over the past five years. To create an object, successive layers of wax or plastic powder are rolled out and selectively sintered (fused) by a laser in order to fabricate the part one cross-sectional layer at a time. DTM Corporation's final product, the Sinterstation 2000 System, is shown in Exhibit 1. Some of the parts fabricated by the process are shown in Exhibit 2. The team faced the challenge of establishing a product architecture that would enable them to transform the basic selective laser sintering technology into a commercially successful product. In considering their next steps, the team members asked:

- How would the architecture of the product impact their ability to complete the design within 12 months?
- How could they most effectively engage external suppliers in the development process?
- How would the architecture of the product influence their ability to manage the development process?
- How could they retain maximum flexibility for future model changes?

Product architecture is the arrangement of the functional elements of a product into physical blocks. A product's architecture begins to emerge during concept development. This happens informally—in the sketches, function diagrams,

EXHIBIT 2   Parts made by the SLS selective laser sintering process. (Courtesy of DTM Corp.)

and proof-of-concept prototypes of the concept development phase. However, the architectural decisions must be formalized after the product concept has been selected but before the detail design of the product begins. This occurs during the system-level design phase of development. In fact, creation of the product architecture is the dominant activity of the system-level design phase. In addition to establishing the product architecture during system-level design, the team also typically works to model, analyze, and test the system-level performance of the product; chooses values for key design variables (voltages, speeds, temperature, etc.); and selects key components and suppliers.

We focus this chapter on the task of establishing the product architecture. The purpose of the product architecture is to define the basic physical building blocks of the product in terms of what they do and what their interfaces are to the rest of the device. Architectural decisions allow the detailed design and testing of these building blocks to be assigned to teams, individuals, and/or suppliers, such that development of different portions of the product can be carried out simultaneously.

In the next two sections of this chapter, we define product architecture and illustrate the profound implications of architectural decisions, using examples from the Sinterstation 2000 System and several other products. We then present a methodology for establishing the product architecture and focus on the Sinterstation 2000 System for illustration.

WHAT IS PRODUCT ARCHITECTURE?

A product can be thought of in both functional and physical terms. The *functional elements* of a product are the individual operations and transformations that contribute to the overall performance of the product. For the Sinterstation 2000 System, some of the functional elements are "deliver powder" and "control atmosphere temperature." Functional elements are usually described in schematic form before they are reduced to specific technologies, components, or physical working principles.

The *physical elements* of a product are the parts, components, and subassemblies that ultimately implement the product's functions. The physical elements become more defined as development progresses. Some physical elements are dictated by the product concept, and others become defined during the detail design phase. For example, the Sinterstation 2000 System embodies a product concept involving powder, a "part piston," and a laser. These physical elements are inextricably linked to the product concept and are defined at the time of concept selection. However, the physical implementation of the atmospheric temperature control function and other functions remains unspecified until the detailed design phase.

The physical elements of a product are typically organized into several major physical building blocks, which we call *chunks*. (This term is attaining some pop-

EXHIBIT 3   Two models of bicycle brake and shifting controls. The product on the left exemplifies a modular architecture; the product on the right has a more integral architecture. (Courtesy of Shimano.)

ularity within major U.S. manufacturing firms.) Each chunk is then made up of a collection of components that implement the functions of the product. The *architecture* of a product is the scheme by which the functional elements of the product are arranged into physical chunks and by which the chunks interact.

Perhaps the most important characteristic of a product's architecture is its modularity. Consider the two different designs for bicycle braking and shifting controls shown in Exhibit 3. In the traditional design (left), the shifting function and the braking function are allocated to separate chunks, which in fact are mounted in separate locations on the bicycle. This design exhibits a modular architecture. In the novel design on the right, the shifting function and braking function are allocated to the same chunk. This design exhibits an integral architecture—in this case motivated by aerodynamic and ergonomic concerns.

A *modular architecture* has the following two properties:

- Chunks implement one or a few functional elements in their entirety.
- The interactions between chunks are well defined and are generally fundamental to the primary functions of the product.

The most modular architecture is one in which each functional element of the product is implemented by exactly one physical chunk and in which there are a few well-defined interactions between the chunks. Such a modular architecture allows a design change to be made to one chunk without generally requiring a change to other chunks for the product to function correctly. The chunks may also be designed quite independently of one another.

The opposite of a modular architecture is an *integral architecture*. An integral architecture exhibits one or more of the following properties:

- Functional elements of the product are implemented using more than one chunk.

- A single chunk implements many functional elements.

- The interactions between chunks are ill-defined and may be incidental to the primary functions of the products.

A product embodying an integral architecture will often be designed with the highest possible performance in mind. Implementation of functional elements may be distributed across multiple chunks. Boundaries between the chunks may be difficult to identify or may be non existent. Many functional elements may be combined into a few physical components to optimize certain dimensions of performance; however, modifications to any one particular component or feature may require extensive redesign of the product.

Modularity is a relative property of a product architecture. Products are rarely strictly modular or integral. Rather, we can say that they exhibit either more or less modularity than a comparative product, as in the brake and shifter controls example in Exhibit 3.

IMPLICATIONS OF THE ARCHITECTURE

Decisions about how to divide the product into chunks and about how much modularity to impose on the architecture are tightly linked to several issues of importance to the entire enterprise: product performance, product change, product variety, component standardization, manufacturability, and project management. The architecture of the product therefore is closely linked to decisions about marketing strategy, manufacturing capabilities, and product development management.

Product Change

Chunks are the physical building blocks of the product, but the architecture of the product defines how these blocks relate to the function of the product. The architecture therefore also defines how the product can be changed. Modular chunks allow changes to be made to a few isolated functional elements of the product without necessarily affecting the design of other chunks. Changing an integral chunk may influence many functional elements and require changes to several related chunks.

Some of the motives for product change are:

- *Upgrade:* As technological capabilities or user needs evolve, some products can accommodate this evolution through upgrades. Examples include changing the processor board in a computer printer or replacing a pump in a cooling system with a more powerful model.

- *Add-ons:* Many products are sold by a manufacturer as a basic unit, to which the user adds components, often produced by third parties, as needed. This type of change is common in the personal computer industry (e.g., third-party mass storage devices may be added to a basic computer).

- *Adaptation:* Some long-lived products may be used in several different use environments, requiring adaptation. For example, machine tools may need to be converted from 220-volt to 110-volt power. Some engines can be converted from a gasoline to a propane fuel supply.

- *Wear:* Physical elements of a product may deteriorate with use, necessitating replacement of the worn components to extend the useful life of the product. For example, many razors allow dull blades to be replaced, tires on vehicles can usually be replaced, most rotational bearings can be replaced, and many appliance motors can be replaced.

- *Consumption:* Some products consume materials which can then be easily replenished. For example, copiers and printers frequently contain toner cartridges, cameras take film cartridges, glue guns consume glue sticks, torches have gas cartridges, and watches contain batteries, all of which are generally replaceable.

- *Flexibility in use:* Some products can be configured by the user to exhibit different capabilities. For example, many 35mm cameras can be used with different lens and flash options, some boats can be used with several awning options, and fishing rods may accommodate several rod-reel configurations.

- *Reuse:* In creating subsequent products, the firm may wish to change only a few functional elements while retaining the rest of the product intact. For example, manufacturers of consumer electronics may wish to update the product line by changing only the user interface and enclosure while retaining the inner workings from a previous model.

In each of these cases, a modular architecture allows the firm to minimize the *physical* changes required to achieve a *functional* change.

Product Variety

Variety refers to the range of product models the firm can produce within a particular time period in response to market demand. Products built around modular product architectures can be more easily varied without adding tremendous complexity to the manufacturing system. For example, Swatch produces hundreds of different watch models, but can achieve this variety at relatively low cost by assembling the variants from different combinations of standard chunks (Exhibit 4). A large number of different hands, faces, and wristbands can be combined with a relatively small selection of movements and cases to create seemingly endless combinations.

EXHIBIT 4   Swatch uses a modular architecture to enable high-variety manufacturing. (Stuart Cohen)

Component Standardization

Component standardization is the use of the same component or chunk in multiple products. If a chunk implements only one or a few widely useful functional elements, then the chunk can be standardized and used in several different products. Such standardization allows the firm to manufacture the chunk in higher volumes than would otherwise be possible. This in turn may lead to lower costs and increased quality. For example, the watch movement in Exhibit 4 is identical for many Swatch models. Component standardization may also occur outside the firm when several manufacturers' products all use a chunk or component from the same supplier. For example, the watch battery in Exhibit 4 is made by a supplier and standardized across several manufacturers' product lines.

Product Performance

We define *product performance* as how well a product implements its intended functions. Typical product performance characteristics are speed, efficiency, life, accuracy, and noise. To the extent that a product performance characteristic depends on the size, shape, or mass of a product, it generally can be enhanced through an integral architecture.

Consider, for example, a motorcycle. A conventional motorcycle architecture

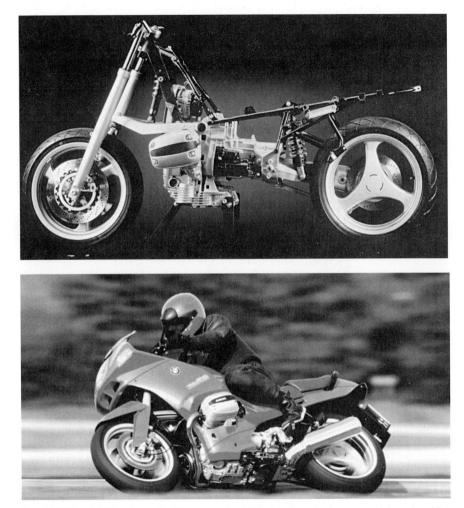

EXHIBIT 5 The BMW R1100RS motorcycle. This product exhibits function sharing and an integral architecture with the design of its transmission chunk. (Courtesy of BMW.)

assigns the structural-support functional element to a frame chunk and the power-conversion functional element to a transmission chunk. Exhibit 5 shows a photograph of the BMW R1100RS. The architecture of this motorcycle assigns both the structural-support function and the power-conversion function to the transmission chunk. This integral architecture allows the motorcycle designers to exploit the secondary structural properties of the transmission casing in order to eliminate the extra size and mass of a separate frame. The practice of implementing multiple functions using a single physical element is called *function sharing*.

An integral architecture facilitates the optimization of those performance characteristics that are driven by the size, shape, and mass of a product. Such characteristics include acceleration, energy consumption, aerodynamic drag, noise, and aesthetics. An integral architecture allows for redundancy to be eliminated through function sharing (as in the case of the motorcycle) and allows for geometric nesting of components to minimize the volume a product occupies. Such function sharing and nesting also allows materials use to be minimized, potentially reducing the cost of manufacturing the product.

Manufacturability

In addition to the cost implications of product variety and component standardization described above, the product architecture also directly affects the ability of the team to design each chunk to be produced at low cost. One important design for manufacturing (DFM) strategy involves the minimization of the number of parts in a product through *component integration*. However, to maintain a given architecture, the integration of physical components can only be easily considered within each of the chunks. Component integration across several chunks is difficult, if not impossible, and would alter the architecture dramatically. Since the product architecture constrains subsequent detail design decisions in this way, the team must consider the manufacturing implications of the architecture. For this reason DFM begins during the system-level design phase while the layout of the chunks is being planned. For details about the implementation of DFM, see the chapter "Design for Manufacturing."

Product Development Management

Responsibility for the detail design of each chunk is usually assigned to a relatively small group within the firm or to an outside supplier. Chunks are assigned to a single individual or group because their design requires careful resolution of interactions, geometric and otherwise, among components within the chunk. With a modular architecture, the group assigned to design a chunk deals with known, and relatively limited, functional interactions with other chunks. If a functional element is implemented by two chunks, as in some integral architecture, detail design will require close coordination between two different groups. This coordination is likely to be substantially more involved and challenging than the coordination required between two groups designing two different chunks in a modular design. For this reason, teams relying on outside suppliers or on a geographically dispersed team often opt for a modular architecture in which development responsibilities can be split according to the chunk boundaries. Another possibility is to have several functional elements allocated to the same chunk. In this case, the work of the group assigned to that chunk involves a great deal of internal coordination across a larger group.

Modular and integral architectures also demand different project management styles. Modular approaches require very careful planning during the system-level design phase, but detail design is largely concerned with ensuring that the teams assigned to chunks are meeting the performance, cost, and schedule requirements for their chunks. An integral architecture may require less planning and specification during system-level design, but such an architecture requires substantially more integration, conflict resolution, and coordination during the detail design phase.

ESTABLISHING THE ARCHITECTURE

Because the product architecture will have profound implications for subsequent product development activities and for the manufacturing and marketing of the completed product, it should be established in a cross-functional effort by the development team. The end result of this activity is an approximate geometric layout of the product, descriptions of the major chunks, and documentation of the key interactions among the chunks. We recommend a four-step methodology to structure the decision process, which is illustrated using the Sinterstation 2000 System example. The steps are:

1 Create a schematic of the product.
2 Cluster the elements of the schematic.
3 Create a rough geometric layout.
4 Identify the fundamental and incidental interactions.

Step 1: Create a Schematic of the Product

A schematic is a diagram representing the team's understanding of the constituent elements of the product. A schematic for the Sinterstation 2000 System is shown in Exhibit 6. At the end of the concept development phase, some of the elements in the schematic are physical concepts, such as the piston/cylinder containing the part under construction. Some of the elements correspond to critical components, such as the laser the team expects to use. However, some of the elements remain described only functionally. These are the functional elements of the product that have not yet been reduced to physical concepts or components. For example, "deliver powder" is a functional element required for the selective laser sintering concept, but the physical concept of how to deliver the powder has not yet been decided. Those elements that have been reduced to physical concepts or components are usually key to the basic product concept the team has generated and selected. Those elements that remain unspecified in physical terms are usually ancillary functions of the product.

The schematic should reflect the team's best understanding of the state of the product, but it does not have to contain every imaginable detail, such as "lock access doors" or "convert AC power to regulated DC." These and other more detailed functional elements are deferred to a later step. A good rule of thumb is to aim for fewer than 30 elements in the schematic, for the purpose of establishing the product architecture. If the product is complex, involving hundreds of functional elements, then it is useful to omit some of the minor ones and to

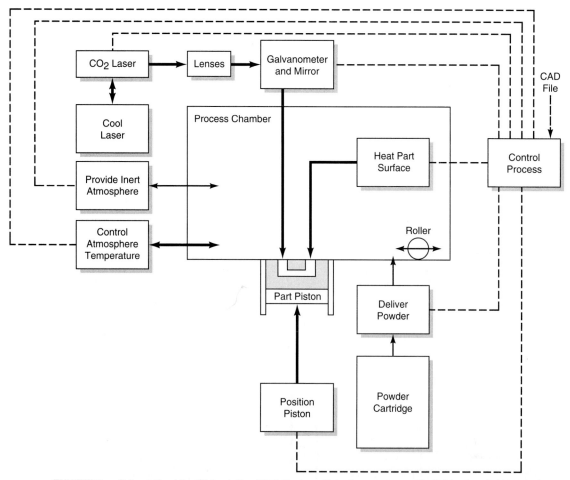

EXHIBIT 6   Schematic of the Sinterstation 2000 System. Note the presence of both functional elements (e.g., "deliver powder") and physical elements (e.g., "part piston"). The lines connecting the elements in the schematic indicate the flow of forces or energy (thick lines), material (thin lines), and signals or data (dashed lines).

group some others into higher-level functions to be decomposed later. (See "Defining Secondary Systems" later in this chapter.)

The schematic is not unique. The specific choice of certain functional elements and their arrangement partly defines the product architecture. For example, the functional element "control process" is represented as a single centralized element in Exhibit 6. An alternative would be to distribute the control of each of the other elements of the product throughout the system. Because there is usually substantial latitude in the schematic, the team should generate several alternatives and select an approach which will facilitate the consideration of several architectural options.

Step 2: Cluster the Elements of the Schematic

The challenge of step 2 is to assign each of the elements of the schematic to a chunk. One possible assignment of elements to chunks is shown in Exhibit 7, where five chunks are used. Although this was the approach taken by the DTM team, there are several other viable alternatives. At one extreme, each element could be assigned to its own chunk, yielding 14 chunks. At the other extreme, the team could decide that the product would have only one major chunk and then attempt to physically integrate all of the elements of the product. In fact, consideration of all possible clusterings of elements would yield thousands of

EXHIBIT 7   Clustering the elements into chunks. Five chunks, with boundaries represented by dotted lines, make up the architecture of the Sinterstation 2000 System. Note that for this schematic, most of the dashed signal/data flow lines are omitted for clarity.

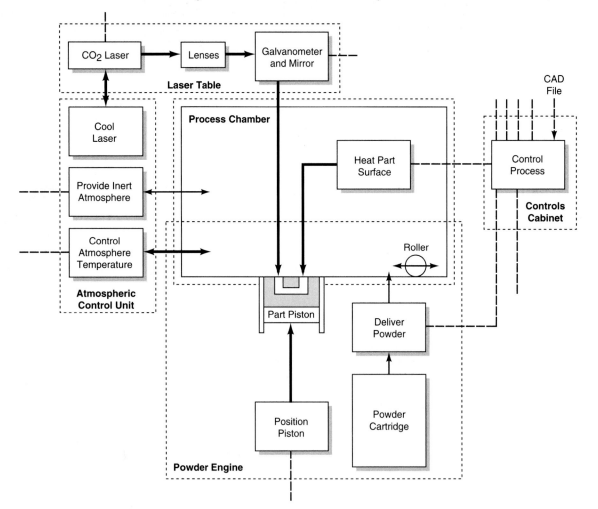

alternatives. One procedure for managing the complexity of the alternatives is to begin with the assumption that each element of the schematic will be assigned to its own chunk, and then to successively cluster elements where advantageous. To determine when there are advantages to clustering, consider these factors, which echo the implications discussed in the previous section:

- *Geometric integration and precision:* Assigning elements to the same chunks allows a single individual or group to control the physical relationships among the elements. Elements requiring precise location or close geometric integration can often be best designed if they are part of the same chunk. For the Sinterstation 2000 System, this would suggest clustering the laser components together because they require precise optical alignment. Because of the necessary precise geometric relationship of the roller and part piston, clustering these two elements would facilitate their design. The need to carefully control the geometric relationship between the laser and the part would also suggest that the laser table and part piston be clustered, although other factors (noted below) may argue against this.

- *Function sharing:* When a single physical component can implement several functional elements of the product, these functional elements are best clustered together. This is the situation exemplified by the BMW motorcycle transmission (Exhibit 5). For the Sinterstation 2000 System, the team believed that laser cooling and atmospheric temperature control could share the same refrigeration unit and therefore decided to cluster these two elements into the same chunk.

- *Capabilities of vendors:* A trusted vendor may have specific capabilities related to a project, and in order to best take advantage of such capabilities a team may choose to cluster those elements about which the vendor has expertise into one chunk. In the case of the Sinterstation 2000 System, this was the reason for the clustering of the laser cooling, atmospheric temperature control, and atmospheric inerting into one chunk, the "atmospheric control unit." The DTM team decided that this chunk would be designed and produced by a single vendor.

- *Localization of change:* When a team anticipates a great deal of change in some element, it makes sense to isolate that element into its own modular chunk, so that required changes to the element can be carried out without disrupting any of the other chunks. The DTM team felt that changes to the controls were highly likely. This factor, among others, drove the team to contain all of the controls in a single chunk, the "controls cabinet." This argument also applies to smaller subassemblies and components. The team knew that lasers would have to be replaced regularly and so chose to design the laser attachment in a way that ensured easy replacement. Similarly, because of anticipated changes, the team chose to design the heater and powder cartridges in a modular way.

- *Accommodating variety:* Elements should be clustered together in a way that enables the firm to vary the product in ways that will have value for customers. DTM anticipated offering several different part material choices for the Sinterstation 2000 System. The atmospheric control unit was one of the chunks the team felt it could simply swap with an alternative in order to create the temperature and atmospheric conditions required for different materials.

- *Enabling standardization:* If a set of elements will be useful in other products, they should be clustered together into a single chunk. This allows the physical elements of the chunk to be produced in higher quantities. Internal standardization was not a major factor in DTM's architectural decisions.

- *Portability of the interfaces:* Some interactions are easily transmitted over large distances. For example, digital signals are much more portable than are mechanical actions. As a result, elements with electronic interactions can be easily separated from one another. This is also true, but to a lesser extent, for fluid connections. This property of fluid and electrical interactions allowed the DTM team to cluster the atmospheric control unit elements together and allowed the controls to all be contained in a single chunk. Conversely, the laser-related elements and the part- and powder-related elements are much more constrained (to be geometrically close) by their necessary interactions.

Step 3: Create a Rough Geometric Layout

A geometric layout can be created in two or three dimensions, using drawings or models (of cardboard or foam, for example). Exhibit 8 shows a rough geometric layout of the Sinterstation 2000 System, positioning the major chunks.

EXHIBIT 8   A rough geometric layout.

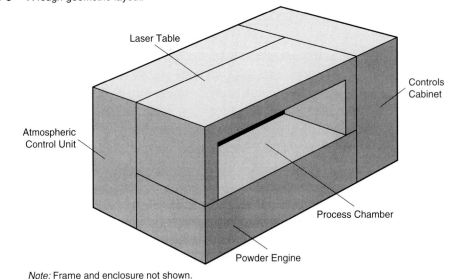

Note: Frame and enclosure not shown.

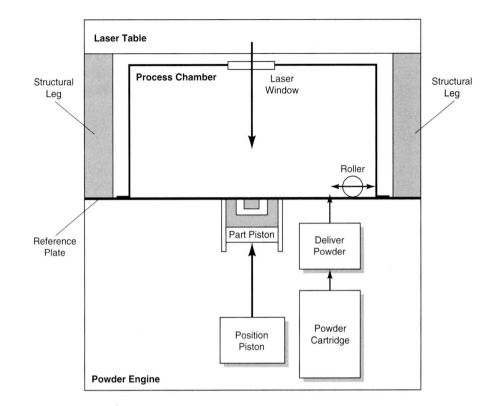

EXHIBIT 9   A more detailed layout of the laser table, powder engine, and process chamber chunks.

Creating a geometric layout forces the team to consider whether the geometric interfaces among the chunks are feasible. For example, during this process, the DTM team discovered that the laser table would have to straddle the process chamber in order to precisely locate the laser table with respect to the powder engine. This discovery would not have been possible without the creation of a three-dimensional geometric layout of the chunks. Recall that the laser elements might have been best clustered with the part-related elements to allow for better precision and alignment. Several other factors made this approach unattractive: the team wished to assign the powder engine design and the laser table design to two different groups, and the team hoped to be able to isolate the laser table from the thermally active part and powder areas. To work out the definition of the chunks, the team created a more detailed layout of just these elements and chunks, as shown in Exhibit 9. They reasoned that they could use "structural legs" to accurately locate the laser table relative to the part. They introduced a key interface they called the "reference plate," to which the laser table, process chamber, and powder engine were all referenced. (Key geometric features such as the reference plate are sometimes called "hard points" because they are features the entire team can reliably assume will not change over time.) They also specified a laser "window" which would allow the laser to reside outside of the atmosphere of the process chamber.

In this step, as in the previous step, the team benefits from generating several alternative layouts and selecting the best one. Layout decision criteria are closely related to the clustering issues in step 2. In some cases, the team may discover that the clustering derived in step 2 is not geometrically feasible and thus some of the elements would have to be reassigned to other chunks. Creating the rough layout should be coordinated with the industrial designers on the team in cases where the aesthetic and human interface issues of the product are important and strongly related to the geometric arrangement of the chunks.

Step 4: Identify the Fundamental and Incidental Interactions

Most likely each chunk will be designed by a different person or group. Because the chunks interact with one another in both planned and unintended ways, these different groups will have to coordinate their activities and exchange information. In order to better manage this coordination process, the team should identify the known interactions between chunks during the system-level design phase.

There are two categories of interactions between chunks. First, *fundamental interactions* are those corresponding to the lines on the schematic that connect the chunks to one another. For example, the energy flow from the laser to the part crosses from the laser table chunk to the process chamber chunk. This interaction is planned for, and it should be well understood, even from the very earliest schematic, since it is fundamental to the system's operation. Second, *incidental interactions* are those that arise because of the particular physical implementation of functional elements or because of the geometric arrangement of the chunks. For example, the process chamber may transfer heat to the legs of the laser table, causing thermal expansion and possible degradation of laser alignment. This interaction is not represented by the schematic and only arises as an incidental consequence of the physical arrangement of the laser table and process chamber. Interactions of this type had to be identified so the DTM team could alleviate any detrimental effects.

While the fundamental interactions are explicitly represented by the schematic showing the clustering of elements into chunks, the incidental interactions must be documented in some other way. For a small number of interacting chunks (less than about 10), an *interaction graph* is a convenient way to represent the incidental interactions. Exhibit 10 shows the interaction graph for the Sinterstation 2000 System, representing the known incidental interactions. For larger systems this type of graph becomes confusing, and an *interaction matrix* is useful instead. See Pimmler and Eppinger (1994) for an example of using such a matrix, which is also used to cluster the functional elements into chunks based on quantifications of their interactions.

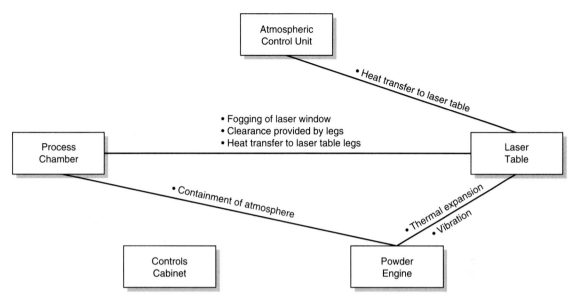

EXHIBIT 10   Incidental interaction graph.

The graph in Exhibit 10 suggests that the laser table chunk involves several important incidental interactions with other chunks. These interactions represent challenges in the development of the system, requiring focused coordination efforts within the team.

We can use the mapping of the interactions between the chunks to provide guidance for structuring and managing the remaining development activities. Chunks with important interactions should be designed by groups with strong communication and coordination between them. Conversely, chunks with little interaction can be designed by groups with less coordination. McCord and Eppinger (1993) describe a matrix-based method for prescribing such system-level coordination needs in larger projects.

It is also possible, through careful advance coordination, to develop two interacting chunks in a completely independent fashion. This is facilitated when the interactions between the two chunks can be reduced in advance to a completely specified interface that will be implemented by both chunks. For example, the laser and its cooling system can be developed by two different suppliers, once the key interactions are specified (amount of heat to be dissipated, fluid flow rate, etc.). It is relatively easy to specify interfaces to handle the fundamental interactions, while it can be difficult to do so for incidental interactions.

Knowledge of the incidental interactions (and sometimes of the fundamental interactions as well) develops as system-level and detail design progress. The schematic and the interaction graph or matrix can be used for documenting this information as it evolves.

RELATED SYSTEM-LEVEL DESIGN ISSUES

The four-step methodology for establishing the product architecture guides the early system-level design activities, but many more detailed activities remain. Here we discuss some of the issues that frequently arise during subsequent system-level design activities and their implications for the product architecture.

Defining Secondary Systems

The schematic in Exhibit 6 shows only the key elements of the product. There are many other functional elements that are not shown, some of which will only be conceived as the system-level design evolves. These additional functional elements make up the "secondary systems" of the product. Examples include safety systems, power systems, status monitors, structural supports, and enclosures. Some of these systems, such as safety systems, will have to cut across chunks. Fortunately, secondary systems usually involve flexible interfaces such as wiring and tubing and can be considered after the major architectural decisions have been made. Secondary systems cutting across the boundaries of chunks present a special management challenge: should a single group or individual be assigned to design a secondary system even though the system will be made up of components residing in several different chunks? Or should the group or individuals responsible for the chunks be responsible for coordinating among themselves to ensure that the secondary systems will work as needed? The former approach is more typical, where specific individuals or sub-teams are assigned to focus on the secondary systems.

Establishing the Architecture of the Chunks

Some of the chunks of a complex product may be very complex systems in their own right. For example, every chunk in the Sinterstation 2000 System involves hundreds of parts. Each of these chunks may have its own architecture—the scheme by which it is divided into smaller chunks. This problem is essentially identical to the architectural challenge posed at the level of the entire product. Careful consideration of the architecture of the chunks is nearly as important as the creation of the architecture of the overall product.

Migration of Functionality across Chunk Interfaces

As system-level and detail design of the product progresses, decisions will have to be made about where to locate specific individual components implementing the functional elements of the product. Some single functional elements, like those shown in Exhibit 7, end up being implemented by dozens or hundreds of physical components. Often there is migration of some of these components back and forth across the boundaries of chunks. For example, the team may wish to move a power supply for the piston drive into the controls cabinet instead of leaving it in the powder engine with the other components of the piston drive. A strictly modular architecture requires that all of the components implementing a functional element reside in the same chunk. For this reason, each potential migration of a component across chunk boundaries should be considered carefully in terms of its implications for product change, standardization, variety, performance, manufacturability, and project management.

Creating Detailed Interface Specifications

As the system-level design progresses, the fundamental interactions indicated by lines on the schematic in Exhibit 6 become much more detailed collections of specific signals, material flows, and exchanges of energy. As this refinement occurs, the specification of the interfaces between chunks should also be clarified. For example, Exhibit 11 shows a refined schematic of the piston drive sys-

EXHIBIT 11 Schematic of the piston drive system. This diagram specifies the interfaces between the relevant chunks. (Courtesy of DTM Corp.)

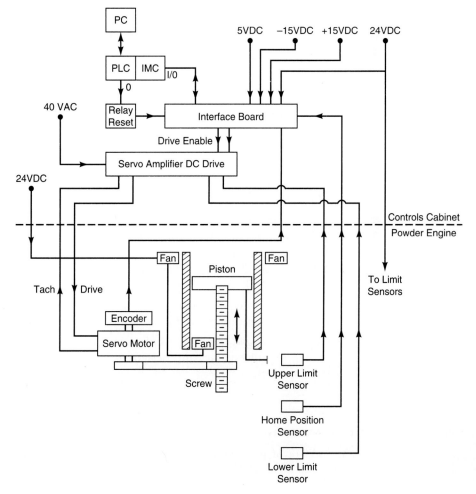

tem of the Sinterstation 2000 System, indicating the detailed interactions among components. Each line in the schematic which crosses a chunk boundary corresponds to a specific interaction between the chunks. These interactions are detailed in an associated interface specification document.

SUMMARY

Product architecture is the scheme by which the functional elements of the product are arranged into physical chunks. The architecture is established during the system-level design phase of development.

- Product architecture decisions have far-reaching implications, affecting such things as product performance, product change, product variety, component standardization, manufacturability, and product development management.

- A key characteristic of a product architecture is the degree to which it is modular or integral.

- Modular architectures are those in which each physical chunk implements a specific set of functional elements and has well-defined interactions with the other chunks.

- Integral architectures are those in which the implementation of functional elements is spread across chunks, resulting in ill-defined interactions between the chunks.

- We recommend a four-step methodology for establishing the product architecture:

    1 Create a schematic of the product.
    2 Cluster the elements of the schematic.
    3 Create a rough geometric layout.
    4 Identify the fundamental and incidental interactions.

- This methodology leads the team through the preliminary architectural decisions. Subsequent system-level and detail design activities will contribute to a continuing evolution of the architectural details.

- Due to the broad implications of architectural decisions, inputs from marketing, manufacturing, and design are essential in this aspect of product development.

REFERENCES AND BIBLIOGRAPHY

The concept of product architecture and its implications are treated more thoroughly and theoretically by Ulrich in the following article:

Ulrich, Karl, "The Role of Product Architecture in the Manufacturing Firm," *Research Policy*, Vol. 24, 1995.

Many of the issues involved in establishing a product architecture are treated from a slightly different perspective in the systems engineering literature. One relatively recent book with good references to earlier work is the following:

Hall, Arthur D., III, *Metasystems Methodology: A New Synthesis and Unification*, Pergamon Press, Elmsford, NY, 1989. ISBN 0-08-036956-1.

The linkage between product variety and product architecture is discussed by Pine in the context of *mass customization*, or very high variety manufacturing.

Pine, B. Joseph, II, *Mass Customization: The New Frontier in Business Competition*, Harvard Business School Press, Boston, MA, 1992. ISBN 0-87584-372-7.

Clark and Fujimoto discuss the practice of "black box" supplier interactions in their book on product development in the automobile industry. In this situation, the manufacturer specifies only the function and interface of a chunk or component and the supplier handles the detailed implementation issues.

Clark, Kim B., and Takahiro Fujimoto, *Product Development Performance: Strategy, Organization, and Management in the World Auto Industry*, Harvard Business School Press, Boston, MA, 1991. ISBN 0-87584-245-3.

Alexander's book is an early research monograph on partitioning a design into minimally interacting chunks.

Alexander, Christopher, *Notes on the Synthesis of Form*, Harvard University Press, Cambridge, MA, 1964. ISBN 0-67462-750-4.

McCord and Eppinger discuss the relationship between problem partitioning and product development project management. They present a method for identifying the needs for integration across chunks within complex development projects.

McCord, Kent R., and Steven D. Eppinger, "Managing the Integration Problem in Concurrent Engineering," MIT Sloan School of Management, Working Paper #3594-93-MSA, Cambridge, MA, August 1993.

Pimmler and Eppinger present a methodology to cluster functional elements into chunks based on quantification of the interactions between the elements. By using the interaction information early in the process, a team can choose an architecture that minimizes the complexity of the coordination required to develop the system.

Pimmler, Thomas, U., and Steven D. Eppinger, "Integration Analysis of Product Decompositions," ASME Design Theory and Methodology Conference, Minneapolis, MN, September 1994.

EXERCISES

1 Draw a schematic for a wristwatch, using only functional elements (without assuming any particular physical working principles or components).
2 Describe the architecture of a Swiss Army knife. What advantages and disadvantages does this architecture provide?

3 Take apart a small electromechanical product (which you are willing to sacrifice if necessary). Draw a schematic including the essential functional elements. Identify two or three possible clusterings of these elements into chunks. Is there any evidence to suggest which architecture was chosen by the development team?

THOUGHT QUESTIONS

1 Do service products, such as bank accounts or insurance policies, have architectures?

2 Can a firm achieve high product variety without a modular product architecture? How (or why not)?

3 The argument for the motorcycle architecture shown in Exhibit 5 is that it allows for a lighter motorcycle than the more modular alternative. What are the other advantages and disadvantages? Which approach is likely to cost less to manufacture?

4 There are thousands of architectural decisions to be made in the development of an automobile. Consider all of the likely fundamental and incidental interactions that any one functional element, say safety restraints, would have with the others. How would you use the documentation of such interactions to guide the decision about what chunk to place this functional element in?

5 The schematic shown in Exhibit 6 includes 14 functional and physical elements. Consider the possibility of assigning each element to its own chunk. What are the strengths and weaknesses of such an architecture?

INDUSTRIAL DESIGN

Developed in collaboration with Paul Brody.

EXHIBIT 1   Motorola portable cellular telephones. These are
the 1989 original MicroTAC (right) and the more
traditional DynaTAC design it replaced (left).
(Courtesy of Motorola Inc.)

In the mid-1980s, Motorola launched a product development effort to replace its original DynaTAC line of cellular phones, which were deemed too large, too heavy, and too difficult to manufacture to remain competitive in the marketplace. With their electronics getting smaller every year, phones were becoming slimmer and lighter. The project team had considered several phone design concepts that were a great deal smaller than the DynaTAC.

The project was well under way and a sleek new phone design had been selected, and it looked like the engineers would indeed be able to fit the electronics into the smaller package. Motorola's top managers, however, were still concerned that the phone was not exciting enough to be considered a true breakthrough. So, even though the project was quite far along, they asked the industrial design group to propose some more innovative design concepts.

The proposed design departed radically from the "yet slimmer" direction that had become the norm. The unique folding design finally allowed the phone to actually fit into a shirt pocket, rather than requiring storage in a briefcase or a special carrying bag. When the industrial design group showed off the folding design, it immediately turned the project completely around, literally overnight. The first folding design (shown later in Exhibit 4) was considered so radical that it was worth redirecting the project to focus upon this new concept. The resulting MicroTAC design, shown in Exhibit 1, incorporated the latest technology into an aesthetic and functional package.

After its introduction in 1989, MicroTAC sales reached over $1 billion in just the first two years. A product design analysis performed by the Corporate Design Foundation (Kamm and Poklop, 1992) attributed the MicroTAC's success to the following:

- **Small size and weight:** With its slimline battery pack installed, the MicroTAC has a volume of 220 cubic centimeters and a weight of 300 grams, making it the smallest and lightest cellular phone on the market at the time. The MicroTAC can be folded in one hand, like a wallet, and placed into a pocket. It can literally be taken anywhere.

- **Performance features:** The MicroTAC incorporates all the features of its predecessor, yet in a much smaller package. Important features include a continuous talk time of 30 minutes with the slimline battery pack (70 minutes with a standard battery pack), an alphanumeric memory to store numbers and names, and a constant memory to recall any of the last ten numbers dialed.

- **Superior ergonomics:** The MicroTAC's sleek, ergonomic design complements the human face. The shape of the handset, particularly the angle and position of the ear piece and mouthpiece, conform to the user for superior comfort. The spacing and position of the buttons on the keypad are based on accepted standards allowing for fast and accurate dialing. The folding design allows the user to answer or end calls by flipping the mouthpiece open or closed.

152

- *Durability:* As with all Motorola products, the MicroTAC was designed to meet military specifications. It can be dropped from a height of four feet onto a cement floor or sat upon in the open position without sustaining any visible or operational damage. The MicroTAC can also withstand temperature extremes, humidity, shock, dust, and vibration.

- *Ease of manufacture:* The MicroTAC consists of 400 parts that can be robotically assembled in two hours. The entire unit snaps together using no screws. For comparison, earlier Motorola cellular phones consisted of over 3,000 parts and required up to 40 hours to assemble.

- *Appearance:* The sleek appearance and black color gave the MicroTAC a futuristic look associated with innovation. Because of its aesthetic appeal the MicroTAC has become somewhat of a status symbol that evokes strong feelings of pride among owners.

The MicroTAC development team included electrical, mechanical, and manufacturing engineers, whose contributions were instrumental in developing the technologies and manufacturing processes that allowed the product to achieve its performance, size, and weight. However, without the contributions of industrial designers, who helped to define the size, shape, and human factors, the MicroTAC would never have taken its innovative form. In fact, the Motorola team could easily have developed "just another phone," smaller and lighter than the existing DynaTAC model, but a revolutionary concept from industrial design turned the project into a dramatic success.

Industrial designers are primarily responsible for the aspects of a product that relate to the user—the product's aesthetic appeal (how it looks, sounds, feels, smells) and its functional interfaces (how it is used). For many U.S. manufacturers, industrial design has historically been an afterthought. Managers used industrial designers to style or "gift wrap" a product after its technical features were determined. Companies would then market the product on the merits of its technology alone, although customers certainly evaluate a product using more holistic judgments, including ergonomics and style.

Today, a product's core technology is generally not enough to ensure commercial success. The globalization of markets has resulted in the design and manufacture of a wide array of consumer products. Fierce competition makes it unlikely that a company will enjoy a sustainable competitive advantage through technology alone. Accordingly, companies such as Motorola are increasingly using industrial design as an important tool for both satisfying customer needs and differentiating their products from those of their competition.

This chapter introduces engineers and managers to industrial design (ID) and explains how the ID process takes place in relation to other product development activities. We refer to the MicroTAC example throughout this chapter to explain critical ideas. Specifically, this chapter presents:

- A historical perspective on ID and a precise definition of ID
- Statistics on typical investments in ID

- A methodology for determining the importance of ID to a particular product
- The costs and benefits of investing in ID
- How ID helps to establish a corporation's identity
- Specific steps industrial designers follow while designing a product
- A description of how the ID process changes according to product type
- A methodology for assessing the quality of the ID effort for a completed product

WHAT IS INDUSTRIAL DESIGN?

The birth of ID is often traced to western Europe in the early 1900s. [See Lorenz (1986) for an account of the history of ID, which is summarized here.] Several German companies, including AEG, a large electrical manufacturer, commissioned a multitude of craftsmen and architects to design various products for manufacture. Initially, these early European designers had little direct impact on industry; however, their work resulted in lasting theories that have influenced and shaped what is today known as industrial design. Early European theories on ID, such as the Bauhaus movement, went beyond mere functionalism; they emphasized the importance of geometry, precision, simplicity, and economy in the design of products. In short, early European designers believed that a product should be designed "from the inside out." Form should follow function.

In the United States, however, early concepts of ID were distinctly different. While early European industrial designers were architects and engineers, most industrial designers in America were actually theater designers and artist-illustrators. Not surprisingly, ID in the United States was often at the service of sales and advertising, where a product's exterior was all important and its insides mattered little. Pioneers in U.S. industrial design, including Walter Dorwin Teague, Norman Bel Geddes, and Raymond Loewy, emphasized streamlining in product design. This trend is best evidenced in U.S. products of the 1930s. From fountain pens to baby buggies, products were designed with nonfunctional aerodynamic shapes in an attempt to create product appeal. The auto industry provides another example. The shapes of European automobiles of the thirties were fairly simple and smooth, while U.S. cars of the same era were decorated with such nonfunctional features as tailfins and chrome teeth.

By the 1970s, however, the European influence had strongly influenced American ID thinking, largely through the works of Henry Dreyfuss and Eliot Noyes. Heightened competition in the marketplace forced companies to search for ways to improve and differentiate their products. Increasingly, companies accepted the notion that the role of ID needed to go beyond mere shape and appearance. Success stories such as Bell, Deere, Ford, and IBM, all of whom effectively integrated ID into their product development process, helped further this thinking.

Today, the Industrial Designers Society of America (IDSA) defines industrial design as the "professional service of creating and developing concepts and specifications that optimize the function, value and appearance of products and systems for the mutual benefit of both user and manufacturer." This definition is broad enough to include the activities of the entire product development team. In fact, industrial designers focus their attention upon the form and user interaction of products. Dreyfuss (1967) lists five critical goals that industrial designers can help a team to achieve when developing new products:

- *Utility:* The product's human interfaces should be safe, easy to use, and intuitive. Each feature should be shaped so that it communicates its function to the user.
- *Appearance:* Form, line, proportion, and color are used to integrate the product into a pleasing whole.
- *Ease of maintenance:* Products must also be designed to communicate how they are to be maintained and repaired.
- *Low costs:* Form and features have a large impact on tooling and production costs, so these must be considered jointly by the team.
- *Communication:* Product designs should communicate the corporate design philosophy and mission through the visual qualities of the products.

Industrial designers are typically educated in four-year university programs where they study sculpture and form; develop drawing, presentation, and model-making skills; and gain a basic understanding of materials, manufacturing techniques, and finishes. In industrial practice, designers receive additional exposure to basic engineering, advanced manufacturing/fabrication processes, and common marketing practices. Their ability to express ideas visually can facilitate the process of concept development for the team. Industrial designers may create most of the concept sketches, models, and renderings used by the team throughout the development process, even though the ideas come from the entire team.

ASSESSING THE NEED FOR INDUSTRIAL DESIGN

To assess the importance of ID to a particular product, we first review some investment statistics and then define the dimensions of a product which are dependent upon good ID.

Statistics on Expenditures for Industrial Design

Exhibit 2 shows approximate values of investment in ID for a variety of products. Both the total expenditures on ID and the percentage of the product development budget invested in ID are shown for consumer and industrial products spanning various industries. These statistics should give design teams a rough idea of how much ID investment will be required for a new product.

The exhibit shows that the range of expenditures on ID is tremendous. For

EXHIBIT 2   Industrial design expenditures for some consumer and industrial products.

products with relatively little user interaction such as some types of industrial equipment, the cost of ID is only in the tens of thousands of dollars. On the other hand, the development of an intensely interactive product such as an automobile requires millions of dollars of ID effort. The relative cost of ID as a fraction of the overall development budget also shows a wide range. For a technically sophisticated product, such as a new aircraft, the ID cost can be insignificant relative to the engineering and other development expenditures. This does not suggest, however, that ID is unimportant for such products; it suggests only that the other development functions are more costly. Certainly the success of a new automobile design is highly dependent on its aesthetic appeal and the quality of the user interfaces, two dimensions largely determined by ID, yet the ID expense of $7 million is modest, relative to the entire development budget.

How Important Is Industrial Design to a Product?

Most products on the market can be improved in some way or another by good ID, and all products that are used, operated, or seen by people depend critically on ID for commercial success.

With this in mind, a convenient means for assessing the importance of ID to a particular product is to characterize importance along two dimensions:

ergonomics and aesthetics. (Note that we use the term *ergonomics* to encompass all aspects of a product that relate to its human interfaces.) The more important each dimension is to the product's success, the more dependent the product is on ID. Therefore, by answering a series of questions along each dimension we can qualitatively assess the importance of ID.

Ergonomic Needs

- *How important is ease of use?* Ease of use may be extremely important both for frequently used products, such as an office photocopier, and for infrequently used products, such as a fire extinguisher. Ease of use is more important if the product has multiple features and/or modes of operation which may confuse or frustrate the user. When ease of use is an important criterion, industrial designers will need to ensure that the features of the product effectively communicate their function.

- *How important is ease of maintenance?* If the product needs to be serviced or repaired frequently, then ease of maintenance is crucial. For example, a user should be able to clear a paper jam in a printer or photocopier easily. Again, it is critical that the features of the product communicate maintenance/repair procedures to the user. However, in many cases, a more desirable solution is to eliminate the need for maintenance entirely.

- *How many user interactions are required for the product?* In general, the more interactions users have with the product, the more the product will depend on ID. For example, a doorknob typically requires only one interaction, whereas a portable computer may require a dozen or more, all of which the industrial designer must understand in depth. Furthermore, each interaction may require a different design approach and/or additional research.

- *How novel are the user interaction needs?* A user interface requiring incremental improvements to an existing design will be relatively straightforward to design, such as the buttons on a next-generation desktop computer mouse. A more novel user interface may require substantial research and feasibility studies, such as the built-in trackball in the first Macintosh PowerBook notebook computer.

- *What are the safety issues?* All products have safety considerations. For some products, these can present significant challenges to the design team. For example, the safety concerns in the design of a child's toy are much more prominent than those for a new computer mouse.

Aesthetic Needs

- *Is product differentiation required?* Products with stable markets and technology are highly dependent upon ID to create aesthetic appeal and, hence, differentiation. In contrast, a product such as a computer's internal disk drive, which is differentiated by its technology, is less dependent on ID.

- *How important are pride of ownership, image, and fashion?* A customer's perception of a product is in part based upon its aesthetic appeal. An attractive product may be associated with high fashion and image and will likely create a strong sense of pride among its owners. This may similarly be true for a product that looks and feels rugged or conservative. When these characteristics are important, ID will play a critical role in determining the product's ultimate success.

- *Will an aesthetic product motivate the team?* A product that is aesthetically appealing can generate a sense of "team pride" among the design and manufacturing staff. Team pride helps to motivate and unify everyone associated with the project. An early ID concept gives the team a concrete vision of the end result of the development effort.

To demonstrate this method, we can use the above questions to assess the importance of industrial design in the development of the Motorola MicroTAC. Exhibit 3 displays the results of such analysis. We find that both ergonomics and aesthetics were extremely important for the MicroTAC. Accordingly, ID did indeed play a large role in determining many of the product's critical success factors.

THE IMPACT OF INDUSTRIAL DESIGN

The previous section focused primarily upon the importance of ID in satisfying customer needs. Next we explore both the direct economic impact of investing in ID as well as the impact ID has upon corporate identity.

Is Industrial Design Worth the Investment?

Managers will often want to know, for a specific product or for a business operation in general, how much effort should be invested in industrial design. While it is difficult to answer this question precisely, we can offer several insights by considering the costs and benefits.

The costs of ID include direct cost, manufacturing cost, and time cost, described below:

- *Direct cost* is the cost of the ID services. This quantity is determined by the number of designers used, duration of the project and number of models required, plus material costs and other related expenses. In 1994, consulting services cost $75 to $125 per hour plus costs for models, photos, etc. The true cost of internal corporate design services is generally about the same.

- *Manufacturing cost* is the expense incurred to implement the product details created through ID. Surface finishes, stylized shapes, rich colors, and many

Needs	Level of Importance			Explanation of Rating
	Low	Medium	High	
Ergonomics				
Ease of use			○	Critical for a portable telephone since it can be operated by motorists while driving. The product's function must be communicated through its design.
Ease of maintenance	○			Of little importance for the MicroTAC. As with many integrated electronics products, there is very little maintenance required.
Quantity of user interactions		○		There are many important user interactions, such as changing the battery, dialing, setting the volume, sending and receiving calls.
Novelty of user interactions		○		Design solutions that satisfy some of the customer interactions are straightforward, such as the numeric keypad, since there is a wealth of human factors data which dictate the basic dimensions. However, other interfaces, such as the unique folding joint for the mouthpiece, had never been incorporated into a Motorola product and therefore required careful study.
Safety	○			There were few safety issues for ID to consider on the MicroTAC. However, for engineering there were several safety issues to be considered carefully.
Aesthetics				
Product differentiation			○	There were 10 models of cellular phones on the market when the MicroTAC was introduced. Its appearance (including its size and shape) was essential for differentiation.
Pride of ownership, fashion, or image			○	The MicroTAC was intended to be a highly visible product used by people for business and personal communication in public areas. It had to be physically attractive for everyday use.
Team motivation		○		The MicroTAC's novel form turned out to be an important inspiration to the development team.

EXHIBIT 3 Assessing the importance of industrial design for the MicroTAC.

other design details can increase tooling cost and/or production cost. Note, however, that many ID details can be implemented at practically no cost, particularly if ID is involved early enough in the process (see below). In fact, some ID inputs can actually reduce manufacturing costs—particularly when the industrial designer works closely with the manufacturing engineers.

- *Time cost* is the penalty associated with extended lead time. As industrial designers attempt to refine the ergonomics and aesthetics of a product, multiple design iterations and/or prototypes will be necessary. This may result in a delay in the product's introduction, which will likely have an economic cost.

The benefits of using ID include increased product appeal and greater customer satisfaction through additional or better features, strong brand identity, and product differentiation. These benefits usually translate into a price premium and/or increased market share (as compared to marketing the product without the ID efforts).

These costs and benefits of ID were estimated as part of a study conducted at MIT that assessed the impact of detail design decisions on product success factors for a set of competing products in the market (automatic drip coffee makers). Although the relation is difficult to quantify precisely, this study found a significant correlation between product aesthetics (as rated by practicing industrial designers) and the retail price for each product, but no correlation between aesthetics and manufacturing cost. The researchers could not conclude whether the manufacturers had priced their products optimally, nor could they determine if aesthetics of the products enabled manufacturers to garner higher prices. However, the study suggests that an increase in price of $1 per unit, for typical sales volumes, would be worth several million dollars in profits over the life of these products. Industrial designers asked to price design services for such products gave a range from $75,000 to $250,000, suggesting that if ID could add even one dollar's worth of perceived benefit to the consumer, it would pay back handsomely (Pearson, 1992).

A second study, conducted at the Open University in England, also suggests that investing in ID yields a positive return. This study tracked the commercial impact of investing in engineering and ID for 221 design projects at small and medium-sized manufacturing firms. The study claims that investing in industrial design consultants led to profits in over 90 percent of all implemented projects, and when comparisons were possible with previous, less ID-oriented products, sales increased by an average of 41 percent (Roy and Potter, 1993).

For a specific decision, performing simple calculations and sensitivity analyses can help quantify the likely economic returns from ID. For example, if investing in ID will likely result in a price premium of $10 per unit, what will be the net economic benefit when summed over the original market sales projections? Similarly, if investing in ID will likely result in a greater demand for the product—by, say, 1,000 units per year—what will be the net economic benefit when summed at the original unit price? The rough estimates of these benefits can be compared to the expected cost of the ID effort. Spreadsheet models are commonly used for this kind of financial decision making and can easily be applied to estimate the expected payback of ID for a project. (The chapter "Economics of Product Development Projects" describes a methodology for developing such a financial model.)

How Does Industrial Design Establish a Corporate Identity?

Corporate identity is derived from "the visual style of an organization," a factor that affects the firm's positioning in the market (Olins, 1989). A company's identity emerges primarily through what people see. Consider the following attributes that establish a corporation's identity:

- *Products or services*—what the company makes and sells
- *Environment*—where the company makes or sells its products or services
- *Communication*—how the company presents or promotes what it does

In product-based companies, ID plays an important role in determining the company's identity. Industrial design determines a product's look and feel, which are directly related to the public perception of the firm. Some companies that have effectively used ID to establish corporate identity through their product lines include:

- *Apple Computer, Inc.:* The original Macintosh had a small, upright shape and a benign buff coloring. This design purposely gave the product a non-threatening, user-friendly look that has since been associated with all of Apple's products.
- *Rolex Watch Co.:* The Rolex line of watches maintains a classic look and solid feel that signifies quality and prestige.
- *Braun AG:* Braun kitchen appliances and shavers have clean lines and basic colors. The Braun name is now associated with simplicity and quality.
- *Bang & Olufsen:* B&O high-fidelity consumer electronics systems are designed to have sleek lines and impressive visual displays, providing an image of technological innovation.

THE INDUSTRIAL DESIGN PROCESS

Many large companies have internal industrial design departments. Small companies tend to use contract ID services provided by consulting firms. In either case, industrial designers should participate fully on cross-functional product development teams. Within these teams, engineers will generally follow an established procedure to generate and evaluate concepts for the technical features of a product. In a similar manner, most industrial designers follow an established procedure for designing the aesthetics and ergonomics of a product. Although this approach may vary depending on the firm and the nature of the project, industrial designers also generate multiple concepts and then work with engineers to narrow these options down through a series of evaluation steps.

Specifically, the ID process is made up of the following phases:

1 Investigation of customer needs

2 Conceptualization

3 Preliminary refinement

4 Further refinement and final concept selection

5 Control drawings

6 Coordination with engineering, manufacturing, and vendors

This section discusses each of these phases in order, and the following section will discuss the timing of these phases within the overall product development process.

Investigation of Customer Needs

The product development team begins by documenting customer needs as described in the chapter "Identifying Customer Needs." Since industrial designers are skilled at recognizing issues involving user interactions, ID involvement is crucial in the needs process. For example, in researching customer needs for a new medical instrument, the team would study an operating room, interview physicians, and conduct focus groups. While involvement of marketing, engineering, and ID certainly leads to a common, comprehensive understanding of customer needs for the whole team, it particularly allows the industrial designer to gain an intimate understanding of the interactions between the user and the product.

Unlike many development efforts, on the MicroTAC project the design team did not rely heavily upon focus groups or formal market research. The team believed that the high level of secrecy surrounding the project, and the difficulty in gaining customer input for something that had never been done before, made these techniques impractical. Instead, the team used extensive input from Motorola employees to understand user needs. Working with marketing personnel, industrial designers determined the important user interface needs such as the number of functions which must appear on the keypad. Similarly, engineering supplied information on technical limitations involving geometry and materials. [Obtain the case study by Kamm and Poklop (1992) for additional details.]

Conceptualization

Once the customer needs and constraints are understood, the industrial designers help the team to conceptualize the product. During the concept generation stage engineers naturally focus their attention upon finding solutions to the technical subfunctions of the product. (See the chapter "Concept Generation.") At this time, the industrial designers concentrate upon creating the product's form and user interfaces. Industrial designers make simple sketches, known as *thumbnail sketches*, of each concept. These sketches are a fast and inexpensive medium for expressing ideas and evaluating possibilities. Exhibit 4 shows two such sketches for the MicroTAC.

The proposed concepts may then be matched and combined with the technical solutions under exploration. Concepts are grouped and evaluated by the team according to the customer needs, technical feasibility, cost, and manufacturing considerations. (See the chapter "Concept Selection.")

In some companies, industrial designers unfortunately work quite independently from engineering. When this happens, ID is likely to propose concepts involving strictly form and style, and there are usually numerous iterations when engineering finds the concepts technically infeasible. Firms have therefore found it beneficial to coordinate tightly the efforts of industrial designers and

EXHIBIT 4   Concept sketches showing two of the early concepts in the MicroTAC development project. The more radical design (bottom) was the first "flip concept" considered, which formed the basis of the MicroTAC phone. (Courtesy of Motorola Inc.)

engineers throughout the concept development phase so that these iterations can be more quickly accomplished—even in sketch form.

Preliminary Refinement

In the preliminary refinement phase, industrial designers build models of the most promising concepts. *Soft models* are typically made in full scale using foam or foam-core board. They are the second fastest method—only slightly slower than sketches—used to evaluate concepts.

Although very rough, these models are invaluable because they allow the development team to express and visualize product concepts in three dimensions. Through the process of touching, feeling, and modifying the models created, industrial designers, engineers, marketing personnel, and (at times) potential customers evaluate each concept. Typically, designers will build as many models as possible depending on time and financial constraints. Concepts that are particularly difficult to visualize require more models than do simpler ones.

The MicroTAC industrial designers did not use soft models on this project because they wanted to evaluate models with more realistic feel, particularly since the phone is carried and also held against the face. Thus, they used numerous hard models (described below) for concept refinement.

Further Refinement and Final Concept Selection

At this stage, industrial designers often revert from soft models and sketches to hard models and information-intensive drawings known as *renderings*. Renderings show the details of the design and often depict the product in use. Drawn in two or three dimensions, they convey a great deal of information about the product. Renderings are often used for color studies and for testing customers' reception to the proposed product's features and functionality.

The final refinement step before selecting a concept is to create *hard models*, alluded to previously. These models are still technically nonfunctional yet are

EXHIBIT 5   A hard model. This model from the MicroTAC project has a slight bend in the body of the phone, which was determined to be difficult to manufacture. (Courtesy of Motorola Inc.)

close replicas of the final design. They are made from wood, dense foam, plastic, or metal; are painted and textured; and have some "working" features such as buttons that push or sliders that move. Because a hard model can cost thousands of dollars, a product development team usually has the budget to make only a few. Exhibit 5 shows one of the several hard models built during the MicroTAC development process.

Hard models can be used to gain additional customer feedback in focus groups, to advertise and promote the product at trade shows, to sell the concept to senior management within an organization, and to further refine the final concept.

Control Drawings

Industrial designers complete their development process by making control drawings of the final concept. Control drawings document functionality, features, sizes, colors, surface finishes, and key dimensions. Although they are not detailed part drawings (known as engineering drawings), they can be used to fabricate final design models and other prototypes. Typically, these drawings are given to the detailed part designers for completion. Exhibit 6 shows a control drawing of the (almost) final MicroTAC design.

Coordination with Engineering, Manufacturing, and External Vendors

The industrial designers must continue to work closely with engineering and manufacturing personnel throughout the subsequent product development process. Some companies now even use industrial design consulting firms that offer quite comprehensive engineering services, including detail design and the selection and management of outside vendors of materials, tooling, or components, as well as vendors to perform the final assembly of the product.

The Impact of Computer-Based Tools on the ID Process

In recent years, new computer-aided industrial design (CAID) tools have begun to have a significant impact on industrial designers and their work. Using CAID tools, industrial designers can generate three-dimensional designs on a computer screen and rapidly modify them. In this manner, ID can potentially generate a greater number of detailed concepts more quickly, which may lead to more innovative design solutions. The visual realism of CAID can enhance communication within the product development team and eliminate much of the inaccuracy of the manually generated sketches historically provided by industrial designers (Cardaci, 1992). Furthermore, data from a CAID system can be transferred into engineering design (solids modeling) systems allowing the entire development process to be more easily integrated. Exhibit 7 shows a CAID rendering of the MicroTAC.

EXHIBIT 6   MicroTAC control drawing showing the final MicroTAC shape and dimensions. Only the keypad is slightly different in the production model shown in Exhibit 1. (Courtesy of Motorola Inc.)

EXHIBIT 7   Computer-generated concept image. This design was created using CAID software by Alias Research Inc. (Courtesy of Motorola Inc.)

MANAGEMENT OF THE INDUSTRIAL DESIGN PROCESS

Industrial design may be incorporated into the overall product development process at any time during a development program. The timing of the ID effort depends upon the nature of the product being designed. To explain the timing of the ID effort it is convenient to classify products according to the nature of the dominant challenges facing the development team: achieving technological performance, designing the exterior and user interfaces, or both.

Technology-Driven Products

The primary characteristic of a technology-driven product is that its core benefit is based on its technology, or its ability to accomplish a specific technical task. While such a product may still have important aesthetic or ergonomic requirements, consumers will most likely purchase the product primarily for its technical performance.

It follows that for the development team of a technology-driven product, the engineering or technical requirements will be paramount and will dominate development efforts. Accordingly, the role of ID is often limited to packaging the core technology. This entails determining the product's external appearance and ensuring that the product communicates its technological capabilities and modes of interaction to the user.

User-Driven Products

The core benefit of a user-driven product is derived from the functionality of its interface and/or its aesthetic appeal. Typically there is a high degree of user interaction for these products. Accordingly, the user interfaces must be safe, easy to use, and easy to maintain. The product's external appearance is often important to differentiate the product and to create pride of ownership. While these products may be technically sophisticated, the technology does not differentiate the product; thus, for the product development team, the ID considerations will be more important than the technical requirements. The role of engineering may still be important to determine any technical features of the product; however, since the technology is often already established, the development team focuses on the user aspects of the product.

Technology-and-User-Driven Products

A technology-and-user-driven product is simply the combination of the above two categories. These products have a high degree of user interaction and have stringent technical performance requirements.

Exhibit 8 classifies a variety of familiar products. Rarely does a product fit exactly into a given category. Instead, most products fall somewhere along the continuum.

These classifications can be dynamic. For example, when a company develops a product based on a new core technology, the company is often interested in bringing the product to market as quickly as possible. Since little emphasis is placed on how the product looks or is used, the initial role of ID is small.

EXHIBIT 8 Classification of some common products on the continuum from technology-driven product to user-driven product.

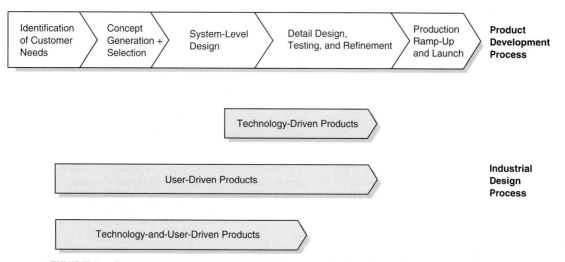

EXHIBIT 9   Relative timing of the industrial design process for three types of products.

However, as competitors enter the market, the product may need to compete more along user or aesthetic dimensions. The product's original classification shifts, and ID assumes an extremely important role in the development process. One example is the Sony Walkman. The core benefit of the first Walkman model was its technology (miniature tape player). As competition entered this market, however, Sony relied heavily on ID to create aesthetic appeal and enhanced utility, adding to the technical advantages of subsequent models.

Timing of Industrial Design Involvement

Typically, ID is incorporated into the product development process during the later phases for a technology-driven product, during the earlier phases for a technology-and-user-driven product, and throughout the entire product development process for a user-driven product. Exhibit 9 illustrates these timing differences. Note that the ID process is a subprocess of the product development process; it is parallel but not separate. As shown in the exhibit, the ID process described above may be rapid relative to the overall development process. The technical nature of the problems that confront engineers in their design activities typically demands substantially more development effort than do the issues considered by ID.

Exhibit 9 shows that for a technology-driven product, ID activities may begin fairly late in the program. This is because ID for such products is focused primarily on packaging issues. For a user-driven product, ID is involved much more fully. In fact, the ID process may dominate the overall product development process for many user-driven products. For a technology-and-user-driven product, the ID process must also begin quite early to investigate the user interac-

Product Development Phase	Type of Product		
	Technology-Driven	**User-Driven**	**Technology-and-User Driven**
Identification of customer needs	ID typically has no involvement	ID works closely with marketing to identify customer needs. Industrial designers participate in focus groups or one-on-one customer interviews.	ID works closely with marketing and engineering to identify customer needs. industrial designers participate in focus groups or one-on-one customer interviews.
Concept generation and selection	ID works with marketing and engineering to assure that human factors and user-interface issues are addressed. Safety and maintenance issues are often of primary importance.	ID generates multiple concepts according to the industrial design process flow described earlier.	ID generates multiple concepts according to the industrial design process flow described earlier. ID must work closely with engineering during this phase.
System-level design	ID typically has little involvement.	ID narrows down the concepts and refines the most promising approaches.	The team narrows down the concepts, selects a final approach, and then finalizes the design.
Detail design	ID is responsible for packaging the product once most of the engineering details have been addressed. ID receives product specifications and constraints from engineering and marketing.	ID selects a final concept, then coordinates with engineering, manufacturing, and marketing to finalize the design.	ID participates in a quality assurance role to affirm that engineering changes do not create ergonomic or aesthetic problems. Typically ID will work closely with engineering and marketing to resolve any design conflicts.

EXHIBIT 10   The role of industrial design according to product type.

tions. ID may largely complete its task during the concept and system-level design phases, even though many technical tasks remain to be completed in the detail design phase. It is not uncommon, however, for ID to make minor modifications (to the surface details, for example) after more of the detailed engineering is completed.

Exhibit 10 describes the responsibilities of ID during each phase of the product development process and how they relate to the other activities of the development team. As with the timing of ID involvement, the responsibilities of ID may also change according to product type.

Exhibit 11 shows actual data from development efforts for products in each of the three categories described above. The exhibit shows how the level of activity for each functional group varies according to product type. The data clearly suggest that for a technology-driven product, engineering dominates throughout the product development cycle, as ID's role in packaging the core technology comes in toward the end of the development process. In contrast, for a user-

EXHIBIT 11 Level of development effort by phase for three products. (Courtesy of Product Genesis Inc.)

driven product, much of the development effort is performed by either ID, marketing, or the support functions. In this example, engineering became more active in the detailed design phase to help with fabrication, testing, and evaluation of prototypes. Finally, for a technology-and-user-driven product, ID dominates the total product development effort during the early phases of the project, while engineering dominates during the later phases. The category labeled "other," which includes marketing and support functions, remains roughly constant throughout most of the process.

ASSESSING THE QUALITY OF INDUSTRIAL DESIGN

Assessing the quality of ID for a finished product is an inherently subjective task. However, we can qualitatively determine whether ID has accomplished its goals by considering each aspect of the product that is influenced by ID. Below are five categories for evaluating a product. These categories roughly match Dreyfuss' five critical goals for ID, presented above. We use these categories to develop specific questions, allowing the product to be rated along five dimensions. Exhibit 12 demonstrates this methodology by showing results for the MicroTAC.

1. Quality of the User Interfaces

This is a rating of how easy the product is to use. Interface quality is related to the product's appearance, feel, and modes of interaction.

- Do the features of the product effectively communicate their operation to the user?
- Is the product's use intuitive?
- Are all features safe?
- Have all potential users and uses of the product been identified?

Examples of product-specific questions include:

- Is the grip comfortable?
- Does the tuning knob turn easily and smoothly?
- Is the power switch easy to locate?
- Is the display easy to read and understand?

2. Emotional Appeal

This is a rating of the overall consumer appeal of the product. Appeal is achieved in part through appearance, feel, sound, and smell.

- Is the product attractive? Is it exciting?
- Does the product express quality?

Assessment Category	Level of Importance			Explanation of Rating
	Low	Medium	High	
1. Quality of the user interfaces	H———————O———H			In general, the MicroTAC is both easy to use and comfortable. For example: calls can be answered by simply flipping open the hinged mouthpiece, numbers can be readily dialed into the keypad, and the visual display is easy to read. The MicroTAC's main drawbacks include: the battery charger is cumbersome to use and lacks a charge-level meter, and many of the software features are too complicated.
2. Emotional appeal	H————————————O—H			The MicroTAC has a high emotional appeal which stems from its sleek appearance and solid feel.
3. Ability to maintain and repair the product	H————————————O——H			Although maintenance and repair are not of primary importance to the customer, the MicroTAC rates high in this category. The battery packs can be removed and replaced easily. Customers can install the slim line or regular pack depending on their preference for size, weight, and talk time.
4. Appropriate use of resources	H————————————O——H			The final design only included features that satisfied real customer needs. Materials were selected to satisfy manufacturing constraints, to withstand extreme environmental conditions, and to meet strict appearance criteria.
5. Product differentiation	H——————————————O—H			The MicroTAC's appearance is clearly unique. It is easily identified when viewed in a public area or next to a competitor's product.

EXHIBIT 12   Assessment of industrial design's role in the MicroTAC.

- What images come to mind when viewing it?
- Does the product inspire pride of ownership?
- Does the product evoke feelings of pride among development team and sales staff?

Examples of product-specific questions include:

- How does the car door sound when slammed?
- Does the hand tool feel solid and sturdy?
- Does the coffee maker look good on the kitchen counter?

3. Ability to Maintain and Repair the Product

This is a rating of the ease of product maintenance and repair. Maintenance and repair should be considered along with the other user interactions.

- Is the maintenance of the product obvious? Is it easy?
- Do product features effectively communicate disassembly and assembly procedures?

Examples of product-specific questions include:

- How easy and obvious is it to clear a paper jam in the copier?
- How difficult is it to disassemble and clean the food processor?
- How difficult is it to change the batteries in the Walkman, a remote controller, a digital watch?

4. Appropriate Use of Resources

This is a rating of how well resources were used in satisfying the customer requirements. Resources typically refer to the dollar expenditures on ID and other functions. These factors tend to drive costs such as manufacturing. A poorly designed product, one with unnecessary features, or a product made from an exotic material will affect tooling, manufacturing processes, assembly processes, and the like. This category asks whether these investments were well spent.

- How well were resources used to satisfy the customer requirements?
- Is the material selection appropriate (in terms of cost and quality)?
- Is the product over- or underdesigned (does it have features that are unnecessary or neglected)?
- Were environmental/ecological factors considered?

5. Product Differentiation

This is a rating of a product's uniqueness and consistency with the corporate identity. This differentiation arises predominantly from appearance.

- Will a customer who sees the product in a store be able to single it out because of its appearance?
- Will it be remembered by a consumer who has seen it in an advertisement?
- Will it be recognized when seen on the street?
- Does the product fit with or enhance the corporate identity?

From an ID perspective, as shown in Exhibit 12, the MicroTAC is an excellent product. It is durable, easy to fabricate, and has strong customer appeal. Since these features are extremely important to the consumer, ID played a critical role in determining the immediate market success of the product.

SUMMARY

This chapter introduces the topic of industrial design, explains its benefits to product quality, and illustrates how the ID process takes place.

- The primary mission of ID is to design the aspects of a product that relate to the user: aesthetics and ergonomics.
- Most products can benefit in some way or another from ID. The more a product is looked at or used by people, the more it will depend on good ID for its success.
- For products that are characterized by a high degree of user interaction and the need for aesthetic appeal, ID should be involved throughout the product development process. Early involvement of industrial designers will ensure that critical aesthetic and user requirements will not be overlooked or ignored by the technical staff.
- When a product relies more on technology, ID can be integrated into the development process later.
- Active involvement of ID on the product development team can help to promote good communication between functional groups. Such communication facilitates coordination and ultimately translates into higher-quality products.

REFERENCES AND BIBLIOGRAPHY

For more information about industrial design—its history, impact, future, and practice—the following books and articles are recommended. The brief history of ID presented in this chapter was adapted from Lorenz's book.

Lorenz, Christopher, *The Design Dimension: Product Strategy and the Challenge of Global Marketing*, Basil Blackwell Ltd., Oxford, UK, 1986. ISBN 0-631-13747-5.

Caplan, Ralph, *By Design: Why There Are No Locks on the Bathroom Doors in the Hotel Louis XIV, and Other Object Lessons*, St. Martin's Press, New York, NY, 1982 (out of print). ISBN 0-312-11085-5.

Lucie-Smith, Edward, *A History of Industrial Design*, Van Nostrand Reinhold Company, New York, NY, 1983. ISBN 0-442-25804-6.

Dreyfuss, Henry, *Designing for People*, New York: Paragraphic Books, 1967 (out of print).

Dreyfuss, Henry, "The Industrial Designer and the Businessman," *Harvard Business Review*, November 1950, pp. 77–85.

Harkins, Jack, "The Role of Industrial Design in Developing Medical Devices," *Medical Device and Diagnostic Industry*, September 1992, p. 51.

Cardaci, Kitty, "CAID: A Tool for the Flexible Organization," *Design Management Journal*, Design Management Institute, Boston, MA, Vol. 3, No. 2, Spring 1992, pp. 72–75.

The following studies are among the very few which have critically assessed the value of ID to products and their manufacturers. An issue of *Design Management Journal* was devoted to this topic.

Pearson, Scott, "Using Product Archaeology to Understand the Dimensions of Design Decision Making," S.M. Thesis, MIT Sloan School of Management, May 1992.

Roy, Robin, and Stephen Potter, "The Commercial Impacts of Investment in Design," *Design Studies*, Vol. 14, No. 2, April 1993.

Design Management Journal, Vol. 5, No. 2, Spring 1994.

Olins describes how a firm develops a corporate identity through design and communication.

Olins, Wally, *Corporate Identity: Making Business Strategy Visible through Design*, Harvard Business School Press, Boston, MA, 1989. ISBN 0-87584-250.

Several excellent case studies involving the ID process and product development issues surrounding ID have been written by the Corporate Design Foundation and the Design Management Institute. The Kamm and Poklop study describes the MicroTAC development.

Kamm, Jennifer, and Laurie Poklop, *Motorola MicroTAC*, case study available from Corporate Design Foundation, Boston, MA, 1992.

Freeze, Karen J., *Braun AG: The KF 40 Coffee Machine*, case study available from Design Management Institute, Boston, MA, 1990.

Svengren, Lisbeth, *AB Bahco Tools—The Development of a Design Strategy at a Tool Company*, case study available from Design Management Institute, Boston, MA, 1991.

While industrial designers are best found through personal referral, IDSA can provide a list of ID consultants in any geographic region.

Industrial Design Society of America (IDSA), "Directory of Industrial Designers," 1992–1993. ISBN 0-31823-072-0.

EXERCISES

1 Visit a local specialty store (e.g., kitchen supplies, tools, office supply, gifts) and photograph (or purchase) a set of competing products. Assess each one in terms of the five ID quality categories as shown in Exhibit 12. Which product would you purchase? Would you be willing to pay more for it than for the others?

2 Develop several concept sketches for a common product. Try designing the product form both "from the inside out" and "from the outside in." Which is easier for

you? Possible simple products include a stapler, a garlic press, an alarm clock, a reading light, a telephone.

3 List some firms that you feel have a strong corporate identity. What aspects of their products helped to develop this identity?

THOUGHT QUESTIONS

1 By what cause-and-effect mechanism does ID affect a product's manufacturing cost? Under what conditions would ID increase or decrease manufacturing cost?

2 What types of products might not benefit from ID involvement in the development process?

3 The term *visual equity* is sometimes used to refer to the value of the distinctive appearance of a firm's products. How is such equity obtained? Can it be "purchased" over a short time period, or does it accrue slowly?

DESIGN FOR MANUFACTURING

EXHIBIT 1   The General Motors 3.8-liter V6 engine. (Courtesy of General Motors Corp.)

General Motors Powertrain Division manufactures about 3,500 3.8-liter V6 engines every day (Exhibit 1). Facing such high production volumes, the company had a strong interest in reducing the cost of the engine, while simultaneously enhancing its quality. A team was formed to improve one of the most expensive subassemblies in the engine: the air intake manifold. (The intake manifold's primary function is to route air from the throttle to the intake valves at the cylinders.) The original and redesigned intake manifold assemblies are shown in Exhibit 2. This chapter presents a methodology for design for manufacturing using the GM V6 intake manifold as an example.

EXHIBIT 2   The original and redesigned air intake manifolds. The body of the original manifold (top) is made of cast aluminum. The redesigned manifold (bottom) is made of molded thermoplastic composite. (Stuart Cohen)

DESIGN FOR MANUFACTURING DEFINED

Customer needs and product specifications are useful for guiding the concept phase of product development; however, during the later development activities teams often have difficulty linking needs and specifications to the specific design issues they face. For this reason, many teams practice "design for X" (DFX) methodologies, where X may correspond to one of dozens of quality criteria such as reliability, robustness, serviceability, environmental impact, or manufacturability. The most common of these methodologies is *design for manufacturing* (DFM), which is of primary importance because it directly addresses manufacturing costs.

This chapter is primarily about DFM, but it is also intended to illustrate, by example, these general principles which apply to methodologies for achieving any of the Xs in DFX:

- Detail design decisions can have substantial impact on product quality and cost.
- Development teams face multiple, and often conflicting, goals.
- It is important to have metrics with which to compare alternative designs.
- Dramatic improvements often require substantial creative efforts early in the process.
- A well-defined methodology assists the decision-making process.

Manufacturing cost is a key determinant of the economic success of a product. In simple terms, the economic success of a product depends on the profit margin earned on each sale of the product and on how many units of the product the firm can sell. Profit margin is the difference between the manufacturer's selling price and the cost of making the product. The number of units sold and the sales price are to a large degree determined by the overall quality of the product. Economically successful design is therefore about ensuring high product quality while minimizing manufacturing cost. DFM is one methodology for achieving this goal; effective DFM practice leads to low manufacturing costs without sacrificing product quality. (See the chapter "Economics of Product Development Projects" for a more detailed discussion of how manufacturing cost relates to economic success.)

DFM Requires a Cross-Functional Team

Design for manufacturing is one of the very integrative methodologies involved in product development. DFM utilizes information of several types, including (1) sketches, drawings, product specifications, and design alternatives; (2) a detailed understanding of production and assembly processes; and (3) estimates of manufacturing costs, production volumes, and ramp-up timing. DFM therefore requires the contributions of most members of the development team as well as outside experts. DFM efforts commonly draw upon expertise from manufacturing engineers, cost accountants, and production personnel, in addition to product designers. Many companies use structured, team-based workshops to facilitate the integration and sharing of views required for DFM.

DFM Is Performed Throughout the Development Process

DFM begins during the concept development phase, when the product's functions and specifications are being determined. When choosing a product concept, cost is almost always one of the criteria on which the decision is made—even though cost estimates at this phase are highly subjective and approximate. When product specifications are refined, the team makes trade-offs between desired performance characteristics, for example, weight reduction may increase manufacturing costs. At this point, the team may have an approximate bill of materials (a list of parts) with estimates of costs. During the system-level design phase of development, the team makes decisions about how to break up the product into individual components, based in large measure on the expected cost and manufacturing complexity implications. Accurate cost estimates finally become available during the detail design phase of development, when many more decisions are driven by manufacturing concerns.

Overview of the DFM Methodology

Our DFM methodology is illustrated in Exhibit 3. It consists of five parts:

1 Estimate the manufacturing costs.
2 Reduce the costs of components.
3 Reduce the costs of assembly.
4 Reduce the costs of supporting production.
5 Consider the impact of DFM decisions on other factors.

As shown in Exhibit 3, the DFM methodology begins with the estimation of the manufacturing cost of the proposed design. This helps the team to determine at a general level which aspects of the design—components, assembly, or support—are most costly. The team then directs its attention to the appropriate areas in the subsequent steps. This methodology is iterative. It is not unusual to recompute the manufacturing cost estimate and to improve the design of the product dozens of times before agreeing that it is good enough. As long as the product design is improving, these DFM iterations may continue even until pilot production begins. At some point, the design is "frozen" (or "released"), and any further modifications are considered formal "engineering changes" or become part of the next generation of the product.

In the next section, we use the original GM V6 intake manifold as an example and explain how manufacturing costs are determined. Then, recognizing that accurate cost estimates are difficult (if not impossible) to obtain, we present several useful methods for reducing the costs of components, assembly, and production support. We use the redesigned intake manifold and other products as

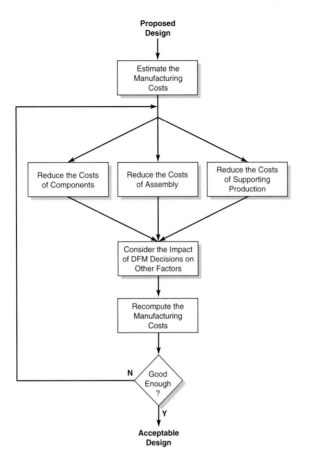

EXHIBIT 3   The design for manufacturing (DFM) methodology.

examples to illustrate these DFM principles. Finally, we discuss the results achieved through DFM and some of the broader implications of DFM decisions.

ESTIMATE THE MANUFACTURING COSTS

Exhibit 4 shows a simple input-output model of a manufacturing system. The inputs include raw materials, purchased components, employees' efforts, energy, and equipment. The outputs include finished goods and waste. Manufacturing cost is the sum of all of the expenditures for the inputs of the system and for disposal of the wastes produced by the system. As the metric of cost for a product, firms generally use *unit manufacturing cost*, which is computed by dividing the total manufacturing costs for some period (usually a quarter or a year) by the number of units of the product manufactured during that period. This simple concept is complicated in practice by several issues:

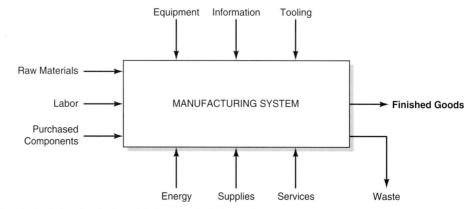

EXHIBIT 4   A simple input-output model of a manufacturing system.

- What are the boundaries of the manufacturing system? Should the field service operations be included? What about product development activities?
- How do we "charge" the product for the use of expensive general-purpose equipment that lasts for many years?
- How are costs allocated among more than one product line in large, multi-product manufacturing systems?

These are issues around which much of the field of managerial accounting is built, and we do not treat them in depth here. Nevertheless, we will be mindful of these complications as we discuss cost and DFM in this chapter.

Exhibit 5 shows one way of categorizing the elements of manufacturing cost. Under this scheme, the unit manufacturing cost of a product consists of costs in three categories:

1 *Component costs:* The *components* of a product (also simply called parts of the product) may include *standard parts* purchased from suppliers. Examples of standard components include motors, switches, electronic chips, and screws. Other components would be *custom parts*, made according to the manufacturer's design from raw materials, such as sheet steel, plastic pellets, or aluminum bars. Some custom components are made in the manufacturer's own plant, while others may be made by suppliers according to the manufacturer's design specifications.

2 *Assembly costs:* Discrete goods are generally assembled from parts. The process of assembling almost always incurs labor costs and may also incur costs for equipment and tooling.

3 *Overhead costs:* Overhead is the category used to encompass all of the other costs. We find it useful to distinguish between two types of overhead: *support costs* and other *indirect allocations*. Support costs are the costs associated with materials handling, quality assurance, purchasing, shipping, receiving, facil-

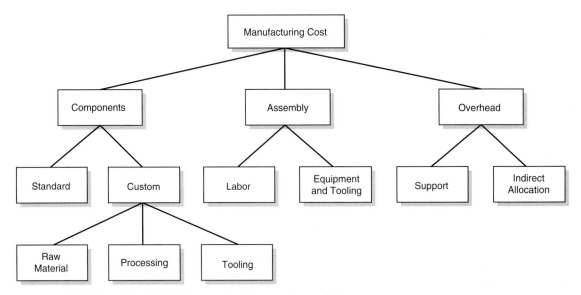

EXHIBIT 5   Elements of the manufacturing cost of a product.

ities, and equipment/tooling maintenance (among others). These are the support systems required to manufacture the product, and these costs do greatly depend upon the product design. Nevertheless, since these costs are often shared by more than one product line, they are lumped together in the category of overhead. Indirect allocations are the costs of manufacturing that cannot be directly linked to a particular product but which must be paid for to be in business. For example, the salary of the security guard and the cost of maintenance to the building and grounds are indirect costs because these activities are shared among several different products and are difficult to allocate directly to a specific product. Because indirect costs are not specifically linked to the design of the product, they are not relevant to DFM, even though they do contribute to the cost of the product.

Fixed Costs versus Variable Costs

Another way to divide manufacturing costs is between *fixed costs* and *variable costs*. Fixed costs are those that are incurred in a predetermined amount, regardless of how many units of the product are manufactured. Purchasing the injection mold required for the new intake manifold is an example of a fixed cost. Whether 1,000 or 1 million units are produced, the fixed cost of the mold is incurred and does not change. Another example is the cost of setting up the factory work area for the intake manifold assembly line. This cost is also fixed, regardless of how many units are produced. Despite the terminology, however, no cost is truly fixed. If we quadruple the production quantity we may have to build another production line. Conversely, we may be able to consolidate two assembly cells if we cannot use all the capacity due to dramatically lower production quantities. When considering a cost as fixed, ranges of production quantities and the assumed time horizon should be specified.

Variable costs are those incurred in direct proportion to the number of units produced. For example, the cost of raw materials is directly proportional to how many intake manifolds are produced, and therefore to how many 3.8-liter V6 engines are made. Assembly labor is sometimes considered a variable cost as well because many firms can adjust the staffing of assembly operations by shifting workers to other areas on short notice.

The Bill of Materials

Since manufacturing cost estimation is fundamental to DFM, it is useful to keep this information well organized. Exhibit 6 shows an information system for recording manufacturing cost estimates. It basically consists of a bill of materials (BOM) augmented with cost information. The BOM (usually pronounced "bomb") is a list of each individual component in the product. Frequently the BOM is created using an indented format in which the assembly "tree structure" is illustrated by the indentation of components and subassembly names.

The columns of the BOM show the cost estimates broken down into fixed and

EXHIBIT 6 Indented bill of materials showing cost estimates for the original intake manifold and related components. The EGR (exhaust gas recirculation), PCV (positive crankcase ventilation), and vacuum block components are included here to facilitate comparison with the redesigned manifold assembly.

Component	Purchased Materials	Processing (Machine + Labor)	Assembly (Labor)	Total Unit Variable Cost	Tooling and Other NRE, K$	Tooling Lifetime, K units	Total Unit Fixed Cost	Total Cost
Manifold machined casting	12.83	5.23		18.06	1960	500+	0.50	18.56
EGR return pipe	1.30		0.15	1.45				1.45
PCV assembly								
Valve	1.35		0.14	1.49				1.49
Gasket	0.05		0.13	0.18				0.18
Cover	0.76		0.13	0.89				0.89
Screws (3)	0.06		0.15	0.21				0.21
Vacuum source block assembly								
Block	0.95		0.13	1.08				1.08
Gasket	0.03		0.05	0.08				0.08
Screw	0.02		0.09	0.11				0.11
Column Totals (Direct Costs)	17.35	5.23	0.95	23.53	1960		0.50	24.03
Overhead Charges	2.60	9.42	1.71				0.75	14.48
Total Cost								**38.51**

variable costs. The variable costs may include materials, machine time, and labor. Fixed costs consist of tooling and other nonrecurring expenses (NRE) such as specialized equipment and one-time setup costs. The tooling lifetime is used to compute the unit fixed cost (unless the tool's expected lifetime exceeds the product's lifetime volume, in which case the lower product volume is used). To compute total cost, overhead is added according to the firm's accepted cost accounting scheme. Note that additional fixed costs, such as capital equipment used for several products are often also included in the overhead charge.

Estimating the Costs of Standard Components

The costs of standard components are estimated by either (1) comparing each part to a substantially similar part the firm is already producing or purchasing in comparable volumes or (2) soliciting price quotes from vendors or suppliers. The costs of minor components (e.g., bolts, springs, and inserts) are usually obtained from the firm's experience with similar components, while the costs of major components are usually obtained from vendor quotes.

In obtaining price quotes, the estimated production quantities are extremely important. For example, the unit price on a purchase of a dozen screws or inserts may be 10 times higher than the unit prices paid by GM when purchasing 100,000 of these parts every month. If the anticipated production quantities are high enough, an application engineer or sales engineer is usually quite willing to work with the development team to specify a component properly. For internally fabricated standard components, if the required quantities are high, there may not be available production capacity, necessitating the purchase of additional equipment or the use of outside suppliers.

Some suppliers will design and fabricate a custom variation to a standard component if production quantities are high enough. For example, small electric motors, such as those found in powered hand tools, are often designed and built specifically for the product application. If the production quantities are high enough (say, 100,000 per year in this case), these custom motors are quite economical ($1 to $5 per unit, depending on the performance characteristics). For the intake manifold, the volumes are sufficiently high that custom studs, bushings, and other parts may not cost much more than standard components. However, as we discuss later, introducing new parts can add substantial cost and complexity to the production system and field service operations, which increases the support costs.

Vendors for most standard components can be found in the *Thomas Register of American Manufacturers* or by looking for company names on components used in related products. To obtain a price quote, first request a catalog or product literature. Then, either choose a part number or, if a custom component will be used, write a one-page description of the requirements of the component. Next, telephone the vendor, ask to speak to someone in "sales," and request price information. Make sure to inform vendors that the information is for estimation purposes only; otherwise, they may claim they do not have enough information to determine exact prices.

Estimating the Costs of Custom Components

Custom components, which are parts designed especially for the product, are made by the manufacturer or by a supplier. Most custom components are produced using the same types of production processes as standard components (e.g., injection molding, stamping, machining); however, custom parts are typically special-purpose parts, useful only in a particular manufacturer's products.

When the custom component is a single part, we estimate its cost by adding up the costs of raw materials, processing, and tooling. In cases where the custom component is actually an assembly of several parts, then we consider it a "product" in and of itself; to arrive at the cost of this "product" we estimate the cost of each subcomponent and then add assembly and overhead costs (these costs are described below). For the purposes of this explanation, we assume the component is a single part.

The raw materials costs can be estimated by computing the mass of the part, allowing for some scrap (e.g., 5 percent to 50 percent for an injection molded part, and 25 percent to 100 percent for a sheet metal part), and multiplying by the cost (per unit mass) of the raw material. A table of raw material costs is given in Appendix A (Exhibit A1).

Processing costs include costs for the operator(s) of the processing machinery as well as the cost of using the equipment itself. Most standard processing equipment costs between $25 per hour (a simple stamping press) and $75 per hour (a medium-sized, computer-controlled milling machine) to operate, including depreciation, maintenance, utilities, and labor costs. Estimating the processing time generally requires experience with the type of equipment to be used. However, it is useful to understand the range of typical costs for common production processes. For this purpose, tables of approximate processing times and costs are given in Appendix B for a variety of stampings, castings, injection moldings, and machined parts.

Tooling costs are incurred for the design and fabrication of the cutters, molds, dies, or fixtures required to use certain machinery to fabricate parts. For example, an injection molding machine requires a custom injection mold for every different type of part it produces. These molds range in cost from $10,000 to $500,000. Approximate tooling costs are also given for the parts listed in Appendix B. The unit tooling cost is simply the cost of the tooling divided by the number of units to be made over the life of the tool. A high-quality injection mold or stamping die can usually be used for a few million parts.

The cost of the original intake manifold's machined casting is estimated as shown in Exhibit 7. Note that the estimate reveals that the cost is dominated by the expense of the aluminum material. We will see that the redesign using composite material not only reduced the material costs but also eliminated machining and allowed many features to be formed into the molded body.

Variable Cost		
Materials	5.7 kg aluminum at $2.25/kg	$12.83
Processing (casting)	150 units/hr at $530/hr	3.53
Processing (machining)	200 units/hr at $340/hr	1.70
Fixed Cost		
Tooling for casting	$160,000/tool at 500K units/tool (lifetime)	0.32
Machine tools and fixtures	$1,800,000/line at 10M units (lifetime)	0.18
Total Direct Cost		**$18.56**
Overhead charges		$12.09
Total Unit Cost		**$30.65**

EXHIBIT 7   Cost estimate for the original intake manifold. Note that the processing costs for casting and machining reflect the costs for a complete casting line and several machining stations.

Estimating the Cost of Assembly

Products made of more than one part require assembly. For products made in quantities of less than several hundred thousand units per year, this assembly is almost always performed manually. One exception to this generalization is the assembly of electronic circuit boards, which is now almost always done automatically, even at relatively low volumes. There will likely be more exceptions in the coming years, as flexible, precision automation becomes more common.

Manual assembly costs can be estimated by summing the estimated time of each assembly operation and multiplying by a labor rate. Assembly operations require from about 4 seconds to about 60 seconds each, depending upon the size of the parts, the difficulty of the operation, and the production quantities. At high volumes, workers can specialize in a particular set of operations, and special fixtures and tools can assist the assembly. Appendix C contains a table of approximate times for manual assembly of various products, which is helpful in estimating the range of times required for assembly operations. A popular method for estimating assembly times has been developed over the past 20 years and is now available as a software tool (Boothroyd and Dewhurst, 1989). This system involves a tabular information system for keeping track of the estimated assembly times for each part. The system is supported by a comprehensive database of standard handling and insertion times for a wide range of situations. Special software is also available for estimating the assembly cost of electronic circuit boards.

Assembly labor can cost from less than $1 per hour in low-wage countries to more than $40 per hour in some industrialized nations. In the United States, assembly labor is likely to cost between $10 and $20 per hour. (Each firm has different assembly labor cost structures, and some industries, such as the automobile and aircraft industries, have substantially higher cost structures.) These figures include an allowance for benefits and other worker-related expenses and are meant to reflect the true cost to the firm of assembly labor.

Component	Quantity	Handling Time	Insertion Time	Total Time
Valve	1	1.50	1.50	3.00
O-rings	2	2.25	4.00	12.50
Spring	1	2.25	6.00	8.25
Cover	1	1.95	6.00	7.95
Total Time (seconds)				**31.70**
Assembly Cost at $45/hour				**$0.40**

EXHIBIT 8   Assembly cost estimation for the PCV valve assembly of the redesigned intake manifold. (From manual assembly tables in Geoffrey Boothroyd and Peter Dewhurst, *Product Design for Assembly*, Boothroyd Dewhurst, Inc., Wakefield, RI, 1989.)

Consider the redesigned intake manifold. The assembly cost of the PCV (positive crankcase ventilation) valve assembly is estimated as shown in Exhibit 8.

Estimating the Overhead Costs

Accurately estimating overhead costs for a new product is difficult, and the industry practices are not very satisfying. Nevertheless, we will describe the standard industry practice here and identify some of its problems. Applying the overhead estimation schemes used by most firms is simple. Estimating the actual overhead costs incurred by the firm due to a particular product is not. The indirect costs of supporting production are very difficult to track and assign to particular product lines. The future costs of supporting production are even more difficult to predict for a new product.

Most firms assign overhead charges by using *overhead rates* (also called burden rates). Overhead rates are typically applied to one or two *cost drivers*. Cost drivers are parameters of the product which are directly measurable. Overhead charges are added to direct costs in proportion to the drivers. Common cost drivers are the cost of any purchased materials, the cost of assembly labor, and the number of hours of equipment time the product consumes. For example, the overhead rate for purchased materials might be 10 percent and the overhead rate for assembly labor might be 80 percent. (Of course, purchased components already have the vendor's overhead included in the price; we only add the purchasing overhead.) Under these conditions, a product containing $100 of purchased components and $10 of assembly labor would incur $18 of overhead costs (10 percent of $100 plus 80 percent of $10). Some typical overhead structures are given in Appendix D for different types of products and firms.

The problem with this scheme is that it implies that overhead costs are directly proportional to the cost drivers. A thought experiment reveals that this cannot always be so: Most firms use "cost of purchased materials" as one cost driver, yet why would any of their overhead costs actually change if a vendor of a $50 component raises its price to $60? The answer is that they would not change at all.

Overhead rates are used as a convenient way to account for overhead costs, but this scheme can yield inaccurate estimates of the true costs experienced by the manufacturer to support production.

This problem is partially addressed by activity-based costing (ABC) methods (Kaplan, 1990). Under the ABC approach, a firm utilizes more and different cost drivers and allocates all indirect costs to the associated cost drivers where they fit best. As a result, the firm may have overhead rates applied to various dimensions of product complexity (such as the number of different machining operations required or the number of different components or suppliers needed), in addition to overhead on tooling, materials, machine time, and direct labor. For the purposes of estimating manufacturing costs, the use of more cost drivers not only allows more accurate overhead cost estimates to be made but also provides important insights for reducing overhead costs by focusing attention on the cost drivers.

REDUCE THE COMPONENT COSTS

For most highly engineered discrete goods the cost of purchased components will be the most significant element of the manufacturing cost. This section presents several strategies for minimizing these costs. Many of these strategies can be followed even without the benefit of accurate cost estimates. In this case, these strategies become *design rules*, or rules of thumb, to guide DFM cost reduction decisions.

Understand the Process Constraints and Cost Drivers

Some component parts may be costly simply because the designers did not understand the capabilities, cost drivers, and constraints of the production process. For example, a designer may specify a small internal corner radius on a machined part without realizing that physically creating such a feature requires an expensive electro-discharge machining (EDM) operation. A designer may specify dimensions with excessively tight tolerances, without understanding the difficulty of achieving such accuracy in production. Sometimes these costly part features are not even necessary for the component's intended function; they arise out of lack of knowledge. It is often possible to redesign the part to achieve the same performance while avoiding costly manufacturing steps; however, to do this the design engineer needs to know what types of operations are difficult in production and what drives their costs.

In some cases, the constraints of a process can be concisely communicated to designers in the form of design rules. For example, the capabilities of an automatic laser cutting machine for sheet metal can be concisely communicated in terms of allowable material types, material thicknesses, maximum part dimensions, and minimum slot widths. When this is possible, part designers can avoid exceeding the normal capabilities of a process and thereby avoid incurring unusually high costs.

For some processes, the cost of producing a part is a simple mathematical function of some attributes of the part, which would be the cost drivers for the process. For example, a welding process could have a cost directly proportional to two attributes of the product: (1) the number of welds and (2) the total length of welds the machine creates.

For processes whose capabilities are not easily described, the best strategy is to work closely with the people who deeply understand the part production process. These manufacturing experts will generally have plenty of ideas about how to redesign components to reduce production costs.

Redesign Components to Eliminate Processing Steps

Careful scrutiny of the proposed design may lead to suggestions for redesign that can result in simplification of the production process. Reducing the number of steps in the part fabrication process generally results in reduced costs as well. Some process steps may simply not be necessary. For example, aluminum parts may not need to be painted, especially if they will not be visible to the user of the product. In some cases, several steps may be eliminated through substitution of an alternative process step. A common example of this strategy is "net shape" fabrication. A net-shape process is a process that produces a part with the final intended geometry in one manufacturing step. Typical examples include molding, casting, forging, and extrusion. Frequently designers are able to use one of the net-shape processes to create a part that is very close to the final requirement (near net shape) and may demand only minor additional processing (e.g., drilling and tapping a hole, cutting to length, etc.).

The original intake manifold required an expensive casting, followed by several machining operations. The redesigned manifold is molded in two parts to net shape. The cost estimate for these two moldings is shown in Exhibit 9. (Compare with Exhibit 7.)

EXHIBIT 9   Cost estimate for the redesigned intake manifold (two moldings).

Variable Cost		
Materials (manifold housing)	1.4 kg glass-filled nylon at $2.75/kg	$ 3.85
Materials (intake runner insert)	0.3 kg glass-filled nylon at $2.75/kg	0.83
Molding (manifold housing)	80 units/hr at $125/hr	1.56
Molding (intake runner insert)	100 units/hour at $110/hr	1.10
Fixed Cost		
Mold tooling (manifold housing)	$350,000/tool at 1.5M units/tool	$ 0.23
Mold tooling (intake runner insert)	$150,000/tool at 1.5M units/tool	0.10
Total Direct Cost		**$ 7.67**
Overhead charges		**$ 5.99**
Total Unit Cost		**$13.66**

Choose the Appropriate Economic Scale for the Part Process

The manufacturing cost of a product usually drops as the production volume increases. This phenomenon is labeled *economies of scale*. Economies of scale for a fabricated component occur for two basic reasons: (1) fixed costs are divided among more units and (2) variable costs become lower because the firm can justify the use of larger and more efficient processes and equipment. For example, consider an injection-molded plastic part. The part may require a mold which costs $50,000. If the firm produces 50,000 units of the part over the product's lifetime, each part will have to assume $1 of the cost of the mold. If, however, 100,000 units are produced, each part will assume only $0.50 of the cost of mold. As production volumes increase further, the firm may be able to justify a four-cavity mold, for which each cycle of the molding machine produces four parts instead of one. As shown in Exhibit 9, the tooling costs for the redesigned intake manifold are quite high; however, spread over the life of the tool, the unit fixed cost is small.

Processes can be thought of as incurring fixed and variable costs. Fixed costs are incurred once per part type regardless of how many parts are produced. Variable costs are incurred each time a part is made. Processes with inherently low fixed costs and high variable costs, such as machining, are appropriate when few parts will be made, while processes with inherently high fixed costs and low variable costs, such as injection molding, are appropriate when many parts will be made. This concept is illustrated by the graph in Exhibit 10. As shown in the exhibit, if production volume is expected to be below 1,000 units, machining would be more economical; otherwise, injection molding would incur lower total costs.

Standardize Components and Processes

The principle of economies of scale also applies to the selection of components and processes. As the production volume of a component increases, the unit cost of the component decreases. Quality and performance often increase as well with increasing production quantities because the producer of the component can invest in learning and improvement of the component's design and its production process. For a given expected product volume, the benefits of substantially higher component volumes can be achieved through the use of standard components.

Standard components are those common to more than one product. This standardization may occur within the product line of a single firm or may occur, via an outside supplier, across the product lines of several firms. For example, the use of the 3.8-liter V6 engine in several GM cars is an example of *internal standardization*. The use of a common 10-millimeter socket head cap screw across several auto manufacturers is an example of *external standardization*. In either case, all other things being equal, the component unit cost is lower than if the component were used in only a single product.

EXHIBIT 10 Total cost of a hypothetical part as a function of the number of units produced for injection molding versus machining.

The redesigned intake manifold is used on all of GM's 3.8-liter V6 engines, even though each particular vehicle application requires different EGR (exhaust gas recirculation) return and vacuum hose routings. To accommodate this, the new intake manifold has two standard interfaces, a vacuum port and an EGR port. For each vehicle model, a custom vacuum block and EGR adapter are used. This allows the major component, the intake manifold, to be standardized internally, rather than using a different manifold for each vehicle.

Components may also be standardized within the same model. For example, most auto manufacturers use the same type of wheel on the right and left side of their cars, even though this causes directional "spokes" to have different orientations on different sides (Exhibit 11).

Adhere to "Black Box" Component Procurement

A component cost reduction strategy used effectively in the Japanese auto industry is called "black box" supplier design. Under this approach, the team provides a supplier with only a "black box" description of the component; a description of what the component has to do, not how to achieve it (Clark and Fujimoto, 1991). This kind of specification leaves the vendor with the widest possible latitude to design or select the component for minimum cost. An additional advantage of this approach is that it relieves the internal team of the responsibility to engineer and design the component. Successful "black box" development efforts require careful system-level design and extremely clear definitions of the functions, interfaces, and interactions of each component. (See the chapter "Product Architecture.")

For the redesigned intake manifold, the PCV valve assembly was designed by

EXHIBIT 11   An example of standardization within a model. Wheels of the Ford Explorer are the same on the right and left sides of the car. (Courtesy of Ford Motor Co.)

GM's AC Rochester Division, which supplies the component. They were given system-level specifications and complete responsibility for the performance of this subsystem.

REDUCE THE ASSEMBLY COSTS

Design for assembly (DFA) is a fairly well established subset of DFM which involves minimizing the cost of assembly. For most products, assembly contributes a relatively small fraction of the total cost. Nevertheless, focusing attention on assembly costs yields strong indirect benefits. Often as a result of emphasis on DFA, the overall parts count, manufacturing complexity, and support costs are all reduced along with the assembly cost. In this section, we present a few principles useful to guide DFA decisions.

Keeping Score

Boothroyd and Dewhurst (1989) advocate maintaining an ongoing estimate of the cost of assembly. In addition to this absolute score, they propose the concept of *assembly efficiency*. This is measured as an index which is the ratio of the *theoretical minimum assembly time* to an estimate of the actual assembly time for the product. This concept is useful in developing an intuition for what drives the cost of assembly. The expression for the *DFA index* is:

$$\text{DFA index} = \frac{(\text{theoretical minimum number of parts})(3 \text{ seconds})}{\text{estimated total assembly time}}$$

To determine the theoretical minimum number of parts, ask the following three questions of each part in the proposed assembly. Only parts satisfying one of these conditions must "theoretically" be separate.

1 Does the part need to move relative to the rest of the assembly? Small motions that can be accomplished using compliance (for example, elastic hinges or springs) do not count.

2 Must the part be made of a different material from the rest of the assembly for fundamental physical reasons?

3 Does the part have to be separated from the assembly for assembly access, replacement, or repair?

The "3 seconds" in the numerator reflects the theoretical minimum time required to handle and insert a part that is perfectly suited for assembly. One can think of this as the average time (sustainable over a whole work shift) required to assemble a small part that is easy to grasp, requires no particular orientation, and demands no special insertion effort; such an operation is as fast as placing a cylinder into a circular hole with adequate clearance.

Integrate Parts

If a part does not qualify as one of those theoretically necessary, then it is a candidate for physical integration with one or more other parts. The resulting multifunctional component is often very complex as a result of the integration of several different geometric features which would otherwise be separate parts. Nevertheless, molded or stamped parts can often incorporate additional features at little or no added cost. Exhibit 12 shows the throttle-body end of the redesigned intake manifold. Integrated into this component are the attachments for the EGR return and the vacuum source block. These attachments use a molded "push in and turn" geometry, eliminating the need for several threaded fasteners.

Part integration provides several benefits:

• Integrated parts do not have to be assembled. In effect, the "assembly" of the geometric features of the part is accomplished by the part fabrication process.

• Integrated parts are often less expensive to fabricate than are the separate parts they replace. For molded, stamped, and cast parts, this cost savings occurs because a single complex mold or die is usually less expensive than two or more less complex molds or dies and because there is usually less processing time and scrap for the single, integrated part.

EXHIBIT 12 Integration of several features into a single component. The EGR return and vacuum source ports are molded into the redesigned intake manifold. (Stuart Cohen)

- Integrated parts allow the relationships among critical geometric features to be controlled by the part fabrication process (e.g., molding) rather than by an assembly process. This usually means that these dimensions can be more precisely controlled.

Note, however, that part integration is not always a wise strategy and may be in conflict with other sound approaches to minimizing costs. For example, the main intake manifold assembly on the old design was a single cast piece, requiring extensive machining. The team replaced this part with two less-expensive, injection-molded pieces. This is an example of dis-integrating parts in order to achieve benefits in the piece-part production costs.

Maximize Ease of Assembly

Two products with an identical number of parts may nevertheless differ in required assembly time by a factor of two or three. This is because the actual time to grasp, orient, and insert a part depends on the part geometry and the required trajectory of the part insertion. The ideal characteristics of a part for an assembly are [Adapted from Boothroyd and Dewhurst (1989)]:

- *Part is inserted from the top of the assembly.* This attribute of a part and assembly is called *z-axis assembly*. By using z-axis assembly for all parts, the assembly never has to be inverted, gravity helps to stabilize the partial assembly, and the assembly worker can generally see the assembly location.

- *Part is self-aligning.* Parts that require fine positioning in order to be assembled require slow, precise movements on the part of the assembly worker. Parts and assembly sites can be designed to be self-aligning so that fine motor control is not required of the worker. The most common self-alignment feature is the *chamfer*. A chamfer can be implemented as a tapered lead on the end of a peg, or a conical widening at the opening of a hole.

- *Part does not need to be oriented.* Parts requiring correct orientation, such as a screw, require more assembly time than parts requiring no orientation, such as a sphere. In the worst case, a part must be oriented correctly in three dimensions. For example, the following parts are listed in order of increasing requirements for orientation: sphere, cylinder, capped cylinder, capped and keyed cylinder.

- *Part requires only one hand for assembly.* This characteristic relates primarily to the size of the part and the effort required to manipulate the part. All other things being equal, parts requiring one hand to assemble require less time than parts requiring two hands, which in turn require less effort than parts requiring a crane or lift to assemble.

- *Part requires no tools.* Assembly operations requiring tools, such as attaching snap rings, springs, or cotter pins, generally require more time than those that do not.

- *Part is assembled in a single, linear motion.* Pushing in a pin requires less time than driving a screw. For this reason, numerous fasteners are commercially available that require only a single, linear motion for insertion.

- *Part is secured immediately upon insertion.* Some parts require a subsequent securing operation, such as tightening, curing, or the addition of another part. Until the part is secured, the assembly may be unstable, requiring extra care, fixtures, or slower assembly.

Consider Customer Assembly

Customers may tolerate completing some of the product assembly themselves, especially if doing so provides other benefits, such as making the purchase and handling of the packaged product easier. However, designing a product such that it can be easily and properly assembled by the most inept customers, many of whom will ignore directions, is a substantial challenge in itself.

REDUCE THE SUPPORT COSTS

In working to minimize the costs of components and the costs of assembly, the team may also achieve reductions in the demands placed on the production support functions. For example, a reduction in the number of parts reduces the demands on inventory management. A reduction in assembly content reduces the number of workers required for production and therefore reduces the cost of supervision and human resource management. Standardized components reduce the demands on engineering support and quality control. There are, in addition, some direct actions the team can take to reduce the costs of supporting production.

It is important to remember that manufacturing cost estimates are often insensitive to many of the factors that actually drive overhead charges. (Recall the discussion of overhead cost estimation above.) Nevertheless, the goal of the design team in this respect should be to reduce the actual costs of production support, even if overhead cost estimates do not change.

Minimize Systemic Complexity

An extremely simple manufacturing system would utilize a single process to transform a single raw material into a single part—perhaps a system extruding a single diameter of plastic rod from plastic pellets. Unfortunately, few such systems exist. Complexity arises from variety in the inputs, outputs, and transforming processes. Many real manufacturing systems involve hundreds of suppliers, thousands of different parts, hundreds of people, dozens of types of products, and dozens of types of production processes. Each variant of suppliers, parts, people, products, and processes introduces complexity to the system. These variants must usually be tracked, monitored, managed, inspected, handled, and inventoried at tremendous cost to the enterprise. Much of this complexity is driven by the design of the product and can therefore be minimized through smart design decisions.

Exhibit 13 shows a simple "scorecard" of manufacturing complexity useful for reminding designers of how the product design drives the complexity of the manufacturing system. The team establishes a score for the initial design and then uses changes in the score as a measure of success in reducing complexity. Note that the drivers given in the scorecard shown are generic categories. In practice, the team develops this list (and may prioritize it with weightings) based on the realities and constraints of the firm's production environment. Firms that

EXHIBIT 13   Scorecard of manufacturing complexity.

Drivers of Complexity	Rev. 1	Rev. 2
Number of new parts introduced to the manufacturing system	6	5
Number of new vendors introduced to the manufacturing system	3	2
Number of custom parts introduced to the manufacturing system	2	3
Number of new "major tools" (e.g., molds and dies) introduced to the manufacturing system	2	2
Number of new production processes introduced to the manufacturing system	0	0
Total	**13**	**12**

use activity-based costing usually know quite well their primary drivers of complexity, as these are the cost drivers they use in allocating overhead. As a simple substitute for an accurate support cost model, such a scorecard allows the team to make informed decisions without formally estimating the indirect costs of production.

Error Proofing

An important aspect of DFM is to anticipate the possible failure modes of the production system and to take appropriate corrective actions early in the development process. This strategy is known as *error proofing*. One type of failure mode arises from having slightly different parts that can be easily confused. Examples of slightly different parts are screws differing only in the pitch of the threads (e.g., 4 × .70 mm and 4 × .75 mm screws) or in the direction of turning (left- and right-handed threads), parts which are mirror images of each other, and parts differing only in material composition.

We recommend that either these subtle differences be eliminated or that slight differences be exaggerated. Exhibit 14 shows an example of exaggerating subtle differences between parts: the left and right versions of the reel lock on a videocassette, which are mirror images of each other, are molded in two different colors. Color coding allows the parts to be identified easily and differentiated in materials handling and assembly.

EXHIBIT 14   Left and right reel locks inside a videocassette (*top center*). The two nearly identical parts are color coded to avoid confusion. (Stuart Cohen)

CONSIDER THE IMPACT OF DFM DECISIONS ON OTHER FACTORS

Minimizing manufacturing cost is not the only objective of the product development process. The economic success of a product also depends on the quality of the product, the timeliness of product introduction, and the cost of developing the product. There may also be situations in which the economic success of a project is compromised in order to maximize the economic success of the entire enterprise. In contemplating a DFM decision, these issues should be considered explicitly.

The Impact of DFM on Development Time

Development time can be precious. For a critical auto development project, time may be worth as much as several hundred thousand dollars per day. For this reason, DFM decisions must be evaluated for their impact on development time as well as for their impact on manufacturing cost. While saving $1 in cost on each manifold would be worth perhaps $1 million in annual cost savings, it would almost certainly not be worth causing a six-month delay in an automobile program.

The relationship between DFM and development time is complex. Here, we note a few aspects of the relationship. The application of some of the DFA guidelines may result in very complex parts. These parts may be so complex that their design or the procurement of their tooling becomes the activity that determines the duration of the overall development effort (Ulrich, et al., 1993). The cost benefits of the DFM decision may not be worth the delay in project duration. This is particularly true for products competing in dynamic markets.

The Impact of DFM on Development Cost

Development cost closely mirrors development time. Therefore, the same caution about the relationship between part complexity and development time applies to development cost. In general, however, teams that aggressively pursue low manufacturing costs as an integral part of the development process seem to be able to develop products in about the same time and with about the same budget as teams that do not. Part of this phenomenon certainly arises from the correlation between good project management practices and the application of sound DFM methodology.

The Impact of DFM on Product Quality

Before proceeding with a DFM decision, the team should evaluate the impact of the decision on product quality. Under ideal circumstances, actions to decrease manufacturing cost would also improve product quality. For example, the new GM manifold resulted in cost reduction, weight reduction, and improved engine performance. It is not uncommon for DFM efforts focused primarily on manufacturing cost reduction to also result in improved serviceability, ease of disassembly, and recycling. However, in some cases actions to decrease manufacturing cost can have adverse effects on product quality (such as reliability or robustness), so it is advisable for the team to keep in mind the many dimensions of quality that are important for the product.

The Impact of DFM on External Factors

Design decisions may have implications beyond the responsibilities of a single development team. In economic terms, these implications may be viewed as externalities. Two such externalities are component re-use and life-cycle costs.

- *Component re-use:* Taking time and money to create a low-cost component may be of value to other teams designing similar products. In general, this value is not explicitly accounted for in manufacturing cost estimates. The team may choose to take an action that is actually more costly for their product because of the positive cost implications for other projects.
- *Life-cycle costs:* Throughout their life cycles, certain products may incur some company or societal costs which are not (or are rarely) accounted for in the manufacturing cost. For example, products may contain toxic materials requiring special handling in disposal. Products may incur service and warranty costs. Although these costs may not appear in the manufacturing cost analysis, they should be considered before adopting a DFM decision.

RESULTS

During the 1980s, design for manufacturing practices were put into place in thousands of firms. Today DFM is an essential part of almost every product development effort. No longer can designers "throw the design over the wall" to production engineers. As a result of this emphasis on improved design quality, some manufacturers claim to have reduced production costs of products by up to 50 percent. In fact, comparing current new product designs with earlier generations, one can usually identify fewer parts in the new product, as well as new materials, more integrated and custom parts, higher-volume standard parts and subassemblies, and simpler assembly procedures.

A sketch of the redesigned intake manifold is shown in Exhibit 15. This DFM effort achieved impressive results. Exhibit 16 shows the cost estimate for the redesigned intake manifold. (Compare with Exhibit 6.) The improvements over the previous design include:

- Unit cost savings of 45 percent.
- Mass savings of 66 percent (3.3 kilograms).
- Simplified assembly and service procedures.
- Improved emissions performance due to routing of EGR into the manifold.

1993 3800 V-6 COMPOSITE UPPER INTAKE

EXHIBIT 15 The redesigned intake manifold. (Courtesy of General Motors Corp.)

EXHIBIT 16 (*below*) Cost estimate for the redesigned intake manifold.

Component	Purchased Materials	Processing (Machine + Labor)	Assembly (Labor)	Total Unit Variable Cost	Tooling and Other NRE, K$	Tooling Lifetime, K units	Total Unit Fixed Cost	Total Cost
Manifold housing	3.85	1.56		5.41	350	1500	0.23	5.65
Intake runner insert	0.83	1.10	0.13	2.05	150	1500	0.10	2.15
Steel inserts (16)	0.32		1.00	1.32				1.32
EGR adapter	1.70		0.13	1.83				1.83
PCV valve								
Valve	0.85		0.04	0.89				0.89
O-rings (2)	0.02		0.16	0.18				0.18
Spring	0.08		0.10	0.18				0.18
Cover	0.02		0.10	0.12				0.12
Vacuum source block	0.04		0.06	0.10				0.10
Column Totals (Direct Costs)	7.71	2.66	1.71	12.08	500		0.33	12.41
Overhead Charges	1.16	4.79	3.08				0.50	9.52
Total Cost								**21.93**

- Improved engine performance due to reduced air induction temperatures.
- Reduced shipping costs due to lighter components.
- Increased standardization across vehicle programs.

For this product, the manufacturing cost savings alone amount to several million dollars annually. The other benefits listed above are also significant, although somewhat more difficult to quantify.

SUMMARY

Design for manufacturing (DFM) is aimed at reducing manufacturing costs while simultaneously improving (or at least not inappropriately compromising) product quality, development time, and development cost.

- DFM begins with the concept development phase and system-level design phase; in these phases important decisions must be made with the manufacturing cost implications in mind.
- DFM utilizes estimates of the manufacturing cost to guide and prioritize cost reduction efforts. Cost estimation requires expertise with the relevant production processes. Suppliers and manufacturing experts must be involved in this process.
- Since accurate cost estimation is very difficult, much of DFM practice involves making informed decisions in the absence of detailed cost data.
- Component costs are reduced by understanding what drives these costs. Solutions may involve novel component design concepts or the incremental improvement of existing designs through simplification and standardization.
- Assembly costs can be reduced by following well-established design-for-assembly (DFA) guidelines. Components can be redesigned to simplify assembly operations, or components can be eliminated entirely by integration of their functions into other components.
- Reduction of manufacturing support costs begins with an understanding of the drivers of complexity in the production process. Design decisions have a large impact on the costs of supporting production. Choices should be made with these effects in mind, even though overhead cost estimates are often insensitive to such changes.
- DFM is an integrative methodology taking place throughout the development process and requiring inputs from across the development team.
- DFM decisions can affect product development lead time, product development cost, and product quality. Trade-offs will frequently be necessary between manufacturing cost and these equally important broader issues.

REFERENCES AND BIBLIOGRAPHY

Two articles describing the needs, methods, and success of DFM are:

Dean, James W., Jr., and Gerald I. Susman. "Organizing for Manufacturable Design," *Harvard Business Review,* January-February 1989, pp. 28–36.

Whitney, Daniel E., "Manufacturing by Design," *Harvard Business Review,* July-August 1988, pp. 83–91.

There are numerous documented examples of DFM success. One classic example is the story of the IBM Proprinter, described by Dewhurst and Boothroyd.

Dewhurst, Peter, and Geoffrey Boothroyd, "Design for Assembly in Action," *Assembly Engineering,* January 1987.

There are many references available to aid in component design, manufacturing process selection, and understanding of process capabilities. Here are several sources which offer specific guidelines for hundreds of applications, materials, and processes:

Bralla, James G. (ed.), *Handbook of Product Design for Manufacturing: A Practical Guide to Low-Cost Production,* McGraw-Hill, New York, 1986. ISBN 0-07-007130-6.

Trucks, H. E., *Designing for Economical Production,* Society of Manufacturing Engineers, second edition, Dearborn, MI, 1987. ISBN 0-87263-249-0.

Bolz, Roger W., *Production Processes: The Productivity Handbook,* fifth edition, Industrial Press, New York, 1981. ISBN 0-8311-1088-0.

Farag, Mahmoud M., *Selection of Materials and Manufacturing Processes for Engineering Design,* Prentice-Hall, Englewood Cliffs, NJ, 1989. ISBN 0-13-802208-9.

Cubberly, William H., and Ramon Bakerjian, *Tool and Manufacturing Engineers Handbook,* Society of Manufacturing Engineers, Dearborn, MI, 1989. ISBN 0-87263-351-9.

The *Thomas Register* is useful for identifying suppliers of components, tooling, machinery, and other industrial products.

Thomas Register of American Manufacturers, Thomas Publishing Company, New York, published annually.

The most popular methodology for DFA is by Boothroyd and Dewhurst. Software is also available to aid in estimating costs for both manual and automatic assembly, as well as a wide range of component costs.

Boothroyd, Geoffrey, and Peter Dewhurst, *Product Design for Assembly,* Boothroyd Dewhurst, Inc., Wakefield, RI, 1989.

Boothroyd, Geoffrey, Peter Dewhurst, and Winston A. Knight, *Product Design for Manufacturing,* Marcel Dekker, New York, 1994. ISBN 0-82479-176-2.

Detailed research on automated assembly has resulted in guidelines for designing products suited for assembly automation.

Nevins, James L., and Daniel E. Whitney, *Concurrent Design of Products and Processes,* McGraw-Hill, New York, 1989. ISBN 0-07-046341-7.

Boothroyd, Geoffrey, *Assembly Automation and Product Design,* Marcel Dekker, New York, 1992. ISBN 0-82478-547-9.

Kaplan and others describe the development of activity-based costing systems, which provide insight into a firm's cost drivers and facilitate more accurate cost estimation.

Kaplan, Robert S. (ed.), *Measures for Manufacturing Excellence*, Harvard Business School Press, Boston, MA, 1990. ISBN 0-87584-229-1.

Clark and Fujimoto conducted a comprehensive study of product development in the world automobile industry. They provide an interesting analysis and discussion of the concept of "black box" component design.

Clark, Kim B., and Takahiro Fujimoto, *Product Development Performance: Strategy, Organization, and Management in the World Auto Industry*, Harvard Business School Press, Boston, MA, 1991. ISBN 0-87584-245-3.

Ulrich, et al. describe the trade-off between development time and manufacturing cost. They also describe an effort to model support costs in some detail.

Ulrich, Karl, Scott Pearson, David Sartorius, and Mark Jakiela, "Including the Value of Time in Design-for-Manufacturing Decision Making," *Management Science*, Vol. 39, No. 4, April 1993.

EXERCISES

1 Estimate the product cost for a simple product you may have purchased. Try costing a product with fewer than 10 components, such as floppy disk, a pen, a jack-knife, or a baby's toy. Remember that one reasonable upper bound for your estimate, including overhead, is the wholesale price (between 50 percent and 70 percent of retail).

2 Suggest some potential cost-reducing modifications you could make to improve the product costed above. Compute the DFA index before and after these changes.

3 List 10 reasons why reducing the number of parts in a product might reduce production costs. Also list some reasons why costs might increase.

THOUGHT QUESTIONS

1 Consider the following 10 "design rules" for electromechanical products. Do these seem like reasonable guidelines? Under what circumstances could one rule conflict with another one? How should such a trade-off be settled?

a Minimize parts count.	**f** Use self-fastening parts.
b Use modular assembly.	**g** Use self-locating parts.
c Stack assemblies.	**h** Eliminate reorientation.
d Eliminate adjustments.	**i** Facilitate parts handling.
e Eliminate cables.	**j** Specify standard parts.

2 Is it practical to design a product with 100 percent assembly efficiency (DFA index = 1.0)? What conditions would have to be met? Can you think of any products with very high (greater than 75 percent) assembly efficiency?

3 Is it possible to determine what a product really costs once it is put into production? If so, how might you do this?

4 Can you propose a set of metrics that would be useful for the team to predict changes in the actual costs of supporting production? To be effective, these metrics must be sensitive to changes in the design that affect indirect costs experienced by the firm. What are some of the barriers to the introduction of such techniques in practice?

APPENDIX A: Materials Costs

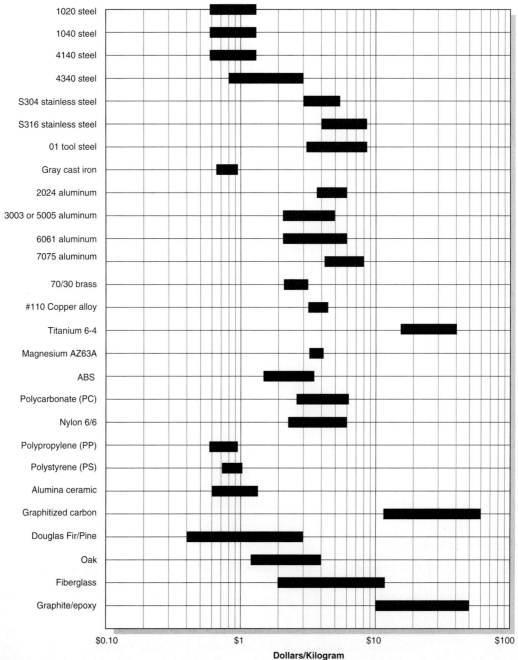

EXHIBIT A1
Range of costs for common engineering materials. Price ranges shown correspond to various grades and forms of each material, purchased in bulk quantities (1994 prices). (Adapted from David G. Ullman, *The Mechanical Design Process,* McGraw-Hill, New York, 1992.)

APPENDIX B: Component Manufacturing Costs

The exhibits in this appendix show example components and their cost data for computer-numerical control (CNC) machining (Exhibit B1), injection molding (Exhibit B2), progressive die stamping (Exhibit B3), and sand casting and investment casting (Exhibit B4). The purpose of these examples is to show, in general terms, what typical operations cost and how the cost structure of each process is affected by part complexity.

Terminology

The following terminology applies to all of the tables in this appendix:

- *Setup* is the work required to prepare the equipment for a production run. Setup costs are charged for each run.

- *Tooling costs* are incurred in advance of the first production run, and tooling can usually be reused for later production runs. However, in very high-volume production runs, tooling wears out and therefore is a recurring expense. Tooling costs may be spread over the entire production volume or may be charged separately. CNC programming time is generally also a one-time expense, like a tooling cost.

- *Material types* are listed for each part. Material weights and costs include processing scrap and waste.

- *Processing costs* vary with the type of manufacturing equipment used and include charges for both machine time and labor.

While fixed costs (setup and tooling) are sometimes billed separately from material and processing costs, for these examples, fixed costs are spread over the production volume shown. Unit costs are calculated as:

$$\text{Total unit cost} = \frac{\text{setup costs} + \text{tooling costs}}{\text{volume}} + \text{variable costs}$$

The cost rates given include overhead charges, so these data are representative of custom components purchased from suppliers.

Description of Processes

CNC machining includes computer-controlled milling and turning processes. CNC machines are highly flexible due to automatic tool-changing mechanisms, multiple work axes, and programmable computer control. To produce a particular part, a machinist must first program the cutting tool trajectories and tool selections into the machine's computer. Also, fixtures or other tooling may be utilized to produce multiple parts more efficiently. Once the program is written and fixtures are made, subsequent productions runs can be set up much more quickly.

Injection molding is the process of forcing hot plastic under high pressure into a mold, where it cools and solidifies. When the part is sufficiently cool, the mold is opened, the part is ejected, the mold closes, and the cycle begins again. Mold complexity depends highly on the part geometry; undercuts (features that would prevent the part from ejecting out of the mold) are achieved using mold "actions" or "retracting pins."

Progressive die stamping is the process of passing a sheet or strip of metal through a set of dies to cut and/or form it to a desired size and shape. While some stampings require only cutting, formed stampings are made by bending and stretching the metal beyond its yield point, thereby causing permanent deformation.

Sand castings are created by forming a sand mold from master patterns (tooling in the shape of the final part). Special binders are mixed with the sand to allow the sand to retain shape when packed around the pattern to create a single-use mold. Internal cavities in a casting can be created using additional sand cores inside the outer mold. Molten metal is then poured into the mold where the metal cools and solidifies. Once cool, the sand is broken off to reveal the metal casting. Sand castings generally require subsequent machining operations to create finished components.

Investment castings are made by first creating a temporary wax pattern, using master tooling. The wax pattern is then dipped or immersed in plaster or ceramic slurry which is allowed to solidify. The form is then heated, melting out the wax, and leaving behind only the thin shell as a mold. Molten metal is then poured into the mold, where it cools and solidifies. When the metal is cool, the mold is broken off to reveal the metal part.

Detailed process descriptions for the above and numerous other processes, as well as more detailed cost estimating techniques, can be found in the reference books listed for this chapter.

	Fixed Costs	Variable Costs	Volume	Total Unit Cost
	Setup: 0.75 hr at $60/hr	Material: $9 ea stock: 1.11 kg of 6061 aluminum	1	$75.00
			10	$21.00
	Tooling: Programming: 0.25 hr at $60/hr	Processing: 6 min/unit at $60/hr	100	$15.50
	Setup: 1.75 hrs at $60/hr	Material: $16 ea stock: 1.96 kg of 6061 aluminum	1	$386.00
			10	$102.50
	Tooling: Programming: 1.0 hr at $60/hr Fixtures: $150	Processing: 55 min/unit at $60/hr	100	$74.15
	Setup: 5.5 hrs at $60/hr	Material: $25 ea stock: 4.60 kg of ultra-high molecular weight polyethylene	1	$646.00
			10	$241.00
	Tooling: Programming: 2.0 hrs at $60/hr	Processing: 2.85 hrs/unit at $60/hr	100	$200.50
	Setup: 2.0 hrs at $60/hr	Material: $12 ea stock: 1.50 kg of 6061 aluminum	1	$612.00
			10	$396.00
	Tooling: Programming: 2.0 hrs at $60/hr	Processing: 6 hrs/unit at $60/hr	100	$374.40

Notes: 1. Programming time is a one-time expense and is included here in tooling costs.
2. Material prices assume low volumes and include cutting charges.
3. Processing costs include overhead charges.

EXHIBIT B1 CNC machining example components and cost data. (Examples and data courtesy of Ramco, Inc. Photos by Stuart Cohen.)

	Fixed Costs		Variable Costs		Volume	Total Unit Cost
	Setup:		Material:	$0.06 ea	10K	$1.890
			45 g of linear low density polyethylene (LLDPF)			
					100K	$0.270
	Tooling:	$18K 8 cavities/mold no actions	Processing:	1000 pcs/hr on an 1800 KN press at $30/hr	1M	$0.108
	Setup:		Material:	$0.147 ea	10K	$1.366
			10 g of steel-filled polycarbonate (PC)			
					100K	$0.466
	Tooling:	$10K 1 cavity/mold no actions	Processing:	160 pcs/hr on a 900 KN press at $35/hr	1M	$0.376
	Setup:		Material:	$0.144 ea	10K	$2.090
			22 g of modified polyphenylene oxide (PPO)			
					100K	$0.470
	Tooling:	$18K 2 cavities/mold no actions 3 retracting pins	Processing:	240 pcs/hr on an 800 KN press at $35/hr	1M	$0.308
	Setup:		Material:	$2.38 ea	10K	$10.801
			227 g of polycarbonate (PC) with 8 brass inserts			
					100K	$3.601
	Tooling:	$80K 1 cavity/mold 1 action 4 retracting pins	Processing:	95 pcs/hr on a 2700 KN press at $40/hr	1M	$2.881

Notes: 1. Setup costs (only a few hours in each case) are negligible for high-volume injection molding.
2. Processing costs include overhead charges.

EXHIBIT B2   Injection molding example components and cost data. (Examples and data courtesy of Lee Plastics, Inc., and Digital Equipment Corporation. Photos by Stuart Cohen.)

	Fixed Costs		Variable Costs		Volume	Total Unit Cost
	Setup:		Material:	$0.035 ea	100K	$0.254
				2.2 g		
				70/30 Brass	1M	$0.074
	Tooling:		Processing:			
		$20K		3000 pcs/hr on a 550 KN press at $57/hr	10M	$0.056
	Setup:		Material:	$0.03 ea	100K	$0.710
				3.5 g		
				304 SST	1M	$0.125
	Tooling:		Processing:			
		$65K		4300 pcs/hr on a 550 KN press at $129/hr	10M	$0.067
	Setup:		Material:	$0.125 ea	100K	$0.234
				19.2 g		
				102 copper	1M	$0.144
	Tooling:		Processing:			
		$10K		4800 pcs/hr on a 650 KN press at $45/hr	10M	$0.135
	Setup:		Material:	$0.25 ea	100K	$2.307
				341 g galvanized steel	1M	$0.687
	Tooling:		Processing:			
		$180K		700 pcs/hr on a 1000 KN press at $180/hr	10M	$0.525

Notes: 1. Setup costs (only a few hours in each case) are negligible for high-volume stamping.
2. Material weights represent the finished stampings. Material costs include scrap.
3. Hourly processing costs are not only driven by press size, but also can include ancillary processing equipment, such as in-die tapping.
4. Processing costs include overhead charges.

EXHIBIT B3   Volume progressive die stamping example components and cost data. (Examples and data courtesy of Brainin Advance Industries and other sources. Photos by Stuart Cohen.)

	Fixed Costs	Variable Costs	Volume	Total Unit Cost
	Setup:	Material: $0.50 ea	10	$180.87
		570 g of gray cast iron	100	$18.87
	Tooling: $1.8K 8 impressions/pattern no cores	Processing: 120 pcs/hr at $44/hr	1000	$2.67
	Setup:	Material: $2.30 ea	10	$243.77
		2,600 g of gray cast iron	100	$27.77
	Tooling: $2.4K 2 impressions/pattern 1 core	Processing: 30 pcs/hr at $44/hr	1000	$6.17

	Fixed Costs	Variable Costs	Volume	Total Unit Cost
	Setup:	Material: $0.713 ea	10	$163.21
		260 g of yellow brass	100	$28.21
	Tooling: $1.5K no cores	Processing: 4 pcs/hr at $50/hr	1000	$14.71
	Setup:	Material: $0.395 ea	10	$750.40
		180 g of 712 aluminum	100	$120.40
	Tooling: $7K 3 cores	Processing: 1 pc/hr at $50 /hr	1000	$57.40

Notes: 1. Setup is not generally charged in costing.
2. Processing costs include overhead charges.

EXHIBIT B4 Sand casting (*top*) and investment casting (*bottom*) example components and cost data. [Examples and data courtesy of Cumberland Foundry Co., Inc. (sand casting) and Castronics, Inc. (investment casting). Photos by Stuart Cohen.]

APPENDIX C: Assembly Costs

Product	Part Data		Assembly Times (seconds)	
	No. of Parts	16	Total	125.7
	No. of Unique Parts	12	Slowest Part	9.7
	No. of Fasteners	0	Fastest Part	2.9
	No. of Parts	34	Total	186.5
	No. of Unique Parts	25	Slowest Part	10.7
	No. of Fasteners	5	Fastest Part	2.6
	No. of Parts	49	Total	266.0
	No. of Unique Parts	43	Slowest Part	14.0
	No. of Fasteners	5	Fastest Part	3.5
	No. of Parts	56/17*	Total	277.0/138.0*
	No. of Unique Parts	44/12*	Slowest Part	8.0/8.0*
	No. of Fasteners	0/0*	Fastest Part	0.75/3.0*

* Data for the mouse are given as: total components (including electronic)/mechanical components only.

Notes: 1. This table gives manual assembly times, which can be converted to assembly costs using applicable labor rates.
2. Assembly times shown include times for individual part handling and insertion, as well as other operations such as subassembly handling and insertion, reorientations, and heat riveting.

EXHIBIT C1 Assembly data for common products. (Data obtained using Boothroyd Dewhurst Inc. DFA software. Photos by Stuart Cohen.)

Component	Time (seconds)		
	Min	Max	Avg
Screw	7.5	13.1	10.3
Snap-fit	3.5	8.0	5.9

Component	Time (seconds)		
	Min	Max	Avg
Pin	3.1	10.1	6.6
Spring	2.6	14.0	8.3

EXHIBIT C2   Typical handling and insertion times for common components. (From manual assembly tables in Geoffrey Boothroyd and Peter Dewhurst, *Product Design for Assembly,* Boothroyd Dewhurst, Inc., Wakefield, RI, 1989.)

APPENDIX D: Cost Structures

Type of Firm	Cost Calculation
Electromechanical products manufacturer (Traditional cost structure)	Cost = (113%) × (Materials Cost) +(360%) × (Direct Labor Cost)
Precision valve manufacturer (Activity-based cost structure)	Cost = (108%) × [(Direct Labor Cost) + (Setup Labor Cost) + (106%) × (Materials Cost) + ($27.80) × (Machine Hours) + ($2,000.00) × (Number of Shipments)]
Heavy equipment component manufacturer (Activity-based cost structure)	Cost = (110%) × (Materials Cost) +(109%) × [(211%) × (Direct Labor Cost) + ($16.71) × (Machine Hours) + ($33.76) × (Setup Hours) + ($114.27) × (Number of Production Orders) + ($19.42) × (Number of Material Handling Loads) + ($487.00) × (Number of New Parts Added to the System)]

Notes: 1. This table shows total cost per customer order.
2. Materials costs include costs of raw materials and purchased components.

EXHIBIT D1   Typical cost structures for manufacturing firms. [From (*top to bottom*): Unpublished company source; Harvard Business School Cases: Destin Brass Products Co. (9-190-089) and John Deere Component Works (9-187-107).]

EFFECTIVE PROTOTYPING

Developed in collaboration with Amy Greenlief.

EXHIBIT 1 Powerbook Duo by Apple Computer, Inc. (Courtesy of Apple Computer.)

$\mathbf{A}$pple Computer sold over 400,000 of the original Powerbook notebook computers in the first year after product launch, making the Powerbook the most successful new product in Apple's history. However, the subsequent model of Powerbook, the Duo, had to be even smaller, lighter, and more powerful in order to remain competitive. One major obstacle to reducing the thickness of the original Powerbook was the thickness of the trackball mechanism, and so a new trackball became one of the key elements of the Duo development effort. A trackball is commonly used in a portable computer as a substitute for a computer mouse. The ball, recessed in a housing, is manipulated by the user in order to control the position of the cursor on the computer screen. Exhibit 1 shows a photograph of the Duo, and Exhibit 2 shows an external view of the trackball. In addition to the dominant goal of reducing the size of the trackball, the development team at Apple hoped to decrease its cost and increase its quality. Throughout the development of the trackball, the team used a variety of prototypes. This chapter defines *prototype*, explains why prototypes are built, and then presents several principles of prototyping practice. The chapter also describes a methodology for planning prototypes before they are built. The Duo trackball is used as an illustrative example throughout.

PROTOTYPE BASICS

What Is a Prototype?

Although dictionaries define *prototype* as a noun only, in product development practice the word is used as a noun, a verb, and an adjective. For example:

EXHIBIT 2   The Duo trackball.   (Stuart Cohen)

- Industrial designers produce *prototypes* of their concepts.
- Engineers *prototype* a design.
- Software developers write *prototype* programs.

We define *prototype* as "an approximation of the product along one or more dimensions of interest." Under this definition, any entity that exhibits some aspect of the product that is of interest to the development team can be viewed as a prototype. This definition is purposely broad and includes prototypes ranging from concept sketches to fully functional artifacts. *Prototyping* is the process of developing such an approximation of the product.

Types of Prototypes

Prototypes can be usefully classified along two dimensions. The first dimension is the degree to which a prototype is *physical* as opposed to *analytical*. Physical prototypes are tangible artifacts created to approximate the product. Aspects of the product of interest to the development team are actually built for testing and experimentation. Examples of physical prototypes include models which look and feel like the product, proof-of-concept prototypes used to test an idea quickly, and experimental hardware used to validate the functionality of a product. Analytical prototypes represent the product in a nontangible, usually mathematical, manner. Interesting aspects of the product are analyzed, rather than built. Examples of analytical prototypes include computer simulations, systems of equations encoded within a spreadsheet, and computer models of three-dimensional geometry.

The second dimension is the degree to which a prototype is *comprehensive* as opposed to *focused*. Comprehensive prototypes implement most, if not all, of the attributes of a product. A comprehensive prototype corresponds closely to the everyday use of the word *prototype*, in that it is a full-scale, fully operational version of the product. An example of a comprehensive prototype is a beta prototype given to customers in order to identify any remaining design flaws before committing to production. In contrast to comprehensive prototypes, focused prototypes implement one, or a few, of the attributes of a product. Examples of focused prototypes include foam models to explore the form of a product, and wire-wrapped circuit boards to investigate the electronic performance of a product design. A common practice is to use two or more focused prototypes together to investigate the overall performance of a product. One of these prototypes is often a "looks like" prototype, and the other is a "works like" prototype. By building two separate focused prototypes, the team may be able to answer its questions much earlier than if it had to create one comprehensive prototype.

Exhibit 3 is a plot with axes corresponding to these two dimensions. Several different example prototypes are shown on this plot. Note that focused prototypes can be either physical or analytical, but that for physical products, fully comprehensive prototypes must generally be physical. Prototypes sometimes contain a combination of analytical and physical elements. For example, a

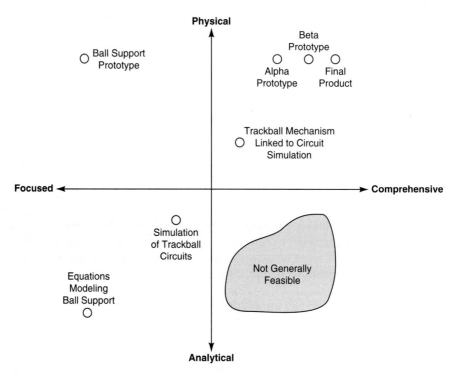

EXHIBIT 3   Types of prototypes. Prototypes can be classified according to the degree to which they are physical and the degree to which they implement all of the attributes of the product.

mechanical trackball could be linked to a software simulation of the circuitry that would eventually be used to monitor the trackball motion. Some analytical prototypes can be viewed as being more "physical" than others. For example, a video animation of a mechanism generated from a detailed simulation of the physical interactions of the elements in the mechanism is, in one sense, more physical than a set of equations approximating the overall motion of the same mechanism.

What Are Prototypes Used For?

Within a product development project, prototypes are used for four purposes: learning, communication, integration, and milestones.

- *Learning:* Prototypes are often used to answer two types of questions: "Will it work?" and "How well does it meet the customer needs?" When used to answer such questions, prototypes serve as learning tools. In developing the trackball, the ball support system was investigated using focused prototypes. The three support pegs were placed at different radii from the center of the ball socket. In Exhibit 4, these support pegs can be seen in the prototype

EXHIBIT 4   Focused physical prototypes of the trackball support. These prototypes were used for learning about trackball "feel."   (Stuart Cohen)

with the 13.00-millimeter radius placement. Other prototypes with spaces for the pegs at different radii are also shown. This is an example of a focused physical prototype used as a learning tool. During the development of the trackball, geometric modeling on a computer was used to check for fit and interference of the trackball components. This is an example of a focused analytical prototype used as a learning tool.

- *Communication:* Prototypes enrich communication with top management, vendors, partners, extended team members, customers, and sources of financing. This is particularly true of physical prototypes: a visual, tactile, three-dimensional representation of a product is much easier to understand than a verbal description or even a sketch of the product. When developing concepts for the Duo trackball, communication between design engineers, industrial designers and customers was enhanced through the use of "look and feel" prototypes. Several such prototypes were used to communicate possible features of the trackball to customers. The customers then gave feedback to the engineers and industrial designers about which features they preferred.

- *Integration:* Prototypes are used to ensure that components and subsystems of the product work together as expected. Comprehensive physical prototypes are most effective as integration tools in product development projects because they require the assembly and physical interconnection of all of the parts and subassemblies that make up a product. In doing so, the prototype forces coordination between different members of the product development team. If the combination of any of the components of the product interferes with the overall function of the product, the problem may only be detected through physical integration in a comprehensive prototype. Common names for these comprehensive physical prototypes are *experimental, alpha, beta,* or *preproduction* prototypes. Two such prototypes (an alpha and a beta) for the Duo trackball are shown in Exhibit 5. In the alpha prototype, actuator arms are visible on the switches (lower-left and upper-right corners). In the beta prototype, the actuator arms have been removed. This change was necessary because a tolerance "stack-up" resulted in poor

EXHIBIT 5   Comprehensive trackball prototypes. The alpha prototype, with the light gray retaining ring, is on the left; the beta prototype, with the dark gray retaining ring, is on the right.   (Stuart Cohen)

actuation of some switches. This problem was detected as a result of the physical integration forced by the assembly and test of the alpha prototype. Prototypes also help to integrate the perspectives of the different functions represented on a product development team (Leonard-Barton, 1991). A simple physical model of the form of a product can be used as the medium through which the marketing, design, and manufacturing functions agree on a basic design decision.

• *Milestones:* Particularly in the later stages of product development, prototypes are used to demonstrate that the product has achieved a desired level of functionality. Milestone prototypes provide tangible goals, demonstrate progress, and serve to enforce the schedule. Senior management (and sometimes the customer) often requires a prototype that demonstrates certain functions before they will allow the project to proceed. For example, in many government procurements, a prototype must pass a "first-article test" before a contractor can proceed with production. A major milestone for the Duo trackball development was the ability to pass a "50-mile test." During this test the ball is moved randomly by automatic test equipment for a total of 50 miles. There can be no failures of the trackball system for the test to be successful.

While all types of prototypes are used for all four of these purposes, some types of prototypes are more appropriate than others for some purposes. A summary of the relative appropriateness of different types of prototypes for different purposes is shown in Exhibit 6.

	Learning	Communication	Integration	Milestones
Focused-Analytical	●	○	○	○
Focused-Physical	●	●	○	○
Comprehensive-Physical	●	●	●	●

EXHIBIT 6 Appropriateness of different types of prototypes for different purposes (● = more appropriate, ○ = less appropriate). Note that comprehensive-analytical prototypes are rarely possible.

PRINCIPLES OF PROTOTYPING

Several principles are useful in guiding decisions about prototypes during product development. These principles inform decisions about what type of prototype to build and about how to incorporate prototypes into the development plan.

Analytical Prototypes Are Generally More Flexible Than Physical Prototypes

Because an analytical prototype is a mathematical approximation of the product, it will generally contain parameters that can be varied in order to represent design alternatives. In most cases, changing a parameter in an analytical prototype is easier than changing an attribute of a physical prototype. For example, consider an analytical prototype of the trackball which includes a set of equations representing the sliding of the ball on its supports. One of the parameters in the equations is the coefficient of friction between the ball material and the support material. Changing this parameter and then solving the equations is much easier than changing the actual materials in the physical prototype. In most cases, the analytical prototype is not only easier to change than a physical prototype but also allows larger changes than could be made in a physical prototype. For this reason, an analytical prototype frequently precedes a physical prototype. The analytical prototype is used to narrow the range of feasible parameters, and then the physical prototype is used to fine-tune or confirm the design.

Physical Prototypes Are Required to Detect Unanticipated Phenomena

A physical prototype often exhibits unanticipated phenomena completely unrelated to the original objective of the prototype. One reason for these surprises is that all of the laws of physics are always operating when the team experiments with physical prototypes. Physical prototypes intended to investigate purely geometric issues will also have thermal and optical properties. Some of the incidental properties of physical prototypes are irrelevant to the final product and act as annoyances during testing. However, some of these incidental properties of physical prototypes will also manifest themselves in the final product. In these cases, a physical prototype can serve as a tool for detecting unanticipated detrimental phenomena that may arise in the final product. Analytical prototypes, in contrast, can never reveal phenomena that are not part of the underlying analytical model on which the prototype is based. For this reason at least one physical prototype is almost always built in a product development effort.

A Prototype May Reduce the Risk of Costly Iterations

Exhibit 7 illustrates the role of risk and iteration in product development. In many situations, the outcome of a test may dictate whether a development task will have to be repeated. For example, if a molded part fits poorly with its mating parts, the mold may have to be rebuilt. In Exhibit 7, a 30 percent risk of returning to the mold-building activity after testing part fit is represented with an arrow labeled with a probability of 0.30. If building and testing a prototype substantially increases the likelihood that the subsequent activities will proceed

EXHIBIT 7   A prototype may reduce the risk of costly iteration. Taking time to build and test a prototype may allow the development team to detect a problem that would otherwise not have been detected until after a costly development activity, such as building an injection mold.

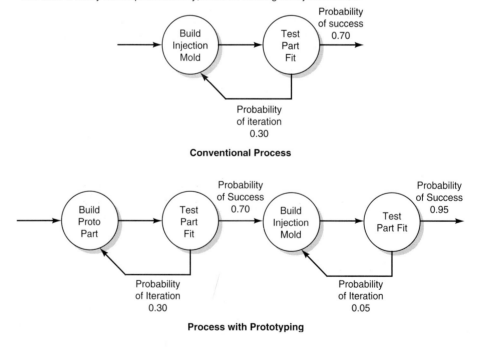

Conventional Process

Process with Prototyping

EXHIBIT 8   Role of a prototype in expediting another step. Taking time to build a prototype may enable more rapid completion of a subsequent step.

without iteration (for example, from 70 percent to 95 percent, as indicated in Exhibit 7), the prototype phase may be justified.

The anticipated benefits of a prototype in reducing risk must be weighed against the time and money required to build and evaluate the prototype. Products which are high in risk or uncertainty, due to high costs of failure, new technology, or the revolutionary nature of the product, will benefit from such prototypes. On the other hand, products for which failure costs are low and the technology is well known do not derive as much risk-reduction benefit from prototyping. Most products fall between these extremes.

A Prototype May Expedite Other Development Steps

Sometimes the addition of a short prototyping phase may allow a subsequent activity to be completed more quickly than if the prototype were not built. If the required time for the prototype phase is less than the savings in duration of the subsequent activity, then this strategy is appropriate. One of the most common occurrences of this situation is in mold design, as illustrated in Exhibit 8. The existence of a physical model of a geometrically complex part allows the mold designer to more quickly visualize and design the mold.

A Prototype May Restructure Task Dependencies

The top part of Exhibit 9 illustrates a set of tasks which are completed sequentially. It may be possible to complete some of the tasks concurrently by building a prototype. For example, a software test may depend on the existence of a physical circuit. Rather than waiting for the production version of the printed circuit

EXHIBIT 9   Use of a prototype to remove a task from the critical path.

board to use in the test, the team may be able to rapidly fabricate a prototype (e.g., a wire-wrapped board) and use it for the test while the production of the printed circuit board proceeds.

PLANNING FOR PROTOTYPES

A potential pitfall in product development is what Clausing calls the "hardware swamp" (Clausing, 1994). The swamp is caused by misguided prototyping efforts, that is, the building and debugging of prototypes (physical or analytical) that do not really contribute to the goals of the overall product development project. One way to avoid the swamp is to define carefully each prototype before embarking on an effort to build and test it. This section presents a four-step methodology for planning a prototype during a product development effort. The methodology applies to all types of prototypes: focused, comprehensive, physical, and analytical. A template for recording the information generated from the methodology is given in Exhibit 10. We use the ball-support prototype shown in Exhibit 4 as an example to illustrate the methodology.

Step 1: Define the Purpose of the Prototype

Recall the four purposes of prototypes: learning, communication, integration, and milestones. In defining the purpose of a prototype, the team lists its specific learning and communication needs. Team members also list any integration needs and whether or not the prototype is intended to be one of the major milestones of the overall product development project.

For the ball-support prototype, the purpose of the prototype was to determine the spacing of the support bearings and the inertia of the ball that would result

Name of Prototype:	Ball Support
Purpose: (Communication, Learning, Integration, Milestones)	What combination of spacing between ball supports and ball inertia yields the best trackball feel? (Learning)
	How much variation is there in users' preferences for feel? (Learning)
Level of Approximation:	Ball surface material as planned for production design.
	Support material as planned for production design.
	Support contact geometry as planned for production design.
Quantity to Be Built (If Physical):	2 sets of 5 different spacings for ball support.
	2 balls with different inertias.
Outline of Test Plan:	Test spacings of 12.75, 13.00, 13.25, 13.50, 13.75 mm for each of two ball inertias.
	Verify that all the spacings provide at least minimally acceptable performance
	Have at least 20 users rank order the prototypes according to feel.
Schedule:	12 August Parts available.
	12 August Parts assembled.
	20 August Tests completed.
	22 August Analysis of results completed.

EXHIBIT 10   Prototype planning template.

in the best ball feel. This "learning" prototype was very focused and there were no other major purposes of the prototype.

Step 2: Establish the Level of Approximation of the Prototype

Planning a prototype requires that the degree to which the final product is approximated be defined. The team should consider whether a physical prototype is necessary or whether an analytical prototype would best meet its needs. In most cases, the best prototype is the simplest prototype that will serve the purposes established in step 1. In some cases, an existing prototype or a prototype being built for another purpose can be borrowed.

For the ball support, the team decided that the only attributes of the product that needed to be approximated were the ball diameter, the ball inertia, the ball material, the bearing support geometry and stiffness, and the bearing support materials. All of the other aspects of the trackball could be ignored, including the color, the surrounding enclosure, the ball retention device, and the position sensing mechanism of the trackball.

A member of the team had previously explored an analytical prototype of the trackball support and felt that the physical prototype was necessary to verify his analysis. He had discovered that there was a basic trade-off between minimizing friction, which would tend to drive the supports closer together, and maximizing the stability of the ball, which would tend to drive the supports farther apart. The team used the analytical prototype to determine the range of ball support dimensions that would be investigated with the physical prototype.

Step 3: Outline an Experimental Plan

In most cases, the use of a prototype in product development can be thought of as an experiment. Good experimental practice helps to ensure the extraction of maximum value from the prototyping activity. The experimental plan includes the identification of the variables of the experiment (if any), the test protocol, an indication of what measurements will be performed, and a plan for analyzing the resulting data. When many variables must be explored, efficient experimental design greatly facilitates this process. Practical statistical methods are available for conducting such experiments (Box and Bisgaard, 1988).

For the ball-support prototype, the team decided to vary only the support spacing and the inertia of the ball. The members of the team agreed that the spacing would be tested at values of 12.75, 13.00, 13.25, 13.50, and 13.75 millimeters. The team also prepared two different balls with different inertias, one with a steel core and one of solid plastic. With only two parameters to explore, the team could test all combinations of diameters and inertias. The test protocol was to have a person subjectively evaluate the feel of the trackball at each of the ten combinations of spacings and inertias and rank them in order of preference. The team agreed to select the setting preferred by the most people. The team members also decided to analyze the variation in the responses as an indication of the degree to which people agree on what constitutes good feel. In an attempt to allow the use of analytical prototypes in the future, the team also planned to measure the ball rolling friction for each of the test conditions and to attempt to model the relationship between the ball and support characteristics and the resulting friction.

Step 4: Create a Schedule for Procurement, Construction, and Test

Because the building and testing of a prototype can be considered a subproject within the overall development project, the team benefits from a schedule for the prototyping activity. Three dates are particularly important in defining a prototyping effort. First, the team defines when the parts will be ready to assemble. (This is sometimes called the "bucket of parts" date.) Second, the team defines the date when the prototype will first be tested. (This is sometimes called the "smoke test" date, because it is the date the team will first apply power and "look for smoke" in products with electrical systems.) Third, the team defines the date when it expects to have completed testing and produced the final results.

For the ball-support prototype, there was little assembly involved, so that when parts were available the prototypes could immediately be assembled and tested. The team planned for eight days of testing and two days of analysis.

Planning Milestones Prototypes

The above methodology for planning a prototype applies to all prototypes, including those as simple as the ball support and those as complex as the beta prototype of the entire trackball. Nevertheless, the comprehensive prototypes the team uses as development milestones benefit from additional planning. This planning activity typically occurs concurrently with the overall product development planning activity at the end of the concept development phase. In fact, planning the milestone dates is an integral part of establishing an overall product development plan. (See the chapter "Managing Product Development Projects.")

All other things being equal, the team would prefer to build as few milestone prototypes as possible because designing, building, and testing prototypes consumes a great deal of time and money. However, in reality, few highly engineered products are developed with fewer than two milestone prototypes, and many efforts require four or more. As a base case, the team should consider using *alpha, beta,* and *preproduction* prototypes as milestones. The team should then consider whether any of these milestones can be eliminated or whether in fact additional prototypes are necessary.

Alpha prototypes are typically used to assess whether the product works as intended. The parts in alpha prototypes are usually similar in material and geometry to the parts that will be used in the production version of the product, but they are usually made with prototype production processes. For example, plastic parts in an alpha prototype may be machined instead of molded as they would be in production.

Beta prototypes are typically used to assess reliability and to identify remaining "bugs" in the product. These prototypes are often given to customers for test in the intended use environment. The parts in beta prototypes are usually made from actual production processes or supplied by the intended parts suppliers, but the product is usually not assembled with the intended final assembly facility. For example, the plastic parts in a beta prototype might be molded with the production injection molds but would probably be assembled by a technician in a prototype shop rather than by production workers or automated equipment.

Preproduction prototypes are the first products produced by the production process. At this point the production process is not yet operating at full capacity but is making limited quantities of the product. These prototypes are used to assess production process capability, are subjected to further testing, and are often supplied to preferred customers. Preproduction prototypes are sometimes called pilot production prototypes.

The most common deviations from the standard prototyping plan are to eliminate one of the standard prototypes or to add additional early prototypes. Eliminating a prototype (usually the alpha) may be possible if the product is very similar to other products the firm has already developed and produced, of if the product is extremely simple. Additional early prototypes are common in situations where the product embodies a new concept or technology. These early prototypes are sometimes called experimental or engineering prototypes. They usually do not look like the final product, and many of the parts of the prototype are not designed with the intention of eventually being produced in quantity.

Once preliminary decisions have been made about the number of prototypes, their characteristics, and the time required to assemble and test them, the team can place these milestones on the overall time line of the project. When the team attempts to schedule these milestones, the feasibility of the overall product development schedule will be tested. Frequently a team will discover, when working backward from the target date for the product launch, that the assembly and test of one milestone prototype overlaps or is perilously close to the design and fabrication of the next milestone prototype. If this overlapping happens in practice, it is the worst manifestation of the "hardware swamp." When prototyping phases overlap, there is little transfer of learning from one prototype to the next, and the team should consider omitting one or more of the prototypes to allow the remaining prototypes to be spread out more in time. During project planning, overlapping prototyping phases can be avoided by beginning the project sooner, delaying product launch, eliminating a milestone prototype, or devising a way to accelerate the development activities preceding each prototype. (See the chapter "Managing Product Development Projects" for some techniques for achieving this acceleration.)

SUMMARY

Product development almost always requires the building and testing of prototypes. A prototype is an approximation of the product on one or more dimensions of interest.

- Prototypes can be usefully classified along two dimensions: (1) the degree to which they are physical as opposed to analytical and (2) the degree to which they are comprehensive as opposed to focused.

- Prototypes are used for learning, communication, integration, and milestones. While all types of prototypes can be used for all of these purposes, physical prototypes are usually best for communication, and comprehensive prototypes are best for integration and milestones.

- Several principles are useful in guiding decisions about prototypes during product development: Analytical prototypes are generally more flexible than physical prototypes. Physical prototypes are required to detect unanticipated phenomena. A prototype may reduce the risk of costly iterations. A prototype may expedite other development steps. A prototype may restructure task dependencies.

- A four-step methodology for planning a prototype is:
  1 Define the purpose of the prototype.
  2 Establish the level of approximation of the prototype.
  3 Outline an experimental plan.
  4 Create a schedule for procurement, construction, and test.
- Milestone prototypes are defined during the project planning phase of development. The number of such prototypes and their timing is one of the key elements of the overall development plan.

REFERENCES AND BIBLIOGRAPHY

Box and Bisgaard provide a good overview of the use of statistical methods, including fractional factorial methods, for experimentation.

> Box, George, and Soren Bisgaard, "Statistical Tools for Improving Designs," *Mechanical Engineering*, January 1988.

Clausing describes some of the pitfalls in prototyping, including the "hardware swamp."

> Clausing, Don, *Total Quality Development*, ASME Press, New York, 1994. ISBN 0-7918-0035-0.

Leonard-Barton describes how prototypes are used for the integration of different product development functions.

> Leonard-Barton, Dorothy, "Inanimate Integrators: A Block of Wood Speaks," *Design Management Journal*, Vol. 2, No. 3, Summer 1991.

Wall, Ulrich, and Flowers provide a formal definition of the quality of a prototype in terms of its fidelity to the production version of a product. They use this definition to evaluate the prototyping technologies available for plastic parts.

> Wall, Matthew B., Karl T. Ulrich, and Woodie C. Flowers, "Evaluating Prototyping Technologies for Product Design," *Research in Engineering Design*, Vol. 3, 1992, pp. 163–177.

Wheelwright and Clark describe the use of prototypes as managerial tools for major product development programs. Their discussion of periodic prototyping cycles is particularly interesting.

> Wheelwright, Stephen C., and Kim B. Clark, *Revolutionizing Product Development: Quantum Leaps in Speed, Efficiency, and Quality*, The Free Press, New York, 1992. ISBN 0-02-905515-6.

EXERCISES

1 A furniture manufacturer was considering a line of seating products to be fabricated by cutting and bending a recycled plastic product available in large sheets. Create a prototype of at least one possible chair design by cutting and bending a sheet of paper or cardboard. (You may wish to design the chair with a sketch first, or just start working with the sheet directly.) What can you learn about the chair

design from your prototype? What can't you learn about the chair design from such a prototype?

2 Position the chair prototype described in Exercise 1 on the plot in Exhibit 3. For which of the four major purposes would a product development team use such a prototype?

3 Devise a prototyping plan (similar to that in Exhibit 10) for investigating the comfort of different types of handles for kitchen knives.

THOUGHT QUESTIONS

1 Many product development teams separate the "looks like" prototype from the "works like" prototype. They do this because integrating both function and form is difficult in the early phases of development. What are the strengths and weaknesses of this approach? For what types of products might this approach be dangerous?

2 Over the past 10 years, several technologies have been developed to create physical parts directly from computer-aided design files (for example, stereolithography and selective laser sintering). How might a team use such rapid prototyping technologies during the concept development phase of the product development process? Might the technologies facilitate identifying customer needs, establishing specifications, generating product concepts, and/or selecting product concepts?

3 Some companies have reportedly abandoned the practice of doing a customer test with the early prototypes of their products, preferring instead to go directly and quickly to market in order to observe the actual customer response. For what types of products and markets might this practice make sense?

4 Is a drawing a physical or analytical prototype?

ECONOMICS OF PRODUCT DEVELOPMENT PROJECTS

Developed in collaboration with Thomas P. Foody.

EXHIBIT 1   Polaroid Corporation's CI-700 Digital PhotoPrinter. (Courtesy of Polaroid Corporation.)

In 1990, Polaroid Corporation was in the midst of developing a new product, the CI-700 Digital PhotoPrinter (Exhibit 1). The CI-700 produces instant full-color photographs from digital images stored in a computer. The primary markets for the product are the graphic arts, insurance, and real estate industries. During the CI-700's development, the Polaroid product development team was faced with several decisions which it knew could have a significant impact on the product's profitability:

- Should the team take more time for development in order to make the product available on multiple computer "platforms," or would a delay in bringing the CI-700 to market be too costly?

- Should the product use print media (instant film) from Polaroid's consumer camera business or new and specialized premium-quality print media?

- Should the team increase development spending in order to increase the reliability of the CI-700?

The product development team needed tools to help it make these and other development decisions. This chapter presents an economic analysis methodology for supporting the decisions of product development teams. The methodology consists of two types of analysis, *quantitative* and *qualitative*. The emphasis in this chapter is on quick, approximate methods for supporting decision making within the project team.

ELEMENTS OF ECONOMIC ANALYSIS
Quantitative Analysis

There are several basic cash inflows (revenues) and cash outflows (costs) in the life cycle of a successful new product. Cash inflows come from product sales. Cash outflows include spending on product and process development; costs of production ramp-up such as equipment purchases and tooling; costs of marketing and supporting the product; and ongoing production costs such as raw materials, components, and labor. The cumulative cash inflows and outflows over the life cycle of a typical successful product are presented schematically in Exhibit 2.

Economically successful products are profitable, that is, they generate more cumulative inflows than cumulative outflows. A measure of the degree to which inflows are greater than outflows is the *net present value* (NPV) of the project, or the value in today's dollars of all of the expected future cash flows. The quantitative part of our economic analysis methodology estimates the NPV of a project's expected cash flows. Our methodology uses NPV techniques because they are easily understood and used widely in business. (The appendix to this chapter is a brief tutorial on NPV.) The value of quantitative analysis is not only in providing objective evaluations of projects and alternatives but also in bringing a measure of structure and discipline to the product development process.

Qualitative Analysis

Quantitative analysis can capture only those factors that are measurable, yet projects often have both positive and negative implications that are difficult to quantify. Also, quantitative analysis rarely captures the characteristics of a dynamic and competitive environment. The chief executive of a major American corporation underscores this point: "I've had MBAs argue with me that a capital expenditure is wrong because it doesn't have a payback within two or three years; they ignore the fact that if we don't make the move, we'll fall behind the rest of our industry in four or five years" (Linder and Smith, 1992). Our methodology uses qualitative analysis to capture some of these issues. Our approach to qualitative analysis is to consider specifically the interactions between the project and (1) the firm, (2) the market, and (3) the macroeconomic environment.

When Should Economic Analysis Be Performed?

Economic analysis, which includes both quantitative and qualitative approaches, is useful in at least two different circumstances:

- *Go/no-go milestones:* For example, should we try to develop a product to meet this market need? Should we proceed with the implementation of a selected concept? Should we launch the product we have developed? These decisions typically arise at the end of each phase of development.

- *Operational design and development decisions:* Typical operational decisions involve questions such as: Should we spend $100,000 to hire an outside firm to develop this component in order to save two months of development

EXHIBIT 2   Typical cash flows for a successful new product.

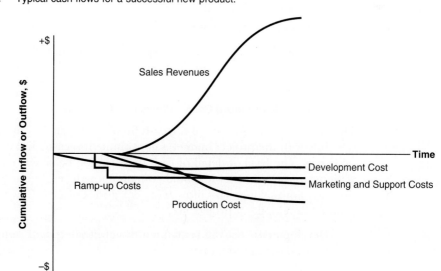

time? Should we launch the product in four months at a unit cost of $450 or wait until six months when we can reduce the cost to $400?

The analysis done at the beginning of a project can usually be updated with current information so that it does not have to be created in its entirety each time. Used in this way, the analysis becomes one of the information systems the team uses to manage the development project.

Economic analysis can be carried out by any member of the development team. In small companies, the project leader or one of the members of the core project team will implement the details of the analysis. In larger companies, a representative from a finance group may be appointed to assist the development team in performing this analysis. We emphasize that even when someone with formal training in financial modeling takes responsibility for this analysis, the entire team should fully understand the analysis and be involved in its formulation and use.

Methodology

We recommend the following four-step methodology for the economic analysis of a product development project:

1 Build a base-case financial model.

2 Perform a sensitivity analysis to understand the relationships between financial success and the key assumptions and variables of the model.

3 Use the sensitivity analysis to understand trade-offs.

4 Consider the influence of the qualitative factors on project success.

The balance of this chapter is organized around these four steps.

STEP 1: BUILD A BASE-CASE FINANCIAL MODEL

Constructing the base-case model consists of estimating the timing and magnitude of future cash flows and then computing the NPV of those cash flows.

Estimate the Timing and Magnitude of Future Cash Inflows and Outflows

The timing and magnitude of the cash flows is estimated by merging the project schedule with the project budget, sales volume forecasts, and estimated production costs. The level of detail of cash flows should be coarse enough to be convenient to work with, yet it should contain enough resolution to facilitate effective decision making. The most basic categories of cash flow for a typical new product development project are:

- Development cost (all remaining design, testing, and refinement costs up to production ramp-up)
- Ramp-up cost

- Marketing and support cost
- Production cost
- Sales revenues

Depending on the types of decisions the model will support, greater levels of detail for one or more areas may be required. More detailed modeling may consider these same five cash flows in greater detail, or it may consider other flows. Typical refinements include:

- Breakdown of production costs into direct costs and indirect costs (i.e., overhead).
- Breakdown of marketing and support costs into launch costs, promotion costs, direct sales costs, and service costs.
- Inclusion of tax effects, including the depreciation tax shield and investment tax credits. (Tax effects are typically considered in even simple financial modeling. For the sake of clarity, however, we omit the tax effects in our examples.)
- Inclusion of such miscellaneous inflows and outflows as working capital requirements, cannibalization (the impact of the new product on existing product sales), salvage costs, and opportunity costs.

The financial model we use in this chapter is simplified to include only the major cash flows that are typically considered in practice, but conceptually it is identical to more complex models. For a good discussion of most of the cash flows that a firm would ever consider in analyzing a product development project, see the discussion of financial analysis in Crawford (1994).

The numerical values of the cash flows come from budgets and other estimates obtained from the development team, the manufacturing organization, and the marketing organization. Exhibit 3 shows the relevant financial estimates for the CI-700. (These data have been disguised to protect Polaroid's proprietary financial information.) For a more detailed discussion of manufacturing costs, see the chapter "Design for Manufacturing." Note that all revenues and expenses to date are *sunk costs* and are irrelevant to NPV calculations. (The concept of sunk costs is reviewed in the appendix.)

EXHIBIT 3   CI-700 project budgets, sales volume forecasts, and production costs.

1. Development cost	$5 million
2. Ramp-up cost	$2 million
3. Marketing and support cost	$1 million/year
4. Unit production cost	$400/unit
5. Sales and production volume	20,000 units/year
6. Unit price	$800/unit

EXHIBIT 4   CI-700 project schedule from inception through market withdrawal.

In order to complete the model, the financial estimates must be merged with timing information. This can be done by considering the project schedule and sales plan. Exhibit 4 shows the project timing information in Gantt chart form for the CI-700. (For most projects, a time increment of months or quarters is most appropriate.) The remaining time to market is estimated to be five quarters, and product sales are anticipated to last 11 quarters.

A common method of representing project cash flow is a table. The rows of the table are the different cash flow categories, while the columns represent successive time periods. Usually this table is encoded in a computer spreadsheet to facilitate further analysis. For this example, we assume that the rate of cash flow for any category is constant across any time period (e.g., total development spending of $5 million over one year is allocated equally to each of the four quarters); however, the values can be arranged in any way that best represents the team's forecast of the cash flows. We multiply unit sales quantity by unit price to find the total product revenues in each period. We also multiply unit production quantity by unit production cost to find the total production cost in each period. Exhibit 5 illustrates the resulting table.

EXHIBIT 5   Merging the project financials and schedule into a cash flow table (all dollar values are in thousands in this and subsequent tables).

($ values in thousands)	Year 1 Q1	Q2	Q3	Q4	Year 2 Q1	Q2	Q3	Q4	Year 3 Q1	Q2	Q3	Q4	Year 4 Q1	Q2	Q3	Q4
Development cost	−1,250	−1,250	−1,250	−1,250												
Ramp-up cost				−1,000	−1,000											
Marketing & support cost					−250	−250	−250	−250	−250	−250	−250	−250	−250	−250	−250	−250
Production cost						−2,000	−2,000	−2,000	−2,000	−2,000	−2,000	−2,000	−2,000	−2,000	−2,000	−2,000
Production volume						5,000	5,000	5,000	5,000	5,000	5,000	5,000	5,000	5,000	5,000	5,000
Unit production cost						−0.4	−0.4	−0.4	−0.4	−0.4	−0.4	−0.4	−0.4	−0.4	−0.4	−0.4
Sales revenue						4,000	4,000	4,000	4,000	4,000	4,000	4,000	4,000	4,000	4,000	4,000
Sales volume						5,000	5,000	5,000	5,000	5,000	5,000	5,000	5,000	5,000	5,000	5,000
Unit price						0.8	0.8	0.8	0.8	0.8	0.8	0.8	0.8	0.8	0.8	0.8

Compute the Net Present Value of the Cash Flows

Computing the NPV requires that the net cash flow for each period be determined, and then that this cash flow be converted to its present value (its value in today's dollars). Consider, for example, the calculations for year 3, first quarter:

1 The period cash flow is the sum of inflows and outflows:

Marketing cost	$-250,000
Product revenues	4,000,000
Production cost	-2,000,000
Period cash flow	$1,750,000

2 The present value of this period cash flow discounted at 10 percent per year (2.5 percent per quarter) back to the first quarter of year 1 (a total of eight quarters) is $1,436,306. (The concepts of *present value* and *net present value* are reviewed in the appendix.)

$$\frac{\$1,750,000}{1.025^8} = \$1,436,306$$

3 Project NPV is the simple sum of the discounted cash flows for each of the periods, or $8,203,000. (Here and in the rest of the chapter we round financial figures to the nearest one thousand dollars.)

The Base-Case Financial Model Can Support Go/No-Go Decisions and Major Investment Decisions

The NPV of this project, according to the base-case model, is positive, so the model supports and is consistent with the decision to proceed with development. Such modeling can also be used to support major investment decisions. Say, for

EXHIBIT 6 Total cash flows, present values, and net present value.

($ values in thousands)	Year 1				Year 2				Year 3				Year 4			
	Q1	Q2	Q3	Q4	Q1	Q2	Q3	Q4	Q1	Q2	Q3	Q4	Q1	Q2	Q3	Q4
Development cost	-1,250	-1,250	-1,250	-1,250												
Ramp-up cost				-1,000	-1,000											
Marketing & support cost				-250	-250	-250	-250	-250	-250	-250	-250	-250	-250	-250	-250	-250
Production cost					-2,000	-2,000	-2,000	-2,000	-2,000	-2,000	-2,000	-2,000	-2,000	-2,000	-2,000	-2,000
Production volume					5,000	5,000	5,000	5,000	5,000	5,000	5,000	5,000	5,000	5,000	5,000	5,000
Unit production cost					-0.4	-0.4	-0.4	-0.4	-0.4	-0.4	-0.4	-0.4	-0.4	-0.4	-0.4	-0.4
Sales revenue					4,000	4,000	4,000	4,000	4,000	4,000	4,000	4,000	4,000	4,000	4,000	4,000
Sales volume					5,000	5,000	5,000	5,000	5,000	5,000	5,000	5,000	5,000	5,000	5,000	5,000
Unit price					0.8	0.8	0.8	0.8	0.8	0.8	0.8	0.8	0.8	0.8	0.8	0.8
Period Cash Flow	-1,250	-1,250	-1,250	-2,250	-1,250	1,750	1,750	1,750	1,750	1,750	1,750	1,750	1,750	1,750	1,750	1,750
PV Year 1, r = 10%	-1,250	-1,220	-1,190	-2,089	-1,132	1,547	1,509	1,472	1,436	1,401	1,367	1,334	1,301	1,269	1,239	1,208
Project NPV	8,203															

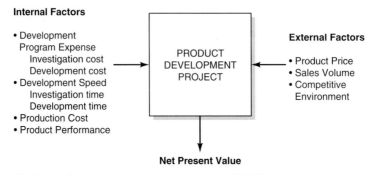

Internal Factors

- Development
  Program Expense
    Investigation cost
    Development cost
- Development Speed
    Investigation time
    Development time
- Production Cost
- Product Performance

PRODUCT
DEVELOPMENT
PROJECT

External Factors

- Product Price
- Sales Volume
- Competitive
  Environment

Net Present Value

EXHIBIT 7   Key factors influencing product development profitability.

example, that Polaroid were deciding between two different production facilities with different ramp-up, production, and support costs. They could develop a model for each of the two scenarios and then compare the NPVs. The scenario with the higher NPV would better support the investment decision. We now consider sensitivity analysis as a technique for readily understanding multiple scenarios for ongoing product development decisions.

STEP 2: SENSITIVITY ANALYSIS

Sensitivity analysis uses the financial model to answer "what if" questions by calculating the change in NPV corresponding to a change in the factors included in the model. Both internal and external factors influence project value. *Internal factors* are those over which the development team has a large degree of influence, including development program expense, development speed, production cost, and product performance. *External factors* are those that the team cannot arbitrarily change, including the competitive environment (e.g., market response, actions of competitors), sales volume, and product price. (There may be disagreement over whether price is an internal or external factor. In either case, there is little disagreement that price is strongly influenced by the prices of competitive products and that it is coupled to sales volume.) While external factors are not directly controlled by product development teams, they are often influenced by the internal factors. The external and internal factors are shown in Exhibit 7.

Development Cost Example

As a first example, let us consider the sensitivity of NPV to changes in development cost. By making incremental changes to development cost while holding other factors constant, we can see the incremental impact on project NPV. For example, what will be the change in NPV if development cost is decreased by 20 percent? A 20 percent decrease would lower the total development spending

($ values in thousands)	Year 1				Year 2				Year 3				Year 4			
	Q1	Q2	Q3	Q4	Q1	Q2	Q3	Q4	Q1	Q2	Q3	Q4	Q1	Q2	Q3	Q4
Development cost	−1,000	−1,000	−1,000	−1,000												
Ramp-up cost				−1,000	−1,000											
Marketing & support cost					−250	−250	−250	−250	−250	−250	−250	−250	−250	−250	−250	−250
Production cost						−2,000	−2,000	−2,000	−2,000	−2,000	−2,000	−2,000	−2,000	−2,000	−2,000	−2,000
Production volume						5,000	5,000	5,000	5,000	5,000	5,000	5,000	5,000	5,000	5,000	5,000
Unit production cost						−0.4	−0.4	−0.4	−0.4	−0.4	−0.4	−0.4	−0.4	−0.4	−0.4	−0.4
Sales revenue						4,000	4,000	4,000	4,000	4,000	4,000	4,000	4,000	4,000	4,000	4,000
Sales volume						5,000	5,000	5,000	5,000	5,000	5,000	5,000	5,000	5,000	5,000	5,000
Unit price						0.8	0.8	0.8	0.8	0.8	0.8	0.8	0.8	0.8	0.8	0.8
Period Cash Flow	−1,000	−1,000	−1,000	−2,000	−1,250	1,750	1,750	1,750	1,750	1,750	1,750	1,750	1,750	1,750	1,750	1,750
PV Year 1, r = 10%	−1,000	−976	−952	−1,857	−1,132	1,547	1,509	1,472	1,436	1,401	1,367	1,334	1,301	1,269	1,239	1,208
Project NPV	9,167															

EXHIBIT 8 CI-700 financial model with 20 percent decrease in development spending.

from $5 million to $4 million. If development time remains one year, then the spending per quarter would decrease from $1.25 million to $1 million. This change is simply entered in the model and the resulting NPV is calculated. This change to the CI-700's base-case model is shown in Exhibit 8.

A 20 percent decrease in development cost will increase NPV to $9,167,000. This represents a dollar increase of $964,000 and a percentage increase of 11.8 in NPV. This is an extremely simple case: we assume we can achieve the same project goals by spending $1 million less on development, and we therefore have increased the project value by the present value of the $1 million in savings accrued over a time period of one year. The CI-700 development cost sensitivity analysis for a range of changes is shown in Exhibit 9. The values in the table are computed by entering the changes corresponding to each scenario into the base-case model and noting the results. It is often useful to know the absolute dollar changes in NPV as well as the relative percentage changes, so we show both in the sensitivity table.

EXHIBIT 9 CI-700's development cost sensitivities.

Change in Development Cost, %	Development Cost, $ Thousands	Change in Development Cost, $ Thousands	Change in NPV, %	NPV, $ Thousands	Change in NPV, $ Thousands
50	7,500	2,500	−29.4	5,791	−2,412
20	6,000	1,000	−11.8	7,238	−964
10	5,500	500	−5.9	7,721	−482
base	5,000	base	0.0	8,203	0
−10	4,500	−500	5.9	8,685	482
−20	4,000	−1,000	11.8	9,167	964
−50	2,500	−2,500	29.4	10,615	2,412

Development Time Example

As a second example, we calculate the development time sensitivities for the CI-700 model. Consider the impact on project NPV of a 25 percent increase in development time. A 25 percent increase in development time would raise the time from four quarters to five quarters. This increase in development time would also delay the start of production ramp-up, marketing efforts, and product sales. To perform the sensitivity analysis, we must make several assumptions about the changes. We assume the same total amount of development cost, even though we will increase the time period over which the spending occurs, thus lowering the rate of spending from $1.25 million to $1.0 million per quarter. We also assume that there is a fixed window for sales which starts as soon as the product enters the market and ends in the fourth quarter of year 4. In effect we assume we can sell product from the time we are able to introduce it until a fixed date in the future. Note that these assumptions are unique to this development project. Different product development projects would require different assumptions as appropriate. For example, we might have instead assumed that the sales window simply shifts in time by one quarter. The change to the CI-700's financial model is shown in Exhibit 10.

Exhibit 11 presents the development time sensitivities for a range of changes. We can see that a 25 percent increase in development time will decrease NPV to $6,764,000. This represents a decrease in NPV of $1,439,000, or 17.5 percent.

We recommend that sensitivities be computed for each of the external and internal factors, with the exception of the competitive environment, which is not explicitly contained in the base-case model. These sensitivity analyses inform the team which factors in the model have a substantial influence on NPV. This information is useful in helping the team understand which factors should be studied

EXHIBIT 10   CI-700 financial model with 25 percent increase in development time.

($ values in thousands)	Year 1 Q1	Q2	Q3	Q4	Year 2 Q1	Q2	Q3	Q4	Year 3 Q1	Q2	Q3	Q4	Year 4 Q1	Q2	Q3	Q4
Development cost	−1,000	−1,000	−1,000	−1,000	−1,000											
Ramp-up cost					−1,000	−1,000										
Marketing & support cost						−250	−250	−250	−250	−250	−250	−250	−250	−250	−250	−250
Production cost							−2,000	−2,000	−2,000	−2,000	−2,000	−2,000	−2,000	−2,000	−2,000	−2,000
Production volume							5,000	5,000	5,000	5,000	5,000	5,000	5,000	5,000	5,000	5,000
Unit production cost							−0.4	−0.4	−0.4	−0.4	−0.4	−0.4	−0.4	−0.4	−0.4	−0.4
Sales revenue							4,000	4,000	4,000	4,000	4,000	4,000	4,000	4,000	4,000	4,000
Sales volume							5,000	5,000	5,000	5,000	5,000	5,000	5,000	5,000	5,000	5,000
Unit price							0.8	0.8	0.8	0.8	0.8	0.8	0.8	0.8	0.8	0.8
Period Cash Flow	−1,000	−1,000	−1,000	−1,000	−2,000	−1,250	1,750	1,750	1,750	1,750	1,750	1,750	1,750	1,750	1,750	1,750
PV Year 1, r = 10%	−1,000	−976	−952	−929	−1,812	−1,105	1,509	1,472	1,436	1,401	1,367	1,334	1,301	1,269	1,239	1,208
Project NPV	6,764															

Change in Development Time, %	Development Time, Quarters	Change in Development Time, Quarters	Change in NPV, %	NPV, $ Thousands	Change in NPV, $ Thousands
50	6	2	−34.6	5,363	−2,840
25	5	1	−17.5	6,764	−1,439
base	4	base	0.0	8,203	0
−25	3	−1	18.0	9,678	1,475
−50	2	−2	36.4	11,190	2,987

EXHIBIT 11 CI-700's development time sensitivities.

in more detail in order to refine and improve the base-case model. The information is also useful in supporting the operating decisions of the team, as discussed in the next step.

STEP 3: USE SENSITIVITY ANALYSIS TO UNDERSTAND PROJECT TRADE-OFFS

Why would a product development team want to change the factors under its control? For instance, why should development time be increased if the change lowers the NPV of the project? Typically, the development team will make such a change only if some other offsetting gain is expected, such as a better-quality product with higher sales volumes. We therefore need to understand the relative magnitude of these financial interactions.

Six Potential Interactions

Development teams attempt to manage six potential interactions between the internally driven factors. These potential interactions are shown schematically in Exhibit 12. The potential interaction between any two internal factors depends on the characteristics of the specific product context. In many cases the interac-

EXHIBIT 12 Potential interactions between internally driven factors. (Adapted from Smith, Preston G., and Donald G. Reinertsen, *Developing Products in Half the Time*, Van Nostrand Reinhold, New York, 1991.)

Change in Sales Volume, %	Sales Volume, $ Thousands	Change in Sales Volume	Change in NPV, %	NPV, $ Thousands	Change in NPV, $ Thousands
30	6,500	1,500	63.0	13,375	5,172
20	6,000	1,000	42.0	11,651	3,448
10	5,500	500	21.0	9,927	1,724
base	5,000	base	0.0	8,203	0
−10	4,500	−500	−21.0	6,479	−1,724
−20	4,000	−1,000	−42.0	4,755	−3,448
−30	3,500	−1,500	−63.0	3,031	−5,172

EXHIBIT 13   CI-700's sales volume sensitivities.

tions are trade-offs. For example, decreasing development time may lead to lower product performance. Increased product performance may require additional product cost. However, some of these interactions are more complex than a simple trade-off. For example, decreasing product development time may require an increase in development spending, yet extending development time may also lead to an increase in cost if the extension is caused by a delay in a critical task rather than by a planned extension of the schedule.

In general these interactions are important because of the linkage between the internal factors and the external factors. For example, increasing development cost or time may enhance product performance and therefore increase sales volume or allow higher prices. Decreasing development time may allow the product to reach the market sooner and thus increase sales volume.

While accurate modeling of externally driven factors (e.g., price, sales volume) is often very difficult, the quantitative model can nevertheless support decision making. Recall from our initial examples that the CI-700 development team was considering increasing development spending in order to develop a higher-quality product, which they hoped would lead to greater sales volume. The quantitative model can support this decision by answering the question of how much the sales volume would have to increase to justify the additional spending on development. We have calculated the sensitivity of NPV to changes in development cost (see Exhibit 9). We can also calculate the sensitivity of NPV to changes in sales volume (Exhibit 13). Say that the CI-700 development team is considering a 10 percent increase in development cost. From Exhibit 9 we found that this increase will decrease NPV by 5.9 percent.

Now, what increase in volume would be necessary to at least compensate for the decrease in NPV? From Exhibit 13 we know that a 10 percent increase in sales volume would increase NPV by 21 percent. It follows, under assumptions of linearity, that a 2.8 percent ($10 \times 5.9/21.0$) increase in sales volume would increase NPV by 5.9 percent. To summarize, a 10 percent *increase* in development cost would *decrease* NPV by 5.9 percent. A 2.8 percent *increase* in sales volume is needed to offset the drop. While the precise impact of the increased development spending upon sales volume is not known, the model does provide a helpful guide for what magnitude of sales volume increase is needed to sustain particular increases in development cost.

Trade-off Rules

The near linearity of many sensitivity analyses allows the team to compute some *trade-off rules* to inform day-to-day decision making. These rules take the form of the cost per unit change in the internal and external factors. For example, what is the cost of a one-month delay in development time? What is the cost of a 10 percent development budget overrun? What is the cost of a $1 per unit increase in manufacturing cost? The trade-off rules are easily computed from the base-case model and can be used to inform the team of the relative magnitude of the sensitivities of the project profitability on factors under its control. Exhibit 14 contains the rules for the CI-700.

The trade-off rules inform the original questions posed in the chapter introduction. The team decided that waiting for the software that would allow the printer to be used with both Apple Macintosh and IBM PC-compatible computers would delay product introduction by two months. It was calculated that the delay would have an approximate cost of $960,000. Rather than wait, the team reasoned that it could introduce the product before all printer drivers were available as long as the drivers were offered as soon as they were available. The film development group at Polaroid estimated that the development of a new print medium would cost more than $1 million and would take at least one year. The team decided that these time and budget penalties did not warrant the marginal increase in print size and quality that would be enabled by the new medium. Finally, the team felt that the reliability of the product could be dramatically improved with the addition of only one engineer and one technician to the team. This additional cost was expected to be approximately $100,000 for the

EXHIBIT 14 Trade-off rules for the CI-700 project.

Factor	Trade-off Rule	Comments
Development time	$480,000 per month change	Assumes a fixed window of opportunity for sales.
Sales volume	$1,724,000 per 10% change	Increasing sales is a powerful way to increase profits; 10% is 500 units/quarter.
Product cost or sales price	$43,000 per $1 change in cost or price	A $1 increase in price or a $1 decrease in cost, each results in a $1 increase in unit profit margins.
Development cost	$482,000 per 10% change	A dollar spent or saved on development is worth the present value of that dollar; 10% is $500,000.

remainder of the project. The team noted that they would have to increase sales by only 0.6 percent to justify this investment. Reliability was identified as a key customer need, and so the team chose to aggressively pursue increased reliability.

Limitations of Quantitative Analysis

Financial modeling and sensitivity analysis are powerful tools for supporting product development decisions, but these techniques have important limitations. One school of thought believes that rigorous financial analyses are required to bring discipline and control to the product development process. However, detractors argue that quantitative analysis suffers from some of the following problems:

- *It focuses only on measurable quantities.* Quantitative techniques like NPV emphasize and rely on that which is measurable. However, many critical factors impacting product development projects are difficult to measure accurately. In effect, quantitative techniques encourage investment in measurable assets and discourage investment in intangible assets.

- *It depends on validity of assumptions and data.* Product development teams may be lulled into a sense of security by the seemingly precise result of an NPV calculation. Financial analyses such as the ones we have performed in this chapter may seem to provide precise estimates of product development project value. However, such *precision in no way implies accuracy*. We can develop a highly sophisticated financial model of a product development project which computes project NPV to the fifth decimal place, yet if the assumptions and data of our model are not correct, the value calculated will not be correct. Consider the CI-700 development time sensitivity example's assumption of a fixed product sales window. This assumption was useful, but its integrity can easily be questioned. Indeed, a different assumption could give dramatically different results.

- *Bureaucracy reduces productivity.* Detractors of financial analysis assert that such activities provide a high level of planning and control at the expense of product development productivity. According to detractors, extensive planning and review guarantees that a brilliantly conceived, well-engineered product will reach the market after its market window has already closed. Detractors also argue that overzealously applied "professional" management techniques stifle the product development process. Potentially productive development time is devoted to preparation of analyses and meetings. The cumulative effect of this planning and review can be a ballooning development process.

These concerns are generally quite valid. However, in our opinion, they are largely associated with the blind application of the results of the quantitative analysis or arise from the combination of financial analysis with an already stifling bureaucracy. We reject the notion that quantitative analysis should not be done just because problems can arise from the blind application of the results. Rather, development teams should understand the strengths and limitations of the techniques and should be fully aware of how the models work and on what assumptions they are based. Furthermore, qualitative analysis, as discussed in the next section, can remedy some of the inherent weaknesses in the quantitative techniques.

STEP 4: CONSIDER THE INFLUENCE OF THE QUALITATIVE FACTORS ON PROJECT SUCCESS

Many factors influencing development projects are difficult to quantify because they are complex or uncertain. We refer to such factors as *qualitative* factors. After providing a conceptual framework for qualitative analysis, we use examples from the CI-700 to illustrate how the analysis is carried out.

Consider the following questions about the CI-700 project: Will knowledge gained from the CI-700 development spill over and be of benefit to other Polaroid development projects? How will competitors react to the introduction of the CI-700? Will competitors modify their own development efforts in response to Polaroid's actions? Will there be significant fluctuations in the dollar/yen exchange rate which change the cost of component parts?

Our quantitative model implicitly accounts for these and many other issues with several broad assumptions. The model assumes that decisions made by the project team do not affect actions of groups external to the project, or alternately that the external forces do not change the team's actions. This important assumption of our model is common to many other financial models and is called the *ceteris paribus* (other things being equal) assumption.

Projects Interact with the Firm, the Market, and the Macro Environment

Decisions made within a project in general do have important consequences for the firm as a whole, for competitors and customers in the market, and even for the macroeconomic (macro) environment in which the market operates (Exhibit 15). Similarly, events and actions outside of a development project often significantly impact its value. Qualitative analysis focuses largely on these interactions. The most basic approach to qualitative analysis is to consider (1) the interactions between the project and the firm as a whole, (2) the interactions between the project and the market in which the product will be sold, and (3) the interactions between the project and the macro environment.

Interactions between the Project and the Firm as a Whole   One assumption embedded in the quantitative model is that firm profit will be maximized if project profit is maximized. However, development decisions must be made in the context of the firm as a whole. The two key interactions between the project and the firm are *externalities* and *strategic fit*.

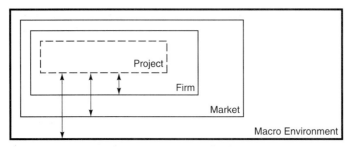

EXHIBIT 15   The broader context of a development project.

- *Externalities:* An externality is an "unpriced" cost or benefit imposed on one part of the firm by the actions of a second; costs are known as negative externalities and benefits as positive externalities. As an example of a positive externality, development learning on one project may benefit other current or future projects but is paid for by the first project. How should the other projects account for such benefits gained at no additional cost? How should the first project account for resources spent which benefit not only itself, but also other current or future projects?

- *Strategic fit:* Decisions of the development team must not only benefit the project, but also be consistent with the firm's technology and competitive strategies. For example, how well does a proposed new product, technology, or feature fit with the firm's resources and objectives? Is it compatible with the firm's emphasis on technical excellence? Is it compatible with the firm's emphasis on uniqueness?

Because of their complexity and uncertainty, externalities and strategic fit are very difficult to quantify. This does not mean these issues should not be considered; rather, they must be considered qualitatively.

Interactions between the Project and the Market   We have modeled explicitly only price and volume as the key externally driven factors. In effect, we have held the actions and reactions of the market constant. To model project value accurately, we must relax the *ceteris paribus* assumption to recognize that a development team's decisions impact the market and that market events impact the development project. The market environment is impacted by the actions of not only the development team but also three other groups:

- *Competitors:* Competitors may provide products in direct competition or products which compete indirectly as substitutes.

- *Customers:* Customers' expectations, incomes, or tastes may change. Changes may be independent or may be driven by new conditions in markets for complementary or substitute products.

- *Suppliers:* Suppliers of inputs to the new product are subject to their own markets' competitive pressures. These pressures may, indirectly through the value chain, impact the new product.

Actions and reactions of these groups most often impact expected price and volume, but they can have second-order effects as well. For example, consider a new competitor that has rapid product development cycles and that seems to value market share rather than short-term profitability. Clearly, the entrance of such a new competitor would change our expected price and volume. Further, we may attempt to accelerate our own development efforts in response. Thus, the competitor's actions may impact not only our sales volume forecasts but also our planned development schedule.

Interactions between the Project and the Macro Environment   We must relax the *ceteris paribus* assumption to take into account key macro factors:

- *Major economic shifts:* Examples of typical major economic shifts which impact the value of development projects are changes in foreign exchange rates or in input prices.
- *Government regulations:* New regulations can destroy a product development opportunity. On the other hand, a shift in the regulatory structure of an industry can also spawn entire new industries.
- *Social trends:* As with government regulations, new social concerns such as increased environmental awareness can destroy existing industries or create new ones.

Macro factors can have important impacts on development project value. However, their effects are difficult to model quantitatively because of inherent complexity and uncertainty.

The product development team for the CI-700 faced many qualitative issues during development of the product. We present three of the key qualitative issues that the Polaroid team encountered and describe the impacts of these issues on the project. The examples illustrate not only the limitations of quantitative analysis but also the importance of qualitative analysis.

Carrying Out Qualitative Analysis

For most project teams, the most appropriate qualitative analysis methodology is simply to consider and discuss the interactions between the project and the firm, the project and the market, and the project and the macro environment. Then the team considers these interactions in concert with the results of the quantitative analysis in order to determine the most appropriate relative emphasis on development speed, development expense, manufacturing cost, and product performance. We provide three examples below of the qualitative analysis for the CI-700.

While we believe this informal approach is most appropriate for decisions made at the level of the project team, more structured techniques are available.

Strategic analysis, game theory, and scenario analysis techniques can assist in carrying out the analysis. References for each of these techniques are included in the bibliography.

Example 1: Decrease in the Price of a Substitute Product

Color laser printers are a substitute product for the CI-700. While color laser printers are much more costly than the CI-700, they limit the potential of the CI-700's market by placing a ceiling on the price Polaroid can charge. During the CI-700 development, manufacturers of color laser printers achieved several important technological breakthroughs. The advances allowed the manufacturers to offer color laser printers at significantly lower prices. The Polaroid team was faced with a change in the competitive environment which was caused by others and which invalidated fundamental assumptions of the financial model for the CI-700.

In this example, it is clear that the CI-700 project cannot be considered in isolation. The original sales volume forecasts incorporated implicit assumptions about the color laser printer market, but the assumptions were invalidated by advances in color laser printer technology. While the color laser printer breakthrough would have been difficult to predict, quantitative analysis helped the CI-700 development team understand the sensitivity of the value of the project to this development. By using the model to estimate the sensitivity of NPV to changes in sales volume, the team was able to grasp quickly the magnitude of the change in project value. The combination of quantitative and qualitative analysis convinced the team they had to move more quickly and to further reduce the cost of the product for the project to remain viable.

Example 2: Increased Competition in a Complementary Product Market

The demand for the CI-700 is closely linked to the prices of personal computers (PCs). PCs are said to be complementary products to the CI-700 because a decrease in the price of PCs increases demand for the CI-700. Cheaper PCs both increase PC sales and allow buyers to afford additional peripheral products such as the CI-700. Thus, a decrease in the price of PCs would increase the value of the CI-700 project.

During the CI-700 development project, intense competition in the PC market further increased with new entrants and the economic recession. In this case, the Polaroid team was faced with a change in the competitive environment caused both by others and by macro factors.

Again, while the changes in the PC market were difficult to predict, quantitative analysis helped the CI-700 development team understand how project value was impacted. By using the model to estimate the sensitivity of NPV to changes in sales volume, the team was able to grasp quickly the magnitude of the change in project value, which they hoped would partially offset the pressure from the falling prices for color laser printers.

Example 3: The "Option" Value of Creating a Good Platform Product

The CI-700 was the first product of its kind produced by Polaroid, and the development team recognized that many of their development decisions would impact potential future generations of the product line. For example, the ease with which future generation products could be built around the same basic technological "platform" depended upon design decisions made in the CI-700 project. The team could choose to increase development spending and development time in order to facilitate the development of potential future generation products, even if doing so would not make economic sense in the context of a single product. They chose, however, to push ahead quickly with the CI-700 without extreme efforts to accommodate future models. The argument was that the future of the market was so uncertain that the risk of not getting to market in time outweighed the potential usefulness of the product as a platform for future products.

SUMMARY

Product development teams must make many decisions in the course of a development project. Economic analysis is a useful tool for supporting this decision making.

- The methodology consists of four steps:
  1 Build a base-case financial model.
  2 Perform a sensitivity analysis to understand the relationships between financial success and the key assumptions and variables of the model.
  3 Use the sensitivity analysis to understand project trade-offs.
  4 Consider the influence of qualitative factors on project success.

- Quantitative analysis using NPV techniques is practiced widely in business. The technique forces product development teams to look objectively at their projects and their decisions. At the very least, they must go through the process of creating realistic project schedules and budgets. Financial modeling provides a method for quantitatively understanding the key profit drivers of the project.

- Quantitative techniques such as financial modeling and analysis rest upon assumptions about the external environment. This environment is constantly changing and may be influenced by a development team's decisions or by other uncontrollable factors. Further, quantitative analysis, by its very nature, considers only that which is measurable; yet, many key factors influencing the project are highly complex or uncertain and are thus difficult to quantify.

- Qualitative analysis emphasizes the importance of such difficult-to-quantify issues by asking specifically what the interactions are between the project and the rest of the firm, the market, and the macro environment.

- Together, quantitative and qualitative techniques can help ensure that the team makes economically sound development decisions.

REFERENCES AND BIBLIOGRAPHY

For an analytical approach to new-product development and a comprehensive view of the cash flows that may be considered in financial analysis, see:

Crawford, Merle C., *New Products Management,* fourth edition, Richard D. Irwin Inc., Homewood, IL, 1994. ISBN 0-256-12152-4.

A more detailed discussion of estimating "cross-factor" effects, especially the time-cost trade-off, is included in:

Graves, Samuel B., "The Time-Cost Tradeoff in Research and Development: A Review," *Engineering Costs and Production Economics,* Vol. 16, 1989, pp. 1–9.

For a thorough review of discounted cash flow techniques as well as option theory from a general financial perspective, the classic text on corporate finance is:

Brealey, Richard A., and Stewart C. Myers, *Principles of Corporate Finance,* fourth edition, McGraw-Hill, New York, 1991. ISBN 0-070-07405-4.

For a thorough discussion of how to model the economics of development time see:

Smith, Preston G., and Donald G. Reinertsen, *Developing Products in Half the Time,* Van Nostrand Reinhold, New York, 1991. ISBN 0-442-00243-2.

Recent management literature has criticized business schools and MBA programs for their lack of relevance. In particular, MBAs are criticized for their reliance on quantitative techniques such as discounted cash flow. An interesting case study reviewing the issues is:

Linder, Jane C., and H. Jeff Smith, "The Complex Case of Management Education," *Harvard Business Review,* September-October 1992, pp. 16–33.

Michael Porter's strategic analysis techniques have become standard fare for business school students. One of his most influential works on strategic analysis is:

Porter, Michael E., *Competitive Strategy: Techniques for Analyzing Industries and Competitors,* The Free Press, New York, 1980. ISBN 0-029-25360-8.

Scenario analysis is a technique originally developed by Royal Dutch Shell for planning under uncertainty. Porter presents a general structured approach to scenario analysis in:

Porter, Michael E., *Competitive Advantage: Creating and Sustaining Superior Performance,* The Free Press, New York, 1985. ISBN 0-029-25090-0.

Game theory can be used to analyze competitive interactions. A view of strategic analysis and game theory from a microeconomic perspective is found in:

Oster, Sharon M., *Modern Competitive Analysis,* Oxford University Press, New York, 1990. ISBN 0-195-05845-3.

EXERCISES

1 List five reasons firms may choose to pursue a product even if the quantitative analysis reveals a negative NPV.

2 Build a quantitative model to analyze the development and sale of a bicycle light. Assume that you could sell 20,000 units per year for five years at a sales price (wholesale) of $20 per unit and a manufacturing cost of $10 per unit. How much development spending could such a project justify? Assume that production ramp-up expenses would be $20,000, ongoing marketing and support costs would be $2,000 per month, and development would take another 12 months.

3 Compute the trade-off rules for the case described in Exercise 2.

THOUGHT QUESTIONS

1 Can you think of successful products that would never have been developed if their creators had relied exclusively on a quantitative financial model to justify their efforts? Do these products share any characteristics?

2 One model of the impact of a delay in product introduction is that sales are simply shifted later in time. Another model is that some of the sales are pushed beyond the "window of opportunity" and are lost forever. Can you suggest other models for the implications of an extension of product development time? Is such an extension ever beneficial?

3 How would you use the quantitative analysis methodology to capture the economic performance of an entire line of products to be developed and introduced over several years?

APPENDIX A: Time Value of Money and the Net Present Value Technique

Net present value (NPV) is an intuitive and powerful concept. In essence, NPV is simply a recognition of the fact that a dollar today is worth more than a dollar tomorrow. NPV calculations evaluate the value today (*present value*) of some future income or expense. Say that a bank will give an interest rate of 8 percent per time period (it may be useful to think of the time period as being a quarter or a year long). If we invest $100 today for one time period at an interest rate of 8 percent, how much will the bank pay out after one time period? If we let r be the interest rate and C be the amount invested, then the amount received after one time period is:

$$(1 + r) \times C = (1 + 0.08) \times 100 = (1.08) \times 100 = \$108$$

Thus, if we invest $100 for one time period at an interest rate of 8 percent, we will receive $108 at the end of the time period. In other words, $100 today is worth $108 received in the next time period.

Now, let's say that we have invested some amount, C', for one time period at an interest rate r. Let's also say that after the one time period, the amount received back is $100, and the interest rate is 8 percent. How much, then, was invested originally? We can find C', the original investment, by doing the reverse of what we did in the previous example:

$$(1 + r) \times C' = \$100$$

$$C' = \frac{\$100}{1 + r} = \frac{\$100}{1 + 0.08} = \frac{\$100}{1.08} = \$92.59$$

Thus, if we invest $92.59 for one time period at an interest rate of 8 percent, we will receive $100 at the end of the time period. In other words, $92.59 today is worth $100 received in the next time period.

We have just shown how a dollar today is worth more than a dollar tomorrow. Of course, $100 today is worth $100. But what is $100 received *next* time period worth in *today's* dollars? The answer is $92.59 as we showed in the last example. Stated another way, the *present value* of $100 received in the next time period is $92.59 at an interest rate of 8 percent. So, present value is the value in today's dollars of some income received or expense paid out in a future period.

Now let's look at the result of investing $100 at 8 percent for longer periods:

One time period: $(1 + r) \times C = (1 + 0.08) \times \$100 = \$108$
Two time periods: $(1 + r) \times (1 + r) \times \$100 = (1 + 0.08)^2 \times \$100 = \$116.64$
Three time periods: $(1 + r) \times (1 + r) \times (1 + r) \times \$100$
                              $= (1 + 0.08)^3 \times \$100 = \$125.97$

As we did earlier, let's find the present value of three separate investments of $100 received after one, two, and three time periods:

One time period: $(1 + r) \times C' = \$100$

$$C' = \frac{\$100}{1 + 0.08} = \$92.59$$

The present value of $100 received next time period is $92.59.

Two time periods: $(1 + r) \times (1 + r) \times C' = \$100$

$$C' = \frac{\$100}{(1 + 0.08)^2} = \$85.73$$

The present value of $100 received after two time periods is $85.73.

Three time periods: $(1 + r) \times (1 + r) \times (1 + r) \times C' = \$100$

$$C' = \frac{\$100}{(1 + 0.08)^3} = \$79.38$$

The present value of $100 received after three time periods is $79.38.

We found the present value of these three separate investments. Let's say instead that we had one investment that paid out $100 in each of time periods one, two, and three. What would that investment be worth today? The answer is simply the sum of the individual present values, or $257.70. The sum of the present values is called the *net present value*, or NPV. NPV is the present value of all cash inflows and all cash outflows. The present value of a cash *outflow* is just the negative of a cash *inflow* of the same amount.

We can summarize the present value calculation into a convenient formula. The present value (PV) of an amount C received (or paid out) t time periods from now is:

$$PV = \frac{C}{(1 + r)^t}$$

Some calculators have a special present value function on them which can do the calculations quickly. Computer spreadsheet programs such as Lotus 1-2-3 and Microsoft Excel have special financial functions which automatically do the present value calculations. The information required for these special functions is the future amount paid out, the interest rate, and the number of time periods of the investment.

What Interest Rate Should We Use?

The interest rate (also called the discount factor or hurdle rate) to use is our own or our company's "opportunity cost of capital." It is called the opportunity cost of capital because it is the return forgone by investing in the project rather than other investments. Stated another way, the discount factor is the reward that investors demand for accepting delayed payment. A project which has a positive NPV must be earning more than the opportunity cost of capital and is thus a "good" investment. Note that many firms apply a constant hurdle rate to all their investment decisions. In the early 1990s most firms were using discount factors of 10 to 20 percent.

Sunk Costs Are Irrelevant for Net Present Value Calculations

In the context of product development decision making, costs that have already been incurred are termed *sunk costs*. Because sunk costs are past and irreversible outflows, they cannot be affected by present or future decisions, so they should be ignored for NPV calculations. To clarify this point, let's consider an example of the familiar "cut our losses" argument: "We've already spent over $600 million and 9 years with no product to show for it, and you want me to approve another $90 million? That's crazy!" While this type of argument might sound logical, in fact the amount of money already spent is not important for the decision of whether or not to spend $90 million more. What is important is how much extra profit will be gained from investing the additional $90 million. Say that the expected profit from product sales is $350 million. Let's look at the NPV of the two options (assume all numbers given are present values):

"Cut Our Losses"		"Invest $90 Million More"	
Additional amount invested:	$0	Additional amount invested:	−$90
Profits from product sales:	0	Profits from product sales:	350
NPV of "cut losses" decision:	$0	NPV of "invest" decision:	$260
Total invested:	−$600	Total invested:	−$690
Total project return:	−$600	Total project return:	−$340

Because the "invest" decision has a positive NPV, the firm should proceed. While it is clear that the firm will lose money on the project in either case, the $600 million already spent is a sunk cost and should not impact the invest-or-cut-losses decision. Of course, the sunk cost argument is a cold analytical perspective; there is a saying that "sunk costs are only relevant to the manager who sunk them." Project managers with a long record of negative total project returns may find that sunk costs are extremely relevant to their ability to get support for future projects.

Dealing with Uncertainty in the Cash Inflow and Outflow Estimates

Product development projects face many perils. For example, we may think that the manufacturing costs for a particular new product will be $40 per unit. However, the cost could be much higher or it might even be lower—we do not know for sure until the product is actually built. We have made sales forecasts for our new product, but the forecasts depend on (among other things) when our competitors get their versions on the market, and we will not know that information until their products are actually introduced. These types of uncertainties that are peculiar to a project are called *project-specific risks*.

How should project-specific risks be accounted for? Some development teams add a "fudge factor" to the discount rate to offset uncertainty about the outcomes. However, such fudge factors are invariably arbitrary and are usually used because of inadequate forecasting of cash flows. Even worse, a fudge factor in the discount rate would be applied uniformly to both certain and uncertain cash flows. Often, fudge factors are used because teams do not want to confront the true probabilities of bad outcomes.

Instead of using such arbitrary adjustments, development teams should perform realistic forecasting of cash flows. Forecasts should be supplemented with careful sensitivity analysis to understand the impact of the full range of possible outcomes for the uncertain factors. In sum, project-specific risks should be considered only in the expected cash flows and not in the discount rate.

Parenthetically, there is a second type of risk, *market risk*, which is not project-specific. Market risk stems from the fact that there are economy-wide perils which threaten all businesses and projects. How should such market risks be accounted for? There are entire books on calculating market risk; however, for our purposes it suffices to say that market risk is typically accounted for by inflating the discount rate.

For a more thorough discussion of present value techniques and related issues, see Brealey and Myers (1991).

MANAGING PRODUCT DEVELOPMENT PROJECTS

Developed in collaboration with Stephen Raab.

EXHIBIT 1   The Cheetah microfilm cartridge. (Courtesy of Eastman Kodak Company.)

A manufacturer of microfilm imaging equipment approached the Eastman Kodak Company to design and supply the microfilm cartridges for use with a new machine under development (Exhibit 1). The target specifications were similar to previous products developed by the cartridge group at Kodak. However, in contrast to the usual 24-month development time, the customer needed prototype cartridges for demonstration at a trade show in just 8 months, and production was to begin 4 months later. Kodak accepted this challenge of cutting its normal development time in half and called its efforts the Cheetah Project. Effective project management was crucial to the successful completion of the project.

For all but the simplest products, product development involves many people completing many different tasks. Successful product development projects result in high-quality, low-cost products while making efficient use of time and money. Project management is the activity of planning and coordinating resources and tasks to achieve these goals.

Project management activities occur during *project planning* and *project execution*. Project planning involves scheduling the project tasks and determining resource requirements. The project plan is first laid out during the concept development phase, although it is a dynamic entity and continues to evolve throughout the development process.

Project execution involves coordinating and facilitating the myriad tasks required to complete the project in the face of inevitable unanticipated events and the arrival of new information. Execution is just as important as planning; many teams fail because they do not remain focused on their goals for the duration of the project.

This chapter contains five remaining sections. We first present the fundamentals of task dependencies and timing, along with three tools for representing relationships among project tasks. In the second section we show how these principles are used to develop an effective product development plan. In the third section we provide a set of guidelines for completing projects more quickly. After that, we discuss project execution, and finally we present ideas about project evaluation and continuous improvement.

UNDERSTANDING AND REPRESENTING TASKS

Product development projects involve the completion of hundreds or even thousands of tasks. This section discusses some of the fundamental characteristics of interacting tasks—the "basic physics" of projects. We also present three ways to represent the tasks in a project.

Sequential, Parallel, and Coupled Tasks

Exhibit 2 displays the tasks for three portions of the Cheetah project. The tasks are represented by boxes and the dependencies among the tasks are represent-

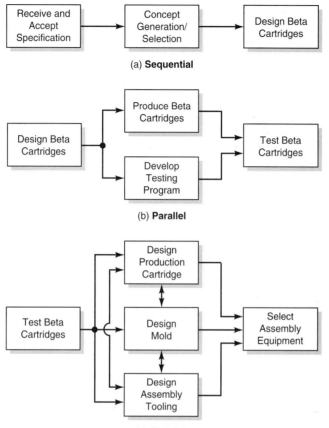

(a) **Sequential**

(b) **Parallel**

(c) **Coupled**

EXHIBIT 2   The three basic types of task dependencies: (a) sequential, (b) parallel, and (c) coupled.

ed by arrows. Task B is dependent on task A if an output of task A is required to complete task B. This dependency is denoted by an arrow from task A to task B.

Exhibit 2(a) shows three tasks, two of which are dependent on the output of another task. These tasks are *sequential*, because the dependencies impose a sequential order in which the tasks must be completed. Exhibit 2(b) shows four development tasks. The middle two tasks depend only on the task on the left, but not on each other. The task on the right depends on the middle two tasks. We call the middle two tasks *parallel* because they are both dependent on the same task but are independent of each other. Exhibit 2(c) shows five development tasks, three of which are *coupled*. Coupled tasks are mutually dependent; each task requires the result of the other tasks in order to be completed. Coupled tasks either must be completed simultaneously with continual exchanges of information or must be carried out in an iterative fashion. When coupled tasks are completed iteratively, the tasks are performed sequentially with the understanding that the results are tentative and that each task will most likely be repeated one or more times until the team converges on a solution.

The Design Structure Matrix

A useful tool for representing and analyzing task dependencies is the *design structure matrix* (DSM). This representation was originally developed by Steward (1981) for the analysis of parametric descriptions of designs and has recently been used to analyze development projects modeled at the task level (Eppinger, 1994). Exhibit 3 shows a DSM for the 14 major tasks of the Cheetah project. (Kodak's actual plan included more than 100 tasks.)

In a DSM, a project task is assigned to a row and a corresponding column. The rows and columns are ordered identically, although generally only the rows are labeled with the names of the tasks. A row, corresponding to one task, is annotated with marks indicating the other tasks (columns) on which it depends. Reading across a row reveals all of the tasks whose output is required to perform the task corresponding to the row. Reading down a column reveals which tasks receive information from the task corresponding to the column. The diagonal elements are usually filled in with dots or the task labels, simply to separate the upper and lower triangles of the matrix and to facilitate tracing dependencies.

The DSM is most useful when the tasks are listed in the order they are to be executed. In most cases, this order will correspond to the order imposed by sequential dependencies. Note that if only sequentially dependent tasks were contained in the DSM, then the tasks could be sequenced such that the matrix would be lower triangular; that is, no marks would appear above the diagonal. A mark appearing above the diagonal has special significance; it indicates that an earlier task is dependent on a later task. An above-diagonal mark could mean that two sequentially dependent tasks are ordered backward, in which case the

EXHIBIT 3 Simplified design structure matrix for the Kodak Cheetah project.

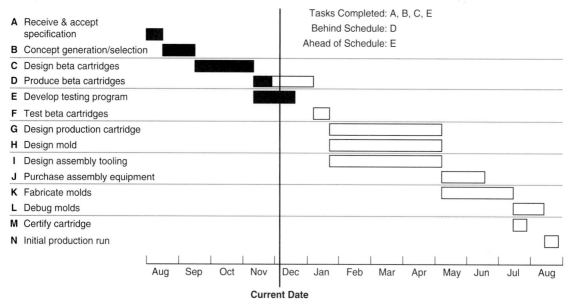

EXHIBIT 4   Gantt chart for the Cheetah project.

order of the tasks can be changed to eliminate the above-diagonal mark. However, when there is no ordering of the tasks that will eliminate an above-diagonal mark, the mark reveals that two or more tasks are coupled.

Changing the order of tasks is called *partitioning*. Simple algorithms are available for partitioning design structure matrices such that the tasks are ordered as much as possible according to the sequential dependencies of the tasks. Inspection of a partitioned DSM reveals which tasks are sequential, which are parallel, and which are coupled and will require simultaneous solution or iteration. In a partitioned DSM, a task is part of a sequential group if its row contains a mark just below the diagonal. Two or more tasks are parallel if there are no marks linking them. As noted, coupled tasks are identified by above-diagonal marks. Exhibit 3 shows how the DSM reveals all three types of tasks.

Gantt Charts

The traditional tool for representing the timing of tasks is the Gantt chart. Exhibit 4 shows a Gantt chart for the Cheetah project. The chart contains a horizontal time line and is created by drawing a horizontal bar representing the start and end of each task. The filled-in portion of each bar represents the fraction of the task that is complete. The vertical line in Exhibit 4 shows the current date, so we can observe directly that task D is behind schedule, while task E is ahead of schedule.

A Gantt chart does not explicitly display the dependencies among tasks. Task dependencies constrain, but do not fully determine, the timing of the tasks. The dependencies dictate which tasks must be completed before others can begin and which tasks can be completed in parallel. When two tasks overlap in time on a Gantt chart, they are usually either parallel or coupled. Parallel tasks can be overlapped in time for convenience in project scheduling because they do not depend on one another. Coupled tasks must be overlapped in time because they must be addressed simultaneously or in an iterative fashion. Under special circumstances, described in the section on accelerating projects, normally sequential tasks can be overlapped somewhat in time.

PERT Charts

PERT (program evaluation and review technique) charts explicitly represent both dependencies and timing, in effect combining some of the information contained in the DSM and Gantt chart. While there are many forms of PERT charts, we prefer the "activities on nodes" form of the chart, which corresponds to the block diagrams that most people are familiar with. The PERT chart for the Cheetah project is shown in Exhibit 5. The blocks in the PERT chart are labeled with both the task and its expected duration. Note that the PERT representation does not allow for loops or feedback and so cannot show coupling explicitly. As a result, the coupled tasks G, H, and I are grouped together into one task. The

EXHIBIT 5   PERT chart for the Cheetah project. The critical path is designated by the thicker lines connecting tasks. Note that tasks, G, H, and I are grouped together because the PERT representation does not depict coupled tasks explicitly.

A	Receive & accept specification	**H**	Design mold
B	Concept generation/selection	**I**	Design assembly tooling
C	Design beta cartridges	**J**	Purchase assembly equipment
D	Produce beta cartridges	**K**	Fabricate molds
E	Develop testing program	**L**	Debug molds
F	Test beta cartridges	**M**	Certify cartridge
G	Design production cartridge	**N**	Initial production run

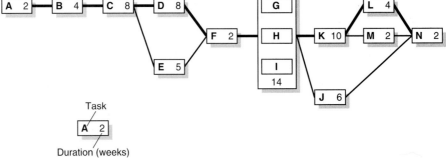

graphical convention of PERT charts is that all links between tasks must proceed from left to right, indicating the temporal sequence in which tasks can be completed.

The Critical Path

The dependencies among several tasks, some of which may be arranged sequentially and some of which may be arranged in parallel, leads to the concept of a *critical path*. The critical path is the single sequence of tasks whose combined required times define the minimum possible completion time for the entire set of tasks. Consider for example the project represented in Exhibit 5. Either the sequence C-D-F or the sequence C-E-F defines how much time is required to complete the four tasks C, D, E, and F. In this case, the path C-D-F requires 18 weeks and the path C-E-F requires 15 weeks, so the critical path for the whole project includes C-D-F. The critical path for the project is denoted by the thick lines in Exhibit 5. Identifying the critical path is important because a delay in any of these *critical tasks* would result in an increase in project duration. All other paths contain some *slack*, meaning that a delay in one of the noncritical tasks does not automatically create a delay for the entire project. Exhibit 4 shows that task D is behind schedule. Because task D is on the critical path, this delay, if not corrected, will result in a delay of the completion of the entire project.

Several software packages are available for producing Gantt charts and PERT charts; these programs can also compute the critical path.

BASELINE PROJECT PLANNING

The project plan is the road map for the remaining development effort. The plan is important in coordinating the remaining tasks and in estimating the required development resources and development time. Some measure of project planning occurs at the earliest stages of product development, but the importance of the plan is highest at the end of the concept development phase, just before significant development resources are committed. This section presents a methodology for creating a *baseline project plan*. After establishing this baseline, the team considers whether it should modify the plan to change the planned development time, budget, or project scope. The results of the concept development phase plus the project plan make up the *contract book*.

The Contract Book

We recommend that a contract book be used to document the project plan and the results of the concept development phase of the development process. The concept of a contract book is detailed by Wheelwright and Clark (1992). The word *contract* is used to emphasize that the document represents an agreement between the development team and the senior management of the company about project goals, direction, and resource requirements. The book is some

Item	Approximate Pages
Mission Statement	1
Customer Needs List	1–2
Competitive Analysis	1–2
Product Specifications	1–3
Sketch of Product Concept	1
Sales Forecast	1–3
Economic Analysis	1–3
Manufacturing Plan	1–5
Project Plan	
Task List	1–5
Team Staffing and Organization	1
Schedule (Gantt and/or PERT)	1–2
Budget	1
Risk Areas	1
Project Performance Measurement Plan	1
Incentives	1
Total Pages	15–32

EXHIBIT 6 Table of contents of a contract book for a project of moderate complexity.

times actually signed by the key team members and the senior managers of the company. A table of contents for a contract book is shown in Exhibit 6.

In the following subsections we discuss each element of the project plan: the project task list, team staffing and organization, the project schedule, the project budget, and the project risk areas.

Project Task List

We have already introduced the idea that a project consists of a collection of tasks. The first step in planning a project is to list the tasks that make up the project. For most product development projects the team will not be able to list every task in great detail; too much uncertainty remains in the subsequent development activities. However, the team will be able to list its best estimate of the remaining tasks at a general level of detail. To be most useful during project planning, the task list should contain from 50 to 200 items. For small projects, such as the development of a hand tool, each task may correspond, on average, to a day or two of work for a single individual. For medium-sized projects, such as the development of a computer printer, each task may correspond to a week of work for a small group of people. For a large project, such as the development of an automobile, each task may correspond to one or more months of efforts for an entire division or subteam. For large projects, each of the tasks identified at this level may be treated as its own development project with its own project plan.

An effective way to tackle the generation of the task list is to consider the tasks in each of the remaining phases of development. For our generic development process, the phases remaining after concept development are system-level design, detail design, testing and refinement, and production ramp-up. (See the chapter "Development Processes and Organizations.") In some cases, the current effort will be very similar to a previous project. In these cases, the actual project tasks from the previous effort are a good starting point for the new task list. The Cheetah project was very similar to dozens of previous efforts. For this reason, the team had no trouble identifying the project tasks (its challenge was to complete them quickly).

After listing all of the tasks, the team estimates the effort required to complete each task. Effort is usually expressed in units of person-hours, person-days, or person-weeks, depending on the size of the project. Note that these estimates reflect the "actual working time" that members of the development team would have to apply to the task and not the "elapsed calendar time" the team expects the task to require. Because the speed with which a task is completed has some influence on the total amount of effort that must be applied to the task, the estimates embody preliminary assumptions about how quickly the team will attempt to complete tasks. These estimates are typically derived from past experience or the judgment of experienced members of the development team. A task list for the Cheetah project is shown in Exhibit 7.

EXHIBIT 7   Task list for the Cheetah project. (This task list is abbreviated for clarity; the actual list contained over 100 tasks.)

Task	Estimated Person-Weeks
Concept Development	
Receive and accept specification	8
Concept generation/selection	16
Detail Design	
Design beta cartridges	62
Produce beta cartridges	24
Develop testing program	24
Testing and Refinement	
Test beta cartridges	20
Design production cartridge	56
Design mold	36
Design assembly tooling	24
Purchase assembly equipment	16
Fabricate molds	16
Debug molds	24
Certify cartridge	12
Production Ramp-Up	
Initial production run	16
Total	354

Team Staffing and Organization

The project team is the collection of individuals who complete project tasks. Whether or not this team is effective depends on a wide variety of individual and organizational factors. Smith and Reinertsen (1991) propose seven criteria as determinants of the speed with which a team will complete product development; in our experience these criteria predict many of the other dimensions of team performance as well:

1 There are 10 or fewer members of the team.
2 Members volunteer to serve on the team.
3 Members serve on the team from the time of concept development until product launch.
4 Members are assigned to the team full-time.
5 Members report directly to the team leader.
6 The key functions, including at least marketing, design, and manufacturing, are on the team.
7 Members are located within conversational distance of each other.

While few teams are staffed and organized ideally, these criteria raise several key issues: How big should the team be? How should the team be organized relative to the larger enterprise? Which functions should be represented on the team? How can the development team of a very large project exhibit some of the agility of a small team? Here we address the issues related to team size. The chapters "Introduction" and "Development Processes and Organizations" address some of the other team and organizational issues.

The minimum number of people required on the project team can be estimated by dividing the total estimated time to complete the project tasks by the planned project duration. For example, the estimated task time for the Cheetah project was 354 person-weeks. The team hoped to complete the project in 12 months (or about 50 weeks), so the minimum possible team size would be seven people. All other things being equal, small teams seem to be more efficient than large teams, so the ideal situation would be to have a team made up of the minimum number of people, each dedicated 100 percent to the project.

Three factors make realizing this ideal difficult. First, specialized skills are often required to complete the project. For example, one of the Cheetah tasks was to design molds. Mold designers are highly specialized, and the team could not use a mold designer for a full year. Second, one or more key team members may have other unavoidable responsibilities. For example, one of the engineers on the Cheetah project was responsible for assisting in the production ramp-up of a previous project. As a result, she was only able to commit half of her time to the Cheetah project initially. Third, the work required to complete tasks on the project is not constant over time. In general, the work requirement increases steadily until the beginning of production ramp-up and then begins to taper off. As a result, the team will generally have to grow in size as the project progresses in order to complete the project as quickly as possible.

After considering the need for specialized people, the reality of other commitments of the team members, and the need to accommodate an increase and subsequent decrease in work load, the project leader, in consultation with his or her management, identifies the full project staff and approximately when each person will join the team. When possible, team members are identified by name, although in some cases they will be identified only by area of expertise (e.g., mold designer, industrial designer). The project staffing for the Cheetah project is shown in Exhibit 8.

Project Schedule

The project schedule is the merger of the project tasks and the project time line. The schedule identifies when major project milestones are expected to occur and when each project task is expected to begin and end. The team uses this schedule to track progress and to orchestrate the exchange of materials and information between individuals. It is therefore important that the schedule is viewed as credible by the entire project team.

We recommend the following steps to create a baseline project schedule:

1 Use the DSM or PERT chart to identify the dependencies among tasks.

2 Position the key project milestones along a time line.

3 Schedule the tasks, considering the project staffing.

4 Adjust the timing of the milestones to be consistent with the time required for the tasks.

Project milestones are useful as anchor points for the scheduling activity. Common milestones include design reviews (also called phase reviews or design gates), comprehensive prototypes (e.g., alpha prototype, beta prototype), and trade shows. Because these events typically require input from almost everyone on the development team, they serve as powerful forces for integration and act

EXHIBIT 8 Project staffing for the Cheetah project. Numbers shown are approximate percentages of full time.

Person	Month: 1	2	3	4	5	6	7	8	9	10	11	12
Team Leader	100	100	100	100	100	100	100	100	100	100	100	100
Schedule Coordinator	25	25	25	25	25	25	25	25	25	25	25	25
Customer Liaison	50	50	50	50	25	25	25	25	25	25	25	25
Mechanical Designer 1	100	100	100	100	100	100	100	100	50	50	50	50
Mechanical Designer 2		50	100	100	100	100	100	100	50			
CAD Technician 1		50	100	100	100	100	100	100	100	50	50	50
CAD Technician 2				50	100	100	100	100	100	50		
Mold Designer 1	25	25	25	25	100	100	100	100	25	25	25	
Mold Designer 2					100	100	100	100				
Assembly Tool Designer	25	25	25	25	100	100	100	100	100	100	50	50
Manufacturing Engineer	50	50	100	100	100	100	100	100	100	100	100	100
Purchasing Engineer		50	50	100	100	100	100	100	100	100	100	100

as anchor points on the schedule. Once the milestones are laid out on the schedule, the tasks can be arranged between these milestones.

The Cheetah schedule was developed by expanding the typical project phases into a set of approximately 100 tasks. The major milestones were the concept approval, the testing of beta prototype cartridges, the trade show demonstration, and production ramp-up. Relationships among these activities and the critical path were documented using a PERT chart.

Project Budget

Budgets are customarily figured and presented using a simple spreadsheet, although many companies have standard budgeting forms for requests and approvals. The major budget items are staff, materials and services, project-specific facilities, and spending on outside development resources.

For most projects the largest budget item is the cost of staff. For the Cheetah project, personnel charges made up 80 percent of the total budget. The personnel costs can be derived directly from the staffing plan by applying the *loaded* salary rates to the estimated time commitments of the staff on the project. Loaded salaries include employee benefits and overhead and are typically between two and three times the actual salary of the team member. Many companies use only one or two different rates to represent the cost of the people on a project. Average staff costs for product development projects range from $2,000 to $5,000 per person-week. For the Cheetah project, assuming an average cost of $3,000 per person-week, the total cost for the 354 person-weeks of effort would be $1,062,000.

Early in the development project, uncertainty of both timing and costs are high and the forecasts may only be accurate within 30 to 50 percent. In the later stages of the project the program uncertainty is reduced to perhaps 5 percent to 10 percent. For this reason some margin should be added to the budget as a contingency. A summary of the Cheetah project budget is shown in Exhibit 9.

EXHIBIT 9 Summary budget for the Cheetah project. The production tooling and equipment are accounted for as manufacturing costs rather than as part of the development project budget. (Kodak figures are disguised and listed here only for illustration.)

Item	Amount
Staff salaries	
354 person-weeks @ $3,000/week	$1,062,000
Materials and Services	125,000
Prototype Molds	75,000
Outside Resources, Consultants	25,000
Travel	50,000
Subtotal	$1,337,000
Contingency (20%)	$267,400
Total	$1,604,400

Risk	Risk Level	Actions to Minimize Risk
Change in customer specifications.	Moderate	• Involve the customer in process of refining specifications. • Work with the customer to estimate time and cost penalties of changes.
Poor feeding characteristics of cartridge design	Low	• Build early functional prototype from machined parts. • Test prototype in microfilm machine.
Delays in mold making shop.	Moderate	• Reserve 25% of shop capacity for May–July.
Molding problems require rework of mold	High	• Involve mold maker and mold designer in the part design. • Perform mold filling computer analysis. • Establish design rules for part design. • Choose materials at end of concept development phase.

EXHIBIT 10   Risk areas for the Cheetah project.

Project Risk Areas

Projects rarely proceed exactly according to plan. Some of the deviations from the plan are minor and can be accommodated with little or no impact on project performance. Other deviations can cause major delays, budget overruns, lapses in product performance, or high manufacturing costs. Often the team can assemble, in advance, a list of what might go wrong, that is, the areas of risk for the project.

We recommend that after identifying each risk, the team assess the level of the risk and then identify the actions the team will take to minimize the risk. In addition to pushing the team to work to minimize risk, the explicit identification of risk during the project planning activity helps to minimize the number of surprises the team will have to communicate to its senior management later in the project. The risk areas for the Cheetah project are shown in Exhibit 10.

Modifying the Baseline Plan

The baseline project plan embodies assumptions about how quickly the project should be completed, about the performance and cost goals for the product, and about the resources to be applied to the project. After completing a baseline plan, the team should consider whether some of these assumptions should be revisited. In particular, the team can usually choose to trade off development time, development cost, product manufacturing cost, product performance, and risk. For example, a project can sometimes be completed more quickly by spending more money. Some of these trade-offs can be explored quantitatively using the economic analysis techniques described in the chapter "Economics of Product Development Projects." The most common desired modification to the baseline plan is to compress the schedule. For this reason, we devote the next section to ways the team can accelerate the project.

ACCELERATING THE PROJECT

Product development time is often the dominant concern in project planning and execution. This section provides a set of guidelines for accelerating product development projects. Most of these guidelines are applicable at the project planning stage, although a few can be applied throughout a development project. Accelerating a project before it has begun is much easier than trying to expedite a project that is already underway.

The first set of guidelines applies to the project as a whole.

- *Start the project early.* Saving a month at the beginning of a project is just as valuable as saving a month at the end of a project, yet teams often work with little urgency before development formally begins. For example, the meeting to approve a project plan and review a contract book is often delayed for weeks because of difficulty in scheduling a meeting with senior managers. This delay at the beginning of a project is exactly as costly as the same delay during production ramp-up. The easiest way to complete a project sooner is to start it early.

- *Manage the project scope.* There is a natural tendency to add additional features and capabilities to the product as development progresses. Some companies call this phenomenon "creeping elegance," and in time-sensitive contexts it may result in an elegant product without a market. Disciplined teams and organizations are able to "freeze the design" and leave incremental improvements for the next generation of the product.

- *Facilitate the exchange of essential information.* As shown in the DSM representation, a tremendous amount of information must be transferred within the product development team. Every task has one or more internal customers for the information it produces. For small teams, frequent exchange of information is quite natural and is facilitated by team meetings and co-location of team members. Larger teams may require more structure to promote rapid and frequent information exchange. Blocks of coupled tasks revealed by the DSM identify the specific needs for intensive information exchange. Computer networks and emerging software technology offer some promise for enhancing this exchange within larger development teams.

The second set of guidelines is aimed at decreasing the time required to complete the tasks on the critical path. These guidelines arise from the fact that the only way to reduce the time required to complete a project is to shorten the critical path. Note that a decision to allocate additional resources to shortening the critical path should be based on the value of accelerating the entire project. For some projects, time reductions on the critical path can be worth hundreds of thousands, or even millions of dollars per day.

- *Complete individual tasks on the critical path more quickly.* The benefit of recognizing the critical path is that the team can focus its efforts on this vital sequence of tasks. The critical path generally only represents a small fraction of the total project effort and so additional spending on completing a critical task more quickly can usually quite easily be justified. Sometimes completing critical tasks more quickly can be achieved simply by identifying a task as critical, so that it gets special attention. Note that the accelerated completion of a critical task may cause the critical path to shift to include previously noncritical tasks.

- *Eliminate some critical path tasks entirely.* Scrutinize each and every task on the critical path and ask whether it can be removed or accomplished in another way.

- *Eliminate waiting delays for critical path resources.* Tasks on the critical path are sometimes delayed by waiting for a busy resource. The waiting time is frequently longer than the actual time required to complete the task. Delays due to waiting are particularly prominent when procuring special components from suppliers. In such cases, purchasing a fraction of the capacity of a vendor's production system in order to expedite the fabrication of prototype parts may make perfect economic sense in the context of the overall development project, even though the expenditure may seem extravagant when viewed in isolation. In other cases, administrative tasks such as purchase order approvals may become bottlenecks. Because in past cartridge development projects periodic budget approvals had caused delays, the Cheetah project leader began early to pursue aggressively the necessary signatures so as not to hold up the activities of the entire team.

- *Overlap selected critical tasks.* By modifying the relationships between sequentially dependent tasks on the critical path, the tasks can sometimes be overlapped or executed in parallel. In some cases, this may require a significant redefinition of the tasks or even changes to the architecture of the product. (See the chapter "Product Architecture" for more details on dependencies arising from the architecture of the product.) In other cases, overlapping entails simply transferring partial information earlier or more frequently between nominally sequential tasks (Krishnan, 1993).

- *Pipeline large tasks.* The strategy of *pipelining* is applied by breaking up a single large task into smaller tasks whose results can be passed along as soon as they are completed. For example, the process of finding and qualifying the many vendors who supply the components of a product can be time consuming and can even delay the production ramp-up if not completed early enough. Instead of waiting until the entire bill of materials is complete before the purchasing department begins qualifying vendors, purchasing could qualify vendors as soon as each component is identified. Pipelining in effect allows nominally sequential tasks to be overlapped.

- *Out-source some tasks.* Project resource constraints are common. When a project is constrained by available resources, assigning tasks to an outside firm or to another group within the company may prove effective in accelerating the overall project.

The final set of guidelines is aimed at completing coupled tasks more quickly. Recall that coupled tasks are those that must be completed simultaneously or iteratively because they are mutually dependent.

- *Perform more iterations quickly.* Much of the delay in completing coupled tasks is in passing information from one person to another and in waiting for a response. If the iteration cycles can be completed at a higher frequency, then the coupled tasks can sometimes be competed more quickly. In the Cheetah project, the mechanical engineer would work closely with the mold designer, who would in turn work closely with the mold maker. In many cases, these three would share a single computer terminal for the purpose of exchanging ideas about how the design was evolving from their three different perspectives.

- *De-couple tasks to avoid iterations.* Iterations can often be reduced or eliminated by taking actions to de-couple tasks. For example, by clearly defining an interface between two interacting components early in the design process, the remaining design of the two components can proceed independently and in parallel. The definition of the interface may take some time in advance, but the avoidance of subsequent iterations may result in net time savings. (See the chapter "Product Architecture" for a discussion of establishing interfaces in order to allow the independent development of components.)

PROJECT EXECUTION

Smooth execution of even a well-planned project requires careful attention. Three problems of project execution are particularly important: (1) What mechanisms can be used to coordinate tasks? (2) How can project status be assessed? and (3) What actions can the team take to correct for undesirable deviations from the project plan? We devote this section to these issues.

Coordination Mechanisms

Coordination among the activities of the different members of the team is required throughout a product development project. The need for coordination is a natural outgrowth of dependencies among tasks. Coordination needs also arise from the inevitable changes in the project plan caused by unanticipated events and new information. Difficulties in coordination can arise from inade-

EXHIBIT 11   Communication frequency versus separation distance. This relationship shown is for individuals with an organizational bond, such as belonging to the same product development team. (Thomas J. Allen, *Managing the Flow of Technology: Technology Transfer and the Dissemination of Technological Information within the R&D Organization,* MIT Press, Cambridge, MA, 1977.)

quate exchanges of information and from organizational barriers to cross-functional cooperation. Mechanisms teams use to address these difficulties and facilitate coordination include informal communication, meetings, and information systems.

- *Informal communication:* A team member engaged in a product development project may communicate with another team member dozens of times per day. Many of these communications are informal; they involve a spontaneous stop by someone's desk or a telephone call to solicit a piece of information. Good informal communication is one of the mechanisms most useful in breaking down individual and organizational barriers to cross-functional cooperation. Informal communication is dramatically enhanced by locating the core members of the development team in the same work space. Allen (1977) has shown that communication frequency is inversely related to physical separation and falls off rapidly when people are located more than a few meters from one another (Exhibit 11). In our experience, electronic mail and, to a lesser extent, voice mail also provide effective means of fostering informal communication among people who are already well acquainted with one another. There are some reports that electronic mail is actually more effective than co-location for fostering communication (Perry, 1992).

- *Meetings:* The primary formal communication mechanism for project teams is meetings. Most teams meet formally at least once each week. Many teams meet twice each week, and some teams meet every day. Teams located in the same work space need fewer formal meetings than those whose members are geographically separated. Time spent exchanging information in meetings is time not spent completing other project tasks. In order to minimize the amount of time wasted in meetings, some teams that hold meetings every day meet standing up to emphasize that the meeting is intended to be quick. Other techniques for controlling the length of meetings include preparing a written agenda, appointing someone to run the meeting, and holding the meeting at lunchtime or near the end of the day when people are anxious to leave. We recommend that team meetings be held at a regular time and place so that no extra effort is expended in scheduling the meeting and in informing the team of its time and location.

- *Information systems:* By information systems we mean all of the structured means the team uses to exchange information, and not only the computer systems used by the team. The most important information system in project execution is the schedule. Most successful projects have a single person who is responsible for monitoring the schedule. On small projects, this is usually the team leader. Larger projects generally have a designated person other than the project leader who watches and updates the schedule regularly. On the Cheetah project, Kodak provided a part-time project analyst who kept the schedule current on a weekly basis and reported to the project team leader. The team members understood the importance of accurate schedule projections and were very cooperative in this effort. Schedule updates are usually displayed in Gantt chart form (Exhibit 4).

Another useful information system is the *weekly status memo.* The memo is written by the project leader and is distributed on paper, in electronic form, or even by voice mail to the entire extended project team, usually on Friday or over the weekend. The memo is usually one or two pages long and lists the key accomplishments, decisions, and events of the past week. It also lists the key events of the coming week. It is sometimes accompanied by an updated schedule.

Each of the methodologies presented in this book also has an associated information system, which aids in project decision making and documentation. For example, the concept selection methodology uses two concept selection matrices to both document and facilitate the selection process. Similarly, each of the other information systems serves both to facilitate the logical execution of the process step and to document its results. Exhibit 12 lists some of the important information systems used at the various stages of the development process.

Assessing Project Status

Project leaders and senior managers need to be able to assess project status to know whether corrective actions are warranted. In projects of modest size (say, fewer than 50 people) project leaders are fairly easily able to assess the status of the project. The project leader assesses project status during formal team meet-

Development Activity	Information Systems Used
Customer needs identification	Customer needs lists
Concept generation	Function diagrams Concept classification tree Concept combination table Concept descriptions and sketches
Concept selection	Concept screening matrix Concept scoring matrix
Product specifications	Needs-metrics matrix Competitive benchmarking charts Specifications lists
System-level design	Schematic diagram Geometric layout
Detailed design	Bill of materials
Industrial design	Aesthetic/ergonomic importance survey
Product development economics	NPV analysis spreadsheet
Project management	Contract book Task list Design structure matrix Gantt chart PERT chart Staffing matrix Risk analysis

EXHIBIT 12   Information systems used to facilitate team consensus and the exchange of information.

ings and also gathers information in informal ways. The leader constantly interacts with the project team, meets regularly with individuals to work through difficult problems, and is able to observe all of the information systems of the project. A team may also engage an expert from outside the core team to review the status of the project. The goal of these reviews is to highlight areas of risk and to generate ideas for addressing these risks areas.

Project reviews, conducted by senior managers, are another common method of assessing progress. These reviews tend to correspond to the end of each phase of development and are key project milestones. These events serve not only to inform senior managers of the status of a project but also to bring closure to a wide variety of development tasks. While these reviews can be useful milestones and can enhance project performance, they can also hinder performance. Detrimental results arise from devoting too much time to preparing formal presentations, from delays in scheduling reviews with busy managers, and from excessive meddling in the details of the project by those reviewing the project.

Corrective Actions

After discovering an undesirable deviation from the project plan, the team attempts to take corrective action. Problems almost always manifest themselves as potential schedule slippage, and so most of these corrective actions relate to arresting potential delays. Some of the possible actions include:

- *Changing the timing or frequency of meetings:* Sometimes a simple change from weekly to daily meetings increases the "driving frequency" of the information flow among team members and enables more rapid completion of tasks. This is particularly true of teams that are not already co-located (although if the team is highly dispersed geographically, meetings can consume a great deal of travel time). Sometimes simply moving a weekly meeting from a Tuesday morning to a Friday afternoon increases the urgency felt by the team to "get it done this week."

- *Changing the project staff:* The skills, capabilities, and commitment of the members of the project team in large measure determine project performance. When the project team is grossly understaffed, performance can sometimes be increased by adding the necessary staff. When the project team is overstaffed, performance can sometimes be increased by removing staff. Note that adding staff in a panic at the end of a project can lead to delays in project completion because the increased coordination requirements may outweigh the increase in human resources.

- *Locating the team together physically:* If the team is geographically dispersed, one way to increase project performance is to locate the team in the same work space. This action invariably increases communication among the team members. Some measure of "virtual co-location" may be possible with electronic mail or video conferencing technologies.

- *Soliciting more time and effort from the team:* If some team members are distributing their efforts among several projects, project performance may be increased by relieving them of their other responsibilities. Needless to say, high-performance project teams include team members who regularly deliver more than a 40-hour work week to the project. If a few critical tasks demand extraordinary effort, most committed teams are willing to devote a few weeks of 14-hour days to get the job done. However, 60- or 70-hour weeks cannot reasonably be expected from most team members for more than a few weeks without causing fatigue and "burnout."

- *Focusing all efforts on the critical tasks:* By definition, only one sequence of tasks forms the critical path. When the path can be usefully attacked by additional people, the team may choose to temporarily drop some or all other noncritical tasks in order to ensure timely completion of the critical tasks.

- *Engaging outside resources:* The team may be able to retain an outside resource such as a consulting firm or a supplier to perform some of the development tasks. Outside firms are typically fast and relatively economical when a set of tasks can be clearly defined and when coordination requirements are not severe.

- *Changing the project scope or schedule:* If all other efforts fail to correct undesirable deviations from the project plan, then the team must either narrow the scope of the project or extend the project schedule. These changes are necessary to maintain a credible and useful project plan.

POSTMORTEM PROJECT EVALUATION

An evaluation of the performance of a project after it has been completed is useful for both personal and organizational improvement. This review is often called a *postmortem project evaluation.* The postmortem project evaluation is usually an open-ended discussion of the strengths and weaknesses of the project plan and execution. This discussion is sometimes facilitated by an outside consultant or by someone within the company who was not involved in the project. Several questions help to guide the discussion:

- Did the team achieve the mission articulated in the mission statement?
- Which aspects of project performance (development time, development cost, product quality, manufacturing cost) were most positive?
- Which aspects of project performance were most negative?
- Which tools, methodologies, and practices contributed to the positive aspects of performance?
- Which tools, methodologies, and practices detracted from project success?
- What problems did the team encounter?
- What specific actions can the organization take to improve project performance?
- What specific technical lessons were learned? How can they be shared with the rest of the organization?

A postmortem report is then prepared as part of the formal closing of the project. These reports are then used in the project planning stage of future projects to help team members know what to expect and to help identify what pitfalls to avoid. The reports are also a valuable source of historical data for studies of the firm's product development practices. Together with the project documentation, and particularly the contract book, they provide "before and after" views of each project.

For the Cheetah project, the postmortem discussion involved six members of the core team and lasted two hours. The discussion was facilitated by a consultant. The project was completed on time, despite the aggressive schedule, so much of the discussion focused on what the team had done to contribute to project success. The team agreed that the most important contributors to project success were:

- Empowerment of a team leader
- Effective team problem solving
- Emphasis on adherence to schedule
- Effective communication links
- Full participation from multiple functions
- Building on prior experience in cartridge development
- Use of computer-aided design (CAD) tools for communication and analysis
- Early understanding of manufacturing capabilities

The Cheetah team also identified a few opportunities for improvement:

- Use of three-dimensional CAD tools and plastic molding analysis tools
- Earlier participation by the customer in the design decisions
- Improved integration of tooling design and production system design

SUMMARY

Successful product development requires effective project management. Some of the key ideas in this chapter are:

- Projects consist of tasks linked to each other by dependencies. Tasks can be sequential, parallel, or coupled.
- Collections of tasks linked by dependencies define a critical path, whose duration defines the minimum possible completion time of a project.
- The design structure matrix (DSM) can be used to represent dependencies. Gantt charts are used to represent the timing of tasks. PERT charts represent both dependencies and timing and are frequently used to compute the critical path.
- Project planning results in a task list, a project schedule, staffing requirements, a project budget, and a risk assessment. These items are key elements of the contract book.
- Most opportunities for accelerating projects arise during the project planning phase. There are many ways to complete development projects more quickly.
- Project execution involves coordination, assessment of progress, and taking action to address deviations from the plan.
- Evaluating the performance of a project encourages and facilitates personal and organizational improvement.

REFERENCES AND BIBLIOGRAPHY

There are many basic texts on project management, although most do not focus on product development projects. PERT and Gantt techniques are described in most texts on project management, including the following:

Kerzner, H., *Project Management: A Systems Approach to Planning, Scheduling, and Controlling*, fourth edition, Van Nostrand Reinhold, New York, 1992. ISBN 0-442-01085-0.

Several authors have written specifically about the management of product development. Wheelwright and Clark discuss team leadership and other project management issues in depth.

Wheelwright, Stephen C., and Kim B. Clark, *Revolutionizing Product Development: Quantum Leaps in Speed, Efficiency, and Quality*, The Free Press, New York, 1992. ISBN 0-02-905515-6.

The design structure matrix (DSM) was originally developed by Donald V. Steward in the 1970s. Recently, this method has been applied to industrial project planning and assessment by Eppinger and his students.

Steward, Donald V., *Systems Analysis and Management: Structure, Strategy, and Design*, Petrocelli Books, New York, 1981. ISBN 0-894-33106-X.

Eppinger, Steven D., et al., "A Model-Based Method for Organizing Tasks in Product Development," *Research in Engineering Design*, vol. 6, no. 1, 1994.

Krishnan, V., S. D. Eppinger, and D. E. Whitney, *A Model-Based Framework to Overlap Product Development Activities*, MIT Sloan School Working Paper No. 3635-93-MSA, November 1993.

Smith and Reinertsen provide many ideas for accelerating product development projects, along with interesting insights on team staffing and organization.

Smith, Preston G., and Donald G. Reinertsen, *Developing Products in Half the Time*, Van Nostrand Reinhold, New York, 1991. ISBN 0-442-00243-2.

Allen discusses communication in R&D organizations at length. He also reports on empirical studies of the influence of physical layout on communication.

Allen, Thomas, J., *Managing the Flow of Technology: Technology Transfer and the Dissemination of Technological Information within the R&D Organization*, MIT Press, Cambridge, MA, 1977. ISBN 0-262-01048-8; paperback edition 1984, ISBN 0-262-51027-8.

Recent work has applied improved information technology using software and networks to enhance the coordination of large project groups.

Applegate, L., J. Cash, and D. Q. Mills, "Information Technology and Tomorrow's Manager," *Harvard Business Review*, November-December 1988, pp. 128–136.

Perry, Tekla S., "E-Mail at Work," *IEEE Spectrum*, October 1992, pp. 24–28.

Sproull, Lee, and Sara Kiesler, *Connections: New Ways of Working in the Networked Organization*, MIT Press, Cambridge, MA, 1991. ISBN 0-262-19306-X.

EXERCISES

1 The tasks for preparing a dinner (along with the normal completion times) might include:
- Wash and cut vegetables for the salad (15 minutes).
- Toss the salad (2 minutes).
- Set the table (8 minutes).
- Start the rice cooking (2 minutes).

- Cook rice (25 minutes).
- Place the rice in a serving dish (1 minute).
- Mix casserole ingredients (10 minutes).
- Bake the casserole (25 minutes).

Prepare a DSM for these tasks.

2 Prepare a PERT chart for the tasks in Exercise 1. How fast can one person prepare this dinner? What if there were two people?

3 What strategies could you employ to prepare dinner more quickly? If you thought about dinner 24 hours in advance, are there any steps you could take to reduce the time between arriving home the next day and serving dinner?

4 Interview a project manager (not necessarily from product development). Ask him or her to describe the major obstacles to project success.

THOUGHT QUESTIONS

1 When a task on the critical path (for example, the fabrication of a mold) is delayed, the completion of the entire project is delayed, even though the total amount of work required to complete the project may remain the same. How would you expect such a delay to impact the total cost of the project?

2 This chapter has focused on the "hard" issues in project management related to tasks, dependencies, and schedules. What are some of the "soft," or behavioral, issues related to project management?

3 What would you expect to be some of the characteristics of individuals who successfully lead project teams?

4 Under what conditions might efforts to accelerate a product development project also lead to increased product quality and/or decreased product manufacturing costs? Under what conditions might these attributes of the product deteriorate when the project is accelerated?

INDEX